APPROACHES
TO
CANADIAN
ECONOMIC
HISTORY

APPROACHES TO
CANADIAN
ECONOMIC
HISTORY

A SELECTION OF ESSAYS
EDITED AND WITH AN INTRODUCTION BY
W.T. EASTERBROOK AND M.H. WATKINS

Carleton Library Series #31

McGill-Queen's University Press
Montreal · Kingston · London · Ithaca

CARLETON LIBRARY SERIES

The Carleton Library Series, funded by Carleton University under the general editorship of the dean of Graduate Studies and Research, publishes material relating to Canadian history, politics, society, economy, geography, and related subjects. It includes important new works as well as reprints of classics in the fields. The editorial committee welcomes manuscripts and suggestions, which should be sent to the dean of Graduate Studies and Research, Carleton University.

© McGill-Queen's University Press 2003
© Carleton University Press Inc. 1984
ISBN 0-88629-021-X

Legal deposit second quarter 2003

Bibliothèque nationale du Québec

Printed in Canada on acid-free paper
Reprinted 1986, 1988, 1991, 1997, 2003

McGill-Queen's University Press acknowledges the support of the Canada Council for the Arts for our publishing program. We also acknowledge the financial support of the Government of Canada through the Book Publishing Industry Development Program (BPIDP) for our publishing activities.

Canadian Cataloguing in Publication Data

Main entry under title:
        Approaches to canadian economic history : a
selection of essays

First published Toronto : McClelland and Stewart Inc., 1967.
        (Carleton library ; no. 31).
Includes bibliographic references.
ISBN 0–88629–021–X

        1. Canada—Economic conditions. I. Easterbrook,
W. T. (William Thomas), 1907- II. Watkins, M. H.
(Melville Henry), 1932- III. Series: The Carleton
library ; no. 31.

HC113.A65 1997   330.971   C97-900914-6

CONTENTS

INTRODUCTION

Neither economics nor history can be properly described as disciplines characterized by definitive and agreed upon methods and conclusions. What is true of these major disciplines is necessarily true of the derivative discipline of economic history. Furthermore, the state of economic history in general is reflected in the state of Canadian economic history in particular. It is therefore appropriate that this collection of readings in Canadian economic history should bear the modest title of *Approaches to Canadian Economic History*.

It is presumably a minimal requirement that editors should justify their title, but it is hardly sufficient to do that alone. The reader is entitled to ask why particular approaches have been emphasized and particular essays chosen. While answers to these questions could perhaps be divined by reading the lengthy review of the literature which is the concluding essay of this volume, some commentary is in order at this point.

Though there are a variety of possible approaches to Canadian economic history, some approaches have proven more popular and durable than others. The most persistent theme of Canadian economic historiography is "the staple approach," and it properly receives pride of place in this volume. Its pioneer exponents are W. A. Mackintosh of Queen's and Harold Innis of Toronto.

Reacting to the constitutional bias of Canadian historians, in 1922 Mackintosh entered a strong plea for the consideration of "Economic Factors in Canadian History." In part, what was needed was greater emphasis on geographic factors and on the role of transport systems moulded thereby. The influence of the American historian Frederick Jackson Turner is evident in Mackintosh's concern with the western frontier and its accessibility, or inaccessibility, in terms of geography and prevailing modes of transport. In part, Canadian developments needed to be considered more in the continental context – where economic factors could not be ignored – and, by implication, less in the imperial context – where political or constitutional factors too easily overshadowed long-run and fundamental determinants. In this insistence on a North American approach, Mackintosh pointed to a deficiency of Canadian historiography that is not yet fully remedied. Mackintosh's greatest contribution, however, is to be found in his explicit recognition of the overriding importance of staple exports, or primary production for external markets, to colonial development. Building on the work of the American economic historian G. S. Callender, Mackintosh writes tersely: "The prime requisite of colonial prosperity is the colonial staple." He thus laid down a unifying theme not only for his seminal essay but for much of Canadian economic historiography down to the present day. His own work as an economic historian – pursued in the midst of the heavy demands of government service and university administration – is highlighted by his definitive study for the Rowell-Sirois Commission on *The Economic Background of Dominion-Provincial Relations* (now available in the Carleton Library). In the midst of the economic catastrophe of the 1930's, Mackintosh excelled in his ability, rare in Canada and elsewhere, to combine the policy implications of the new economics with the historical perspective of the old.

In one of the happy coincidences of Canadian intellectual history, Mackintosh's pioneering work at Queen's in Canadian economic history was being simultaneously matched at Toronto by Innis. Innis too was preoccupied with "The Importance of Staple Products" and by 1940 his staggering output had culminated in massive volumes on the first two great staple trades, *The Fur Trade in Canada* and *The Cod Fisheries*. While Mackintosh's "staple approach" was fundamentally a theory of economic development emphasizing the leading role of exports, Innis made of staple production the central theme around which to write the total history of Canada's economic, political and social institutions. A fundamental insight was Innis' realization of the need to move beyond the recognition of the importance of export-orientation in general to consideration of the decisive importance to historical developments in marginal areas of the peculiar characteristics of each particular export staple. In his own words:

Concentration on the production of staples for export to more highly industrialized areas in Europe and later in the United States had broad implications for the Canadian economic, political and social structure. Each staple in its turn left its

*stamp, and the shift to new staples invariably produced periods
of crises in which adjustments in the old structure were painfully
made and a new pattern created in relation to a new staple.*[1]

Brief excerpts from Innis' work – of which two are found in
this volume, one on staple production and one on the fur trade
in particular – impart something of the flavour of his penetrating
and sweeping powers, but there is no substitute for lengthy
immersion in his writings. His synoptic, even cryptic and hyper-
bolic, style comes to be appreciated, after sufficient exposure,
as the means by which Innis compressed his encyclopedic
learning and generated new insights by juxtaposition and over-
statement. Nor will the rewards from learning to read Innis be
confined only to a deeper understanding of Canada. For after
1940, when Innis turned from Canadian history to universal
history, the method and style remained unchanged. In effect, the
medium of communication became the staple; instead of the
great staple trades of Canada, we now have as the unifying
theme the great media of history such as stone, papyrus, parch-
ment, paper, print and radio.[2] And to have an *entrée* into the
later Innis is to have also an *entrée* into the exciting world of
Marshall McLuhan.[3]

The impact of Mackintosh and Innis on studies in Canadian
political economy and history was pervasive. Amongst the
students of the great staple trades, one of the most distinguished
is the historian A. R. M. Lower, with his studies of the timber
trade and the lumbering industry. His 1932 monograph, "The
Trade in Square Timber," remains the definitive work on this
topic; its brevity permits it to be reprinted here in full. The
timber trade, transitory though it was, spanned a critical gap
between an economy based on trapping and fishing and an
economy based on farming and manufacturing, and revealed
the wealth of forest resources that sustains the Canadian economy down to the present day. While its consequences were
sometimes adverse – as in the excessive specialization which it
engendered in New Brunswick and the Ottawa Valley – it never-

[1] Harold Innis, *Empire and Communications* (London, 1950), pp. 4-5.
[2] Harold Innis, *Empire and Communications; The Bias of Communications* (Toronto, 1951); *Changing Concepts of Time* (Toronto, 1952).
[3] McLuhan has blended Innis' approach with his own highly original
insights to produce some of the most provocative and widely discussed
books of this decade. See his *The Gutenberg Galaxy* (Toronto, 1962)
and *Understanding Media* (New York, 1964).

theless played the important role of encouraging settlement by providing an early cash-crop for farmers and by offering cheap, though hazardous, space for immigrants as return cargo on the timber boats. A staple oriented to the British market, it strengthened imperial ties directly, and also indirectly by provisioning the British Navy which constituted the military power necessary to hold a St. Lawrence polity distinct from the United States. Professor Lower followed his study of the square timber trade with a lengthy and still standard account of Canadian lumbering: *The North American Assault on the Canadian Forest: A History of the Lumber Trade between Canada and the United States.* It is particularly fitting that he should be represented in this part of the collection for he was an early collaborator with Innis in the second volume of the *Select Documents in Canadian Economic History.*

Every economic historian is part economist, part historian, and the trend of the twentieth century has been for the former increasingly to submerge the latter. So it is that the staple approach has been narrowed from a unifying theme for Canadian history into an export-led theory of economic growth; in this sense, Mackintosh's conception now overshadows Innis'. Two representative papers of this phenomenon are those by M. H. Watkins and Gordon Bertram which appeared simultaneously in 1963. Watkins' paper consists of a systematic statement of the staple approach as a theory of economic growth in terms of "linkages" – a concept popular in the literature of economic development – and argues strongly that the pace of Canadian economic growth is still heavily influenced by the ability to export staple products. Professor Bertram – proceeding more from "fact" to "theory" and thereby neatly complementing Watkins – argues that the growth of Canadian industry from 1870 to 1915 is best explained in terms of "the staple model." The data he presents on the evolution of Canadian manufacturing during the critical decades prior to the First World War would itself be reason enough for inclusion of this article; indeed, no separate section on manufacturing is to be found in this collection largely because Professor Bertram so neatly covers the topic.

While the staple approach is undeniably a distinctive Canadian contribution to political economy, it is sometimes alleged that the emphasis it has received has led to a neglect of other topics in Canadian economic history. Though there is some merit in this charge, it has not proved impossible to find excellent studies on a range of topics for inclusion in the collection. Part Two consists of two essays on Land Policy and Agriculture, both dealing with aspects of this topic that tend to receive minimal emphasis from staple theorists. In an article drawn from a larger work, Professor McGuigan shows how the relatively prosaic problem of administering land policy – in this case in the Eastern Townships of Quebec – became the basis for the emergence of the embryonic corporation. Like Bertram's essay, McGuigan's fulfills a dual function: it is a study both in land policy and in corporate history, with the latter area being one of the most neglected in Canadian historical studies. R. L. Jones, whose reputation as an historian of Canadian agriculture rests on the solid foundation of his classic *History of Agriculture in Ontario, 1663-1880*, writes here of developments in the already settled – possibly overpopulated – farmlands of Quebec. To the conventional explanation of Quebec's rural backwardness in terms of the deadweight of the seigneurial system, Jones posits the alternative possibility of a lack of markets, which, while obvious to the economist, is very often given insufficient attention by the historian.

Banking and Capital Formation – the subject matter of Part Three – begins with an excerpt from Bray Hammond's monumental study of *Banks and Politics in America from the Revolution to the Civil War*. A single chapter devoted to developments in British North America is printed here in full despite its length, for no editor could bring himself to tinker with Hammond's reason and rhetoric. Hammond, an American, does for Canadian banking what no Canadian historian has been able to do: he places banking, as cause and effect, squarely in the context of concurrent political and economic development. At the same time, he explicitly contrasts the free-wheeling American banking system, which had been transformed by the tidal wave of Jacksonian democracy, with the staid and "sound" Canadian system, untransformed and in the continuing grip of colonial oligarchies.[4] If Mr. Hammond errs, it is in his readiness to award

[4] For a general discussion contrasting the American "pattern of transformation" of the nineteenth century with the Canadian "pattern of persistence," see W. T. Easterbrook, "Long-Period Comparative Study: Some Historical Cases," *Journal of Economic History*, Dec. 1957, pp. 571-95.

the plaudits to the Canadian system; an economist would note that an over-emphasis on stability may preclude the risk-taking that seems necessary for rapid economic growth to take place along a broad front.

New areas, such as the producing of staples for outside markets, the absorbing of immigrants, the laying down of transport systems, and the opening of frontiers, have historically demonstrated large appetites for capital. Hammond deals with the institutional complex within which capital has been mobilized and allocated, that is, the supply side of the market. Professor Buckley, in a pioneering monograph from which an introduction summarizing his findings is reprinted here, provides not only quantitative estimates of capital formation, aggregate and sectoral, but does so within a framework that delineates the opportunities that induced the capital formation, that is, the demand side of the market. His major conclusion, succinctly stated in his opening sentence: "The production of wheat on the Canadian prairie provided the basic economic opportunity in the economic development of Canada from 1896 to 1930," is given a statistical dress that is all too rare in Canadian historical studies. But staple theorists, who may infer that Buckley has ably demonstrated their case, are warned to read his later provocative and iconoclastic critique of the role of the staple industries in the economic development of Canada.[5]

The most honoured of the themes of Canadian historiography is surely that the state has played an important role in promoting and shaping Canadian economic development. An historical hypothesis becomes a generally accepted truth at great risk to historical research, yet the quantity of writing on the State and Economic Life – Part Four of this collection – has kept up over the years and its quality has been gratifyingly high. Hugh G. J. Aitken, invited to contribute a paper to a general symposium on The State and Economic Life which was organized around a schematic framework, now mostly forgotten, put forward by Bert Hoselitz of Chicago, used the occasion to provide a lengthy and masterful summary of Canadian economic history, with enduring value, written around the unifying theme of what he labelled "defensive expansionism." The role of the state in Canada has been expansionist – pushing frontiers westward, bolstering staple exports, encouraging industrialization, promoting immigration and facilitating capital inflows – but, argues Aitken, expansionism has been mostly a policy of containment in the face of American expansionism. Aitken sticks to his historical last and draws no normative conclusions, but a question that might be put is whether a state that apparently interferes in economic affairs only when threatened externally may not have a too limited vision of the role of government.[6]

In the writings of economic historians the state too often seems to exist as a homogeneous decision-making entity disembodied of the real stuff of political conflict, while in the works of political historians the state too often seems to be the embodiment of great men who have miraculously transcended the basic conflicts of class and section and the exigencies of the business cycle. The brilliant article by Donald Creighton on "The Economic Background of the Rebellion of 1837" provides the needed antidotes. The abortive nature of the rebellion demonstrates not only what Creighton calls "the tragic inexpertness of a farming population which had little but its angry sense of injustice to sustain it" but also the iron fist within the velvet glove of Hammond's benign "colonial oligarchies." Also, in this essay, Creighton gives us glimpses of a unifying theme for Canadian history – the Canadian nation as the political manifestation of the economic magnetism of the St. Lawrence – that is more fully developed in his renowned *The Commercial Empire of the St. Lawrence*. The influence of Innis is clear in Creighton's emphasis on the dictates of geography and the requisites of staple production.[7]

The most famous (or infamous) of the activities of the Canadian government designed to influence economic development is, of course, the protective tariff of 1879 which passes under the name of the National Policy. The literature thereon is large and continues to grow, but no one has said so much on this topic in such a short space as the late Vernon Fowke of Saskatchewan. Two major themes are argued: firstly, the National

---

[6] This issue is discussed in M. H. Watkins, "The 'American System' and Canada's National Policy," a paper presented to the Canadian Association for American Studies, Montreal, October 1966 (forthcoming in *Bulletin* of the C.A.A.S.).

[7] Creighton, as colleague and friend, wrote a perceptive memoir of Innis. See Donald Creighton, *Harold Adams Innis, Portrait of a Scholar* (Toronto, 1957).

Policy should be understood to be not only the protective tariff but the total set of policies pursued by the national government in the interests of promoting economic development; secondly, the first National Policy – of tariffs, railway subsidies, cheap land and an open-door to immigrants – was spent by 1930 and has been replaced, albeit haphazardly, by a second "national policy" centred on public welfare, agriculture, and monetary management. These themes were subsequently elaborated at greater length by Fowke, with particular emphasis on wheat marketing, in *The National Policy and the Wheat Economy*. Fowke's plea for a broader conception of "national policy" has now won general acceptance, but some would argue that he was too kind to Ottawa when he wrote of a discernible "second national policy."

W. T. Easterbrook's comprehensive bibliographical essay on Canadian economic history, originally prepared in 1959, completes the collection. It has been revised by the editors to incorporate significant books and articles published on the subject since that time.

To edit is necessarily to collect, to classify and to rationalize. The inevitable risk is thereby to atrophy the subject being edited, or, at least, to leave the impression with the unwary reader that all is well, that the great books and essays have all been penned. This is most decidedly not the case in Canadian economic history. We hope that this collection will stimulate the reader not only to read more of the same (as editors always say) but to think about new topics that await new economic historians. For example: an Innisian approach to the new staples of this century; an historically-informed application of econometric techniques to a range of controversies in Canadian historiography, from the wisdom of the railway subsidies to the causes of persistent poverty; volumes of good business history; studies of the institutional character of the Canadian economy, from the fur trade to the automobile industry; imaginative comparisons of the economic development of Canada with other countries; probing studies of the Canadian élite; regional and urban studies which consciously eschew a national framework in the interests of a larger perspective; the political economy of Canadian education; and invention versus imitation in Canadian technological history. The interested reader might begin by lengthening this list.

As far as possible, essays and chapters from books included in this collection have been reproduced in their entirety – including footnotes. A self-contained portion of Professor Bertram's essay, dealing with W. W. Rostow's stages of economic growth, has been omitted with the consent of the author. This deletion, together with some other minor ones, has been indicated by ellipses.

W. T. EASTERBROOK
Dar-es-Salaam, Tanzania

M. H. WATKINS
Toronto, Ontario

November 1966

PART ONE

THE STAPLE APPROACH

Economic Factors in Canadian History

W. A. MACKINTOSH

There will be few dissenters from the position that there is
need that more attention should be devoted to the geographic
and economic factors in Canadian history, and that greater
place should be given to the continental aspects of Canadian
history. Up to the present the constitutional bias has been strong,
and for the obvious reason that the most recent and in many
ways the most significant chapter of British constitutional history has been written in Canada. The familiar school-book
periodization of the history of British North America in terms
of succeeding instruments of government is sufficient illustration
of this bias of the British constitutionalist. The artless query of
a high school pupil, "Was everybody a member of parliament
then?" indicates the false picture which has been too frequently

Source: W. A. Mackintosh, "Economic Factors in Canadian History,"
The Canadian Historical Review, Vol. IV, No. 1, March 1923, pp. 12-
25. Reprinted by permission of the University of Toronto Press.
In a footnote to the original publication of this essay in 1923 Dr.
Mackintosh wrote: "The present article contains the substance of two
lectures in Canadian ecomonic history given at the School of Historical
Research at Ottawa during the summer of 1922. The thesis is presented
as one which the writer thinks susceptible of proof, but which cannot
be taken as proved until further research has established it on a sound
basis. Much elaboration and obvious illustration have been omitted in
order that the argument might be presented within reasonable com-
pass. As originally given, the lectures purported to show the relation
of economic and geographic factors to general history, and to suggest
the great need for detailed research in many phases of Canadian
economic history.

"The point of view of the article has been suggested by the writings
of Professor F. J. Turner and the late Professor G. S. Callender."

drawn. It is true that of late years more attention has been given to the economic and geographic factors, but in many cases the chapters on constitutional development have not been in the least influenced by the addenda on "social and economic progress," or by the introduction on "physical characteristics." Constitutional crises lose none of their great importance when viewed as the periodic results of changing conditions, and of the needs and political prepossessions of various elements of the population. History is emphatically not "past politics"; it is the life of yesterday in the present.

The simplest features of American geography are of primary importance in understanding the developing life of the people of this continent. The initial fact to be noted is that for several reasons, structural and climatic, North America faces Europe. That is to say, by far the greater part of this continent is most easily accessible from the Atlantic coast. This has facilitated, though not accounted for, the success of European rather than Asiatic colonization. The evolution of energetic, industrious, forthfaring peoples under the peculiarly favourable climatic conditions of northwestern Europe is the most important element in that success. If then we start with the fact of the European colonization of the Atlantic coast, the structure of American barriers, plains, and waterways takes on a special significance. That structure shaped the course of westward progress; it facilitated or hindered the connection of the frontier with the older settlements and with Europe; it selected to some extent its own settlers; and together with other factors it determined the trend of industrial production.

Structurally, North America, in broad terms, is made up of narrow coastal plains on the Atlantic and the Pacific, the old glaciated Laurentian plateau around Hudson Bay, and a great Central Plain from the Appalachians to the Rockies, with no significant uplift barrier from the Gulf of Mexico to the mouth of the Mackenzie. The presence of the Appalachian barrier to westward movements of population and commerce has given premier importance to the existing gaps in that barrier, of which two, the Mohawk and the St. Lawrence valleys, outrival all others. The partial gaps of Pennsylvania, the Cumberland, and the southwesterly valley of the Shenandoah have all played important parts in American history; but New York today is witness to the significance of the Mohawk valley, as is Chicago to that of the St. Lawrence. When the Dutch and French controlled both gateways to the interior, English colonies built solid communities in the coastal and piedmont regions. Meanwhile the French followed the westward path of the St. Lawrence to discover the basic fact of modern Chicago, viz., that the low watershed causes the St. Lawrence there to pivot on the Mississippi, and on that fact France built a grandiose policy not of settlement but of empire: a policy which failed because of the weakness of the initial settlements.

When the forerunners of British settlement began to enter the central valley and speculative ventures such as that of the Ohio Company about 1745 were set on foot, France and Britain inevitably clashed. They clashed on the upper tributaries of the Ohio where France was busily constructing a line of forts to block British progress into the interior. In later years the war took a European name, the Seven Years' War. Hostilities, however, began earlier in America; they had a distinct American objective, and that objective was not Canada – which was scarcely preferable to Guadeloupe – but the Mississippi valley.

From about 1763 on, the rapidly increasing population of the old colonies overflowed into the Mississippi valley. New England, spreading north and west, entered the valley of the St. Lawrence in the Green Mountain state; and because of its geographical relation to Canada, Vermont did not enter the Union until 1791, ignored the Non-intercourse Act, and was an unwilling and halfhearted partner in the War of 1812. New York and Pennsylvania were already expanding along the Mohawk and the upper Ohio valleys and the men of Virginia occupied the valleys of Tennessee and Kentucky. New problems brought new movements, and the "men of the Western waters" became a significant element in American legislatures.

Later, and with different setting, the same movement into the interior took place in Canada. The American Revolution, the causes of which were not unconnected with the occupation of the west, turned part of the westward movement to the Loyalist settlements of the St. Lawrence valley. At the same time, and later, British immigration augmented the increasing population of the western frontier of Canada. That old West of Canada differed from the settlements of Lower Canada not only in race and religion but in the pioneer problems which it had to face.

In those brilliant introductions to his *Readings in the Eco-*

nomic History of the United States, the late Professor Callender set forth the basis of colonial economy. "Progress does not take place unless the colony possesses markets, where it can dispose of its staple products. The history of modern colonization does not show a single case where a settled country has enjoyed any considerable economic prosperity, or made notable social progress without a flourishing commerce with other communities." The prime requisite of colonial prosperity is the colonial staple. Other factors connected with the staple industry may turn it to advantage or disadvantage, but the staple in itself is the basis of prosperity. The colonies of North America were fortunate in being capable of producing staples which for the most part found ready markets in Europe. Virginia and the other southern colonies found in tobacco, indigo, naval stores, and other products excellent colonial staples, on which the prosperity of the South and southern culture were based. In the north, French furs found ready sale, but the conditions of the industry brought few advantages to the settlement. New England and the Middle Colonies were less favourably endowed. Their products were not dissimilar to those of Europe, and the markets were small and uncertain. Hence the importance to them of the development of the West Indian trade, of which the trade in "rum and niggers" was an important part but by no means the whole, and which brought prosperity to the Boston of commerce and shipping before manufacturing New England had arisen. Nothing is more typical of colonial development than the restless, unceasing search for staples which would permit the pioneer community to come into close contact with the commercial world and leave behind the disabilities of a pioneer existence. Contemporary records abound with the tales of the projects of the faddist and propagandist of new staples, and much money and energy was spent on experiments.

In the tidewater settlements of the British colonies the problem, though not without difficulty, was fairly solved because transport was cheap and Europe and the West Indies comparatively near. In Lower Canada, part of the population was lured by the prizes of the fur trade to the unsettled, vagabond life of the woods, which combined with missionary zeal to spread French names from Acadia to New Orleans and the Mackenzie. The other part, vainly endeavouring to produce an agricultural staple, took on more and more the permanent characteristics of a pioneer community which has failed to rise beyond the stage of primitive diversified agriculture, a self-sufficient, conservative peasantry.

As successive waves of population moved into the Upper St. Lawrence and Mississippi valleys the problem intensified.[1] The Appalachian barrier intervened between the frontier and tidewater, and transportation became a dominant factor in American trade. Not only, however, did the eastern barrier of Appalachia confront the pioneer of the central valley with a new problem, but the possible products of the western country were limited. In spite of innumerable experiments they did not extend beyond grain and timber products, both durable enough but bulky, ill-adapted to the transportation of that day, and with little possibility of becoming profitable staples in any way comparable to southern tobacco or cotton until phenomenal changes had been made in means of transportation. Much might be written of the attempts to establish other staples such as hemp in Lower Canada, or to concentrate the bulk of native products to transportable proportions. The potash trade, partially successful, but handicapped by the smallness of the market, the domestic whiskey manufacturing of Kentucky, still surviving in the hill districts, and the industry which gave to Cincinnati its early nickname of Porkopolis, were all attempts to reduce the bulky products of the Central Valley to transportable size and to establish the greatly-to-be-desired staple.

These obvious facts of the work-a-day colonial world were the conditions upon which colonial policy operated. We have already noted the geographical unity of the two great valleys of the continent and the influence which that unity has had on the history of Canada and of the United States. Up to 1763 the St. Lawrence and Mississippi were linked politically. Marquette and La Salle discovered the easy portages between the river basins and the great river beyond. The Seven Years' War was a war for the central valley which the French had explored, but which the British colonists were ready to occupy. After the conquest, when the Guadeloupe-Canada controversy had been finally decided, the valley was not broken but united with the coast settlements. From 1763 to the Revolutionary War, North America was a free trade area, and the exploitation of it one of

[1] Readers familiar with F. J. Turner's *Rise of the New West* will recognize the writer's indebtedness to it.

the most pressing questions. Disputes between home authorities and the colonies as to the regulation of that exploitation, as shown in the attitude of Shelburne and his successors, in prohibiting settlement west of the Alleghanies in 1763, was one, although only one, of the causes of the American Revolution. With the concession of independence by Great Britain and the establishment of the Mississippi as the western boundary of the United States, the St. Lawrence and Mississippi were divided, and North America fell apart into the protected regions which remained until the Reciprocity Treaty of 1854 partially restored free trade.

This period from 1783 to 1854 (limits more significant than the usual 1791 to 1840) embraces the great age of westward expansion. Though the days of seafaring New Englanders and Nova Scotians were not yet gone, America turned her back on the Atlantic and entered the era of internal expansion. In that expansion, two factors are of prime significance: first, the barriers to westward advance; and second, the barriers making difficult the continued communication with the older settlements. From the first of these the United States in this period was singularly free. Once through the Appalachian barrier the great plain of the Mississippi gave an open road to the Rockies. Formidable obstacles in the shape of dense forests there were indeed until the open prairie was reached, but no great barrier. To the westward, Canadian settlements in the St. Lawrence valley met the impassable barrier of the Laurentian highlands, bordering the Upper Lakes on the north so closely that for half a century progress into the easily settled prairie region beyond was effectually blocked. The immediate consequences of handing over to the United States the Upper Mississippi valley, to which access from the St. Lawrence was easy, were to be seen in the bitter struggles of the fur trade, the vain attempts of Canadian traders to retain the western forts at the time of Jay's Treaty, and the losing fight of the singularly able North West Company with their better personnel of French and Scottish traders against the exclusion policy of John Jacob Astor to the south and the ruthless competition of the Hudson's Bay Company to the north. In 1816 the Exclusion bill was passed, and the company which depended for its existence on the connection of the St. Lawrence with the west, was "submerged" (as one of the partners said) in the Hudson's Bay Company in 1821.

In her communication with the old settlements Canada was more fortunate. The St. Lawrence valley was a line of communication only partially open to the United States. The good fortune was, however, not unmixed. The St. Lawrence linked the frontier of the west, not with expanding, well-developed communities such as the Atlantic states, but with a community whose commerce depended entirely on the interior and which was surrounded by a stable, conservative population, to a large extent self-sustaining, with laws and customs non-commercial, and giving rise to little commerce. There was for the St. Lawrence no manufacturing New England and no cotton-growing South. Further, though the St. Lawrence, the Ottawa, the Trent, and other tributary valleys gave an open road to the voyageur, the fur trader, or even the incoming settler, the way was by no means open for the return traffic of the timber and grain products of the western settlements.

For a period of half a century the scattered Canadian settlements entered into strenuous competition with the other routes from the interior to the seaboard. The Potomac Company, the Pennsylvania route, and the phenomenally successful Erie Canal were met by the stupendous efforts of the St. Lawrence canal system. The Erie had the great advantage of being complete before the British had grasped the problem, and when they were still occupied with the commercially useless Rideau. Most significant of all, the Erie was not a separate system, but a means of linking the upper St. Lawrence system with tidewater at New York. The existing stage communications had made the Albany route familiar to Upper Canadians, and the early opening of the Erie gave to New York a quantity of traffic which Montreal could not hope to equal for many years; and ocean freight rates to and from New York long reflected the better chances of getting both out-going and in-going cargoes.

In Canada of the first half of the nineteenth century we have a country in which population was moving westward to occupy the Upper St. Lawrence and Lower Lake regions at the same time as, at a much more rapid rate, the population of the United States was moving in great waves into the contiguous Mississippi valley. The people of both of these regions, though not of identical origin and with varied equipment for living, faced the same problem, confronted the same deficiency for colonial prosperity, the lack of a compact, saleable, transportable staple. In the case of the United States, however, the early building of the Erie Canal, the effective connection of the Mississippi with the cotton-growing south, and the much greater and more prosperous coast settlements gave a value to grain and timber products not found in Canada. The Canadian settlements in consequence lacked the prosperity which Durham and other observers noted in neighbouring parts of the United States. Not only, then, was Canadian development frustrated geographically at the northwest barrier of the Laurentian plateau, but economic and geographic facts constituted a frustration in the east.

These were the conditions with which commercial policy had to deal. In the United States the producers of bulky products in the upper central valley developed views of commercial policy different from those of the cotton planter of the South with a staple not only readily transported, but with a European market undergoing phenomenal expansion. The course of the tariff history of the United States illustrates the changing policies which these conditions occasioned. Those conditions made the home market argument a powerful one in the middle and western states, while the commercial elements of New England and the planters of the South favoured free trade. It was this growing divergence in economic characteristics which formed the basis for the struggle between North and South whether the specific occasion might be the tariff or the extension of slavery. The divergence was one of conditions rather than of people, though in succeeding generations conditions produced diverging types of people also. Yet families like that of Henry Clay passed from the Carolinas to Kentucky. The Carolinian by descent becomes "Harry of the West" in a western environment. The free-trader by inheritance becomes a protectionist when confronted with a western problem.

The commercial policy of Canada was part of the British Colonial System. It became so in 1763, and after 1783 the system was more carefully applied. The old system, based on a theory of sub-tropical colonial staples, still continued, as seen in the projects in Canada for the growing of hemp and the regulation of the cutting of ships' timber. In addition, however, a newer mercantilism, directed towards cheap food and materials, was finding a limited expression, and the need for building a stable settlement was also apparent. One aspect of British policy is to be found in the attempt to substitute Canada for

New England and the Middle Colonies in the West Indian trade. Another is seen in the encouragement offered by preferential duties on Canadian timber and grain. Both of these policies just failed of success.

Partly because of ill-adjustment of bounties and duties to specific conditions in the West Indian trade, as shown by the numerous complaints from Quebec merchants, and partly because inertia made it difficult to substitute satisfactory trade connections with Canada for the familiar New England trade, the West Indian trade did not take strong root in Canada, though it was somewhat more successful in the Maritime Provinces. The West Indian market for Canada was uncertain and difficult of access. Canadian production responded only slightly to a varying stimulus. In turn, effect became cause, and Canadian grain and lumber, uncertain and variable in supply, was unable to support the irregular West Indian demands. The results were bitter complaints from both colonies. The prohibition of trade with the United States endangered the supplies of the British West Indies and put them at a disadvantage with the other islands depending on United States trade. The advantages of steady supply, of nearness, and of familiarity with the trade were clearly with the New England and the Middle States. When trade relations between the United States and the West Indies were broken off, as between 1826 and 1832, Canadian trade boomed and the western settlements flourished. With, however, the acceptance by Jackson of Huskisson's proposals, and the resumption of trade, the wave of prosperity subsided, and Canada once more strove with the task of Sisyphus.

Less need be said in regard to the failure of the preferential policy toward grain and timber. Dr. Shortt's *Imperial Preferential Trade* and his articles in *Canada and Its Provinces* have made that failure abundantly clear. Before 1825, the complete prohibition of colonial grain (when the price was below 67 shillings) made trade spasmodic and ill-organized. The setting of a fixed duty on colonial grain, and later the adoption of the sliding scale, made matters better, but the direct trade in grain was not great. During the forties, the point of interest was not so much Canadian grain as it was American grain making use of the newly built St. Lawrence canals and obtaining the advantage of the Canadian preference. Montreal interests favoured the free export of American grain through Canada after paying the

Canadian duty. Sir Robert Peel's much-quoted words about Canada being an "integral part of the Empire" were repeated by the Montreal dealers to support their policy; and while the Canada Corn Law did not admit American grain shipped by the St. Lawrence route free, yet flour ground from that grain was freely admitted. This Act, which legalized much that had been carried on extra-legally, gave a fillip to the St. Lawrence flour industry; and the repeal of all duties on wheat and flour some years later was a staggering blow to these interests, since the trade depended on this artificial stimulation. The economic and geographic union of the upper St. Lawrence waterway and the opening grain country of the American west was obvious, but, as Montrealers pointed out, the lower outward rates from New York more than counterbalanced the higher rates from the interior to New York.

The withdrawal of the preferences brought a similar and worse collapse in the timber trade, which had been considerably stimulated by the protection offered, although here too the trade was spasmodic and irregular. Further, the timber trade had some of the peculiarities of the fur trade in its opposition to homemaking and its absentee ownership, and brought some of the same unfortunate results to the regions affected.

From one point of view the preference system was merely a continuation of imperial commercial policy. From the point of view of western Canada, however, it was an attempt to overcome the natural obstacles of the bulky products of the St. Lawrence valley and assure them a European market. More effective than the preference toward this end were the substantially complete St. Lawrence canals. The St. Lawrence lacked some of the advantages of the Erie. The volume of traffic was small and the outward rates from Montreal relatively high. Any considerable stimulus might have brought success, but economic events and conditions combined in the depressing years of the late forties to snatch success away. In 1850 British commercial policy had just failed to attain its object.

As the population of the United States spread across the Mississippi valley to possess it, new problems and new political forces arose in American history. The upper valley faced the same problem of the bulky products which confronted Western Canada. Thanks to the larger population, the rise of manufacturing in New England, the opening of the Erie Canal, the expansion of the cotton staple in the South, and the access to the south by the Mississippi, the United States solved its problem, though not without difficulty. Out of those difficulties in that period arose typical western forces. The adoption of protection, the opposition to "the money power" and the United States banks, the leaning toward "soft" money, and the pressure for internal improvements came out of western conditions of life. Triumphant pioneering democracy rose to its height in the election of Andrew Jackson, important less for himself than for the forces in American life which he represented. Crudities and lack of culture in that period there were, enough to excite the mirth of Goldwin Smith, but strength and national unity were also there. Confronted with nullification in Carolina and the extension of slavery in Kansas, those who stated and enforced the national position, were men of the west and the Mississippi valley, Jackson and Lincoln.

One looks in vain in Canadian history in the first half of the nineteenth century for any such triumphant movement of western forces. In the opposition to the Bank of Upper Canada, the division between the West and commercial Montreal, the disputes over the clergy reserves, and the land policies of the Family Compact, similar situations brought similar reactions, but there was no effective movement. An easy explanation for this difference is the divergence between Canadian and United States "political nature." The Canadian, it is said, has never in politics gone to the extremes of his southern neighbour, nor has he expressed himself so much in popular movements. There is truth in the statement, but the difference is not accounted for. The pioneers of the American and of the Canadian west came from the same sources – the British colonies. It could scarcely be argued that the addition of Scottish elements represented by men such as Gourlay and Mackenzie added soberness to political life. Nor yet did English or Irish immigration bring steadier policies. There was no Jacksonian democracy and no Jackson in Canada because up to 1850 western development in Canada was doubly frustrated, at the east by the difficulties of the St. Lawrence route, and the European market for bulky staples, and at the west by the impassable barrier of the Laurentian highlands. Important as were the constitutional issues of 1837, particularly in the minds of argumentative Scotsmen, there was also a basis of economic failure. Not the least of the distinctions of Durham and Sydenham is that they saw this. Constitutionally, Sydenham was wrong, for he knew little about government. Economically he was right, for he knew much about business. When failure became more apparent in 1849, the Annexation Manifesto was a gesture of despair on the part of the most articulate portion of a frustrated colony.

The middle of the century brought a new era in Canadian history. The Lord Elgin who recognized the necessity of granting responsible government freely was no greater statesman than the Lord Elgin (pupil of the singularly able Hincks) who saw a partial relief from frustration in the Reciprocity Treaty of 1854. What the result of that treaty would have been had outside events been different it is difficult to say. Combined with the improvement of land and water transportation, and the substantial rise in grain prices resulting from the Crimean War, the larger local market, which the treaty gave, brought relief to the blocked colony. For more than half a century Western Canada had striven to reach the goal of colonial existence, the production of a staple export commodity. With this period the country passed from a stage of primitive diversified agriculture to the one-crop stage, the period (in the phrase of the late Mr. C. C. James) "when wheat was king." Though not without its variations that period lasted until the end of the Civil War and the repudiation of the Reciprocity Treaty. The various phases of that period of abounding prosperity, with its railway politics, bank expansion, and incidental protection, are sufficiently well known. Economically, Canada was passing out of the colonial stage.

It would be dangerous to attempt to trace the direct political effects of these conditions. Constitutional difficulties, the supposed menace of an American army, the position of Quebec, and personalities were all solid and significant factors in the coming of Confederation. It is not unfair to say, however, that the dynamic factor which necessitated a constitutional readjustment was the expansion of Canada West in the fifteen years previous. Prosperity and expansion underlay "Representation by Population." The St. Lawrence valley, the Grand Trunk Railway, the grain trade were uniting factors in Canada. The expanding West demanded proportionate weight in a *national* government. Differences of race and of geography necessitated *federal* government.

This period of expansion saw the substantial breaking of the eastern frustration of Canadian development. True, dark days in the seventies and later followed, but once lifted from the frontier stage, the community was changed. The Ontario which turned to cheese, fruit-growing, and small manufacture during the years of trial was a different community from that which had depended on the uncertain support of the British preference fifty years before.

There remained at Confederation the problem of the West. The Laurentian barrier, making impossible the commercial connection of the St. Lawrence with the north central valley, continued to be the solid dominating fact of Canadian development. There could be no Canadian Chicago because there was no meeting of waterway and prairie to the north of the lakes. Grand Portage at the head of Lake Superior, with its well-nigh impassable trail to Winnipeg, was the sorry northern counterpart of Chicago.

In the last half of the nineteenth century, as from the beginning, Canadians found the easiest field of westward expansion in the Upper Mississippi valley. Fifty years before they had hoped that the necessity of St. Lawrence navigation would bring the population of the American west into a working union with Canada. Great as was the effort of the St. Lawrence canals, it failed to accomplish all that was expected. The Upper Mississippi valley was preempted irrevocably by the United States. After the Civil War there could be no question of that. In the years that followed it seemed that the maxim of Henry Tudor would be justified, and that the greater would draw the less. After 1870, the cream of the immigrant and native population was drawn off to the easily settled prairie regions of the Upper Mississippi. The New West of the Canadians was the American North West. The Canadian frontier was the American frontier. In that period all the vitality which a moving frontier absorbs from a people, and gives back again, was lost to the communities of Canada. The export of men was draining the very life-blood of Ontario rural settlements. Canadian development was once more thwarted by geography.

It is this western frustration of Canadian development that furnishes the background for the construction of the Canadian Pacific Railway, and for the "transcontinentalism" of present-day Canadian transportation. As first put forward, the Canadian

Pacific project was an audacious, even foolhardy attempt to bridge the gap between Ontario and British Columbia; and from that point of view the gloomy prophecies that the road would not pay for its axle-grease were "safe and sane" judgments. Though the construction of the railway was a part of a contract with British Columbia, the justification of the railway, and ultimately its salvation, was the north central plain of the prairies. That portion of the railway which links Winnipeg with Lake Superior was and is the most essential part of Canada's transportation system. It gave the St. Lawrence valley access to a country capable of rapid expansion. Other parts of the railway system were important and essential, but none has had the significance of that section which overcomes the Laurentian barrier between the Great Lakes and the prairies. With the building of the Canadian Pacific and its coming to effectiveness in the nineties, just when forces external to Canada were bringing grain prices to higher levels, the western barrier was substantially overcome, and a period of phenomenal expansion set in. Once more a Canadian region by reason of higher prices for grain and improved transportation facilities overcame its physical barriers and entered a one-crop stage of agriculture, the stage of the world staple and of prosperity.

That period of expansion from about 1900 to 1913 was not only a period of growing western settlement, but a time of solid progress in almost all parts of the Dominion. It is as significant for the eastern manufacturer and the Northern Ontario miner as for the western homesteader. Canada had room for expansion within her borders. A staple was exported to world markets; and, as southern cotton started the wheels of American industry and commerce in the nineteenth century, western wheat has permitted the initial step of the Canadian advance in the twentieth. It was only one commodity, and there were many; but it was the basis of that period of prosperity. The world staple primed the pump of Canadian industry.

To Canadians of the present generation political writings of fifty years ago read strangely. Annexation, commercial union, Zollverein, Canada First, Imperial Federation, these have no place in contemporary politics. We are less sensitive on these points. It is difficult to realize that Canadians ever believed in them. The difference is not in Canadians. It is in the economic background. When frustration of Canadian progress was overcome, and a period of expansion resulted, Canadian nationality was assured, and policies which cast doubt upon that nationality fell away. For the first time in Canadian history, powerful and effective western forces made themselves felt. For the first time western problems became capable of solution. The end is not yet; for the West still struggles in time of world-depression with a bulky staple and a long transportation haul. But improvements in transportation have made problems not insoluble. A new factor has arisen in the existence of a manufacturing East. Another is developing in the opening of the Pacific trade; and still another, of unknown significance, will come into play as the forest frontier of the north is attacked in earnest.

Canada is a nation created in defiance of geography, and yet the geographic and economic factors have had a large place in shaping her history. It is not contended that these are the only factors. Others have been often and adequately dealt with. But unless one is to consider Canada merely as a collection of racial types and not as a nation, the basic facts of economic and historical geography can never be ignored. In Canadian history as it is written, there is much of the romance of the individual, sometimes significant and sometimes not. It behooves present-day historians to perceive the romance of a nation in the story of a people facing the prosaic obstacles of a colonial existence, developing national traits, and winning through to nationhood.

The Importance of Staple Products

H. A. INNIS

Fundamentally the civilization of North America is the civilization of Europe and the interest of this volume is primarily in the effects of a vast new land area on European civilization. The opening of a new continent distant from Europe has been responsible for the stress placed by modern students on the dissimilar features of what has been regarded as two separate civilizations. On the other hand communication and transportation facilities have always persisted between the two continents since the settlement of North America by Europeans, and have been subject to constant improvement.

Peoples who have become accustomed to the cultural traits of their civilization – what Mr. Graham Wallas calls the social heritage – on which they subsist, find it difficult to work out new cultural traits suitable to a new environment. The high death rate of the population of the earliest European settlements is evidence to that effect. The survivors live through borrowing cultural traits of peoples who have already worked out a civilization suitable to the new environment as in the case of the Indians of North America, through adapting their own cultural traits to the new environment, and through heavy material borrowing from the peoples of the old land. The process of adaptation is extremely painful in any case but the maintenance of cultural traits to which they have been accustomed is of primary importance. A sudden change of cultural traits can be made only with great difficulty and with the disappearance of many of the peoples concerned. Depreciation of the social heritage is serious.

The methods by which the cultural traits of a civilization may persist with the least possible depreciation involve an

Source: H. A. Innis, *The Fur Trade in Canada: An Introduction to Canadian Economic History*, Revised edition (First edition 1930) Toronto: University of Toronto Press, 1956, pp. 383-386. Reprinted by permission of the publishers.

appreciable dependence on the peoples of the homeland. The migrant is not in a position immediately to supply all his needs and to maintain the same standard of living as that to which he has been accustomed, even with the assistance of Indians, an extremely fertile imagination, and a benevolent Providence such as would serve Robinson Crusoe or the Swiss Family Robinson on a tropical island. If those needs are to be supplied he will be forced to rely on goods which are obtainable from the mother country.

These goods were obtained from the homeland by direct transportation as in the movement of settlers' effects and household goods, involving no direct transfer of ownership, or through gifts and missionary supplies, but the most important device was trade. Goods were produced as rapidly as possible to be sold at the most advantageous price in the home market in order to purchase other goods essential to the maintenance and improvement of the current standard of living. In other words these goods supplied by the home country enabled the migrant to maintain his standard of living and to make his adjustments to the new environment without serious loss.

The migrant was consequently in search of goods which could be carried over long distances by small and expensive sailboats and which were in such demand in the home country as to yield the largest profit. These goods were essentially those in demand for the manufacture of luxuries, or goods which were not produced, or produced to a slight extent, in the home country as in the case of gold and of furs and fish. The latter was in some sense a luxury under the primitive conditions of agriculture in Europe and the demands of Catholic peoples. The importance of metropolitan centres in which luxury goods were in most demand was crucial to the development of colonial North America. In these centres goods were manufactured for the consumption of colonials and in these centres goods produced in the colonies were sold at the highest price. The number of goods produced in a north temperate climate in an area dominated by Pre-Cambrian formations, to be obtained with little difficulty in sufficient quantity and disposed of satisfactorily in the home market under prevailing transport conditions, was limited.

The most promising source of early trade was found in the abundance of fish, especially cod, to be caught off the Grand

Banks of Newfoundland and in the territory adjacent to the Gulf of St. Lawrence. The abundance of cod led the peoples concerned to direct all their available energy to the prosecution of the fishing industry which developed extensively. In the interior, trade with the Indians offered the largest returns in the commodity which was available on a large scale and which yielded substantial profits, namely furs and especially beaver. With the disappearance of beaver in more accessible territory, lumber became the product which brought the largest returns. In British Columbia gold became the product following the fur trade but eventually lumber and fish came into prominence. The lumber industry has been supplemented by the development of the pulp and paper industry with its chief reliance on spruce. Agricultural products – as in the case of wheat – and later minerals – gold, nickel, and other metals – have followed the inroads of machine industry.

The economic history of Canada has been dominated by the discrepancy between the centre and the margin of western civilization. Energy has been directed toward the exploitation of staple products and the tendency has been cumulative. The raw material supplied to the mother country stimulated manufactures of the finished product and also of the products which were in demand in the colony. Large-scale production of raw materials was encouraged by improvement of technique of production, of marketing, and of transport as well as by improvement in the manufacture of the finished product. As a consequence, energy in the colony was drawn into the production of the staple commodity both directly and indirectly. Population was involved directly in the production of the staple and indirectly in the production of facilities promoting production. Agriculture, industry, transportation, trade, finance, and governmental activities tend to become subordinate to the production of the staple for a more highly specialized manufacturing community. These general tendencies may be strengthened by governmental policy as in the mercantile system but the importance of these policies varies in particular industries. Canada remained British in spite of free trade and chiefly because she continued as an exporter of staples to a progressively industrialized mother country.

The general tendencies in the industrial areas of western civilization, especially in the United States and Great Britain, have had a pronounced effect on Canada's export of staples. In these areas machine industry spread with rapidity through the accessibility of the all-year-round ocean ports and the existence of ample supplies of coal and iron. In Great Britain the nineteenth century was characterized by increasing industrialization[1] with greater dependence on the staple products of new countries for raw material and on the population of these countries for a market. Lumber, wheat, cotton, wool, and meat may be cited as examples of staple imports. In the United States[2] the Civil War and railroad construction gave a direct stimulus to the iron and steel industry and hastened industrial and capitalistic growth. These two areas began to draw increasingly on outside areas for staples and even continental United States has found it necessary with the disappearance of free land, the decline of natural resources, and the demand for new industrial materials, notably rubber, to rely on outside areas as shown in her imperialistic policy of the twentieth century. Canada has participated in the industrial growth of the United States, becoming the gateway of that country to the markets of the British Empire. She has continued, however, chiefly as a producer of staples for the industrial centres of the United States even more than of Great Britain making her own contribution to the industrial revolution of North America and Europe and being in turn tremendously influenced thereby.

[1] C. R. Fay, *Great Britain: An Economic and Social Survey from Adam Smith to the Present Day.*
[2] See Chas. A. and Mary R. Beard, *The Rise of American Civilization.*

The Fur Trade

H. A. INNIS

The history of the fur trade in North America has been shown as a retreat in the face of settlement. The strategic campaigns in that retreat include the conquest of New France, the Quebec Act of 1774, the American Revolution, the Jay Treaty of 1794, the amalgamation of 1821, the Oregon Treaty of 1846, and the Rupert's Land Act of 1869. The struggle continues in the newly settled areas of the Dominion. The trade has been conducted by large organizations from the artificial and natural monopolies of New France to the North West Company and the Hudson's Bay Company which still occupies an important position. It has depended on the manufactures of Europe and the more efficient manufactures and cheaper transportation of England. Control of the fur trade was an index of world importance from the standpoint of efficient manufactures, control of markets, and consumption of luxuries. The shift from Paris to London of the fur trade was significant of the industrial growth of France and England – just as possession of Canada after the American Revolution was significant of the industrial limitations of the United States. The demands of the Indians for cheaper and greater quantities of goods were determining factors in the destiny of the northern half of North America.

The crises which disturbed the history of the fur trade were determined finally by various important factors including the geographic background and the industrial efficiency of England. These long-run factors were obscured by a complexity of causes which centred about each crisis. In the first half of the seventeenth century the Indian trading organization was essential to the trade. In the latter part of the century the French trading organization to the interior became more effective and the

Source: H. A. Innis, *The Fur Trade in Canada: An Introduction to Canadian Economic History*, Revised Edition (First edition 1930). Toronto: University of Toronto Press, 1956, pp. 386-392. Reprinted by permission of the publishers.

market became flooded with furs. Finally the geographic limits of the trade with the canoe were reached with the extension of the trade to the Saskatchewan in the first half of the eighteenth century. In the second half of the century transport became more efficient with the development of lake transport supplementary to the canoe and the trade was extended with increased capital resources and efficient business organization to the Pacific. With continued decline in the supply of beaver, the development of a more efficient transport and of a more elastic business organization from Hudson Bay, amalgamation became inevitable and the canoe disappeared as the dominant form of transport in the fur trade. Dependence on the York boat rather than the canoe was symbolic of the increasing importance of capitalism. After the amalgamation improved transport facilities from the south led to the disappearance of monopoly control in 1869 and to the reign of competition which has become increasingly severe since that date. The beaver became less important after the amalgamation and the trade more dependent on other varieties of furs. Supply decreased less rapidly and in spite of competition the trade continued on a more permanent basis. Severe fluctuations were the result, throughout the period, of the discoveries of new territory and new Indians but especially of wars. These fluctuations were more serious in the earlier period of the French régime and occasioned serious results for the colony and the mother country. They became less serious after the Conquest and were less disastrous to the mother country. With the disappearance of these fluctuations, business organization became more efficient. But in the long run improved transport combined with geographic advantages reigned supreme. It was significant, however, that business organization was of vital importance to the trade and, combined with geographic advantages, maintained a strong position. This combination favoured the growth of capitalism which became conspicuous in the later days of the North West Company and in the succeeding Hudson's Bay Company especially after 1869.

The early history of the fur trade is essentially a history of the trade in beaver fur. The beaver was found in large numbers throughout the northern half of North America. The better grades of fur came from the more northerly forested regions of North America and were obtained during the winter season when the fur was prime. A vast north temperate land area with a pronounced seasonal climate was a prerequisite to an extensive development of the trade. The animal was not highly reproductive and it was not a migrant. Its destruction in any locality necessitated the movement of hunters to new areas. The existence of the animal in large numbers assumed a relatively scant population. It assumed an area in which population could not be increased by resort to agriculture. Limitations of geological formation, and climate and a cultural background dependent on these limitations precluded a dense population with consequent destruction of animal life. The culture was dependent on indigenous flora and fauna and the latter was of prime importance. Moose, caribou, beaver, rabbit or hare, and fish furnished the chief supplies of food and clothing. This culture assumed a thorough knowledge of animal habits and the ability of the peoples concerned to move over wide areas in pursuit of a supply of food. The devices which had been elaborated included the snowshoe and the toboggan for the winter and the birch-bark canoe for the summer. This wide area contained numerous lakes and difficult connecting waterways, to which the canoe was adapted for extensive travel. Movement over this area occasioned an extended knowledge of geography and a widespread similarity of cultural traits such as language.

The area which was crucial to the development of the fur trade was the Pre-Cambrian shield of the northern half of the North American continent. It extended northwesterly across the continent to the mouth of the Mackenzie River and was bounded on the north by the northwesterly isothermal lines which determined the limits of the northern forests and especially of the canoe birch (*B. papyrifera*). The fur trade followed the waterways along the southern edge of this formation from the St. Lawrence to the Mackenzie River. In its full bloom it spread beyond this area to the Pacific drainage basin.

The history of the fur trade is the history of contact between two civilizations, the European and the North American, with especial reference to the northern portion of the continent. The limited cultural background of the North American hunting peoples provided an insatiable demand for the products of the more elaborate cultural development of Europeans. The supply of European goods, the product of a more advanced and specialized technology, enabled the Indians to gain a livelihood more easily – to obtain their supply of food, as in the case of moose, more quickly, and to hunt the beaver more effectively. Unfortunately the rapid destruction of the food supply and the revolution in the methods of living accompanied by the increasing attention to the fur trade by which these products were secured, disturbed the balance which had grown up previous to the coming of the European. The new technology with its radical innovations brought about such a rapid shift in the prevailing Indian culture as to lead to wholesale destruction of the peoples concerned by warfare and disease. The disappearance of the beaver and of the Indians necessitated the extension of European organization to the interior. New tribes demanded European goods in increasingly large amounts. The fur trade was the means by which this demand of the peoples of a more limited cultural development was met. Furs were the chief product suitable to European demands by which the North American peoples could secure European goods.

A rapid and extensive development of the trade followed accessibility to the vast areas of the Canadian Shield by the St. Lawrence and its numerous tributaries and by the rivers of the Hudson Bay drainage basin. Following a rapid decline in the supply of beaver in more accessible territory and the necessity of going to more remote areas, the trade began in the Maritime Provinces, extended rapidly by the Saguenay and later by the St. Lawrence and the Ottawa to the Great Lakes, and northwesterly across the headwaters of the rivers of Hudson Bay drainage basin from Lake Superior to Lake Winnipeg, the Saskatchewan, the Churchill, across the headwaters of the Mackenzie River drainage basin to Mackenzie and Peace rivers, and finally to the headwaters of rivers of the Pacific coast to New Caledonia and the Columbia. The waterways along the edge of the Canadian Shield tapped the rich fur lands of that area and in the smaller rivers of the headwaters of four drainage basins provided an environment to which the canoe could be adapted.

The extension of the trade across the northern half of the continent and the transportation of furs and goods over great distances involved the elaboration of an extensive organization of transport, of personnel, and of food supply. The development of transportation was based primarily on Indian cultural growth. The birch-bark canoe was borrowed and modified to suit the demands of the trade. Again, without Indian agriculture, Indian corn, and dependence on Indian methods of capturing buffalo and making pemmican, no extended organization of transport to the interior would have been possible in the early period. The organization of food supplies depended on agricultural development in the more favourable areas to the south and on the abundant fauna of the plains area. Limited transportation facilities, such as the canoe afforded, accentuated the organization and production of food supply in these areas. The extension of the fur trade was supported at convenient intervals by agricultural development as in the lower St. Lawrence basin, in southeastern Ontario, and areas centring about Detroit, and in Michilimackinac and Lake Michigan territory, in the west at Red River, though the buffalo were more important in the plains area in the beginning, and eventually in Peace River. On the Pacific coast an agricultural base was established on the Columbia.

The increasing distances over which the trade was carried on and the increasing capital investment and expense incidental to the elaborate organization of transport had a direct influence on its financial organization. Immediate trade with Europe from the St. Lawrence involved the export of large quantities of fur to meet the overhead costs of long ocean voyages and the imports of large quantities of heavy merchandise. Monopoly inevitably followed, and it was supported by the European institutional arrangements which involved the organization of monopolies for the conduct of foreign trade. On the other hand, internal trade, following its extension in the interior and the demand for larger numbers of voyageurs and canoes to undertake the difficult task of transportation and the increasing dependence on the initiative of the trader in carrying on trade with remote tribes, was, within certain limits, competitive. Trade from Quebec and Montreal with canoes up the Ottawa to Michilimackinac, La Baye, and Lake Superior could be financed with relatively small quantities of capital and was consequently competitive. Further extension of trade through Lake Superior by Grand Portage (later Kaministiquia) to Lake Winnipeg, the Saskatchewan, Athabasca, the Mackenzie River, and New Caledonia and the Pacific coast involved heavy overhead costs and an extensive organization of transportation. But the organization was of a type peculiar to the demands of the fur trade.

Individual initiative was stressed in the partnership agreements which characterized the North West Company. The trade carried on over extended areas under conditions of limited transportation made close control of individual partners by a central organization impossible. The North West Company which extended its organization from the Atlantic to the Pacific developed along lines which were fundamentally linked to the technique of the fur trade. This organization was strengthened in the amalgamation of 1821 by control of a charter guaranteeing monopoly and by the advantages incidental to lower costs of transportation by Hudson Bay.

The effects of these large centralized organizations characteristic of the fur trade as shown in the monopolies of New France, in the Hudson's Bay Company, and in the North West Company were shown in the institutional development of Canada. In New France constant expansion of the trade to the interior had increased costs of transportation and extended the possibilities of competition from New England. The population of New France during the open season of navigation was increasingly engaged in carrying on the trade over longer distances to the neglect of agriculture and other phases of economic development. To offset the effects of competition from the English colonies in the south and the Hudson's Bay Company in the north, a military policy, involving Indian alliances, expenditure on strategic posts, expensive campaigns, and constant direct and indirect drains on the economic life of New France and old France, was essential. As a result of these developments control of political activities in New France was centralized and the paternalism of old France was strengthened by the fur trade. Centralized control as shown in the activities of the government, the church, the seigniorial system, and other institutions was in part a result of the overwhelming importance of the fur trade.

The institutional development of New France was an indication of the relation between the fur trade and the mercantile policy. The fur trade provided an ample supply of raw material for the manufacture of highly profitable luxury goods. A colony engaged in the fur trade was not in a position to develop industries to compete with manufactures of the mother country. Its weakness necessitated reliance upon the military support of the mother country. Finally the insatiable demands of the Indians for goods stimulated European manufactures.

The importance of manufactures in the fur trade gave England, with her more efficient industrial development, a decided advantage. The competition of cheaper goods contributed in a definite fashion to the downfall of New France and enabled Great Britain to prevail in the face of its pronounced militaristic development. Moreover, the importance of manufactured goods to the fur trade made inevitable the continuation of control by Great Britain in the northern half of North America. The participation of American and English merchants in the fur trade immediately following the Conquest led to the rapid growth of a new organization[1] which was instrumental in securing the Quebec Act and which contributed to the failure of the American Revolution so far as it affected Quebec and the St. Lawrence. These merchants were active in the negotiations prior to the Constitutional Act of 1791 and the Jay Treaty of 1794.[2] As prominent members of the government formed under the Quebec Act and the Constitutional Act, they did much to direct the general trend of legislation. The later growth of the North West Company assured a permanent attachment to Great Britain because of its dependence on English manufactures.

The northern half of North America remained British because of the importance of fur as a staple product. The continent of North America became divided into three areas: (1) to the north in what is now the Dominion of Canada, producing furs, (2) to the south in what were during the Civil War the secession states, producing cotton, and (3) in the centre the widely diversified economic territory including the New England states and the coal and iron areas of the middle west demanding raw materials and a market. The staple-producing areas were closely dependent on industrial Europe, especially Great Britain. The fur-producing area was destined to remain British. The cotton-producing area was forced after the Civil War to become subordinate to the central territory just as the northern fur-producing area, at present producing the staples, wheat, pulp and paper, minerals, and lumber, tends to be brought under its influence.

[1] See Mrs. K. B. Jackson (as M. G. Reid), "The Quebec Fur-traders and Western Policy, 1763-1774."
[2] See W. E. Stevens, *The Northwest Fur Trade, 1763-1800.*

The North West Company and its successor the Hudson's Bay Company established a centralized organization which covered the northern half of North America from the Atlantic to the Pacific. The importance of this organization was recognized in boundary disputes, and it played a large role[3] in the numerous negotiations responsible for the location of the present boundaries. It is no mere accident that the present Dominion coincides roughly with the fur-trading areas of northern North America. The bases of supplies for the trade in Quebec, in western Ontario, and in British Columbia represent the agricultural areas of the present dominion. The North West Company was the forerunner of the present confederation.

There are other interesting by-products of the study which may be indicated briefly. Canada has had no serious problems with her native peoples since the fur trade depended primarily on these races. In the United States no point of contact of such magnitude was at hand and troubles with the Indians were a result. The existence of small and isolated sections of French half-breeds throughout Canada is another interesting survival of this contact.[4] The half-breed has never assumed such importance in the United States.

"The lords of the lakes and forest have passed away" but their work will endure in the boundaries of the Dominion of Canada and in Canadian institutional life. The place of the beaver in Canadian life has been fittingly noted in the coat of arms. We have given to the maple a prominence which was due to the birch. We have not yet realized that the Indian and his culture were fundamental to the growth of Canadian institutions. We are only beginning to realize the central position of the Canadian Shield.

[3] *Ibid.*
[4] See Marcel Giraud, *Le Métis canadien*.

The Trade in Square Timber

A. R. M. LOWER

I. THE FOREST IN CANADIAN ECONOMIC LIFE

New countries which rise rapidly to wealth and civilization invariably depend for their progress on the exploitation of some readily available natural resource. Under pioneer conditions there naturally can be no intricate industrial structure and if the capital necessary for the creation of one is to be procured, it can only be procured from older countries in exchange for some commodity of which those countries stand in need. If development is to be rapid, not only must this need be acute but also the supply of the desired commodity must be large, readily obtainable, and of a quality sufficiently uniform to be depended upon.

This dependence of a young country on the development of a satisfactory staple is strikingly illustrated by Canadian history, which in many respects is simply the history of fish, furs, lumber, wheat, and so on. In the supply of these various commodities, it has been no accident that so many of them have been derived directly or indirectly from the forest, for all the eastern half of the country was originally covered with forest and when settlement began it was from the forest that wealth, if it was to be obtained at all, had to be wrung. Thus, for some two centuries, the primary reason for the existence of the country was the presence of fur-bearing animals in the woods. Then for the best part of another century, the main dependence was on the more direct exploitation of the forest in the form of lumbering, while within the present age, the forest transmuted into pulp and paper and in hydro-electric

Source: A. R. M. Lower, "The Trade in Square Timber," University of Toronto Studies, History and Economics, *Contributions to Canadian Economics*, Vol. VI, 1933. Toronto: University of Toronto Press, 1933, pp. 40-61. Reprinted by permission of the publishers. This paper was presented at a meeting of the Royal Canadian Institute in February, 1932.

power, has supplied the foundation for much of the growth of the dominion.

Diagram number 1 illustrates the dominating position which the forest, considered solely in relation to lumbering, has had in Canadian trade. In the period before 1840, wood in various forms was the main item in Canadian exports, exceeding by far even agricultural products. That is, the new wealth on which the country had to rely for further progress, was being obtained abroad – chiefly in the mother country – by the exploitation of the forest at home. After 1840, or thereabouts, owing to the rapid extension of settlement in Upper Canada and the consequent rise of the trade in grain and flour, the proportion (but not the amounts) of forest products declined somewhat, but for another twenty years remained not far from half the total. Until the end of the century, despite the more varied resources which the opening of the west, increasing wealth, and scientific improvement had made available, the forest continued to contribute well over a quarter of the amount contributed from all sources. Of recent years, if paper be included among forest products, the percentage has ranged between twenty and twenty-five of the total exports.

Diagram No. 1

Proportion of Exports of Lumber and Timber etc.
to Total Exports, 1829-1903

II. THE ORIGINS OF THE TRADE IN SQUARE TIMBER:
THE DIFFERENTIAL DUTIES

However valuable the forests of the Atlantic seaboard and of the St. Lawrence valley might potentially be, unless there were opportunities for their profitable use, they were actually worthless. Opportunity was slow to arise. During the French period, attempts had been made to develop an export trade in wood but, owing to the distance of the only market, France, a market which in any case had more readily available supplies of its own at hand, they had come to nothing. After the conquest the width of the Atlantic was not decreased and it remained impossible to ship timber from America to meet the competition of the countries about the Baltic. Had not political events supervened, it is quite possible that the establishment of a vigorous woods industry in British North America would have been indefinitely postponed.

A century and a half ago, in contrast with the present age, which is built on iron, the world was built on wood. It was also more or less permanently at war. The combination of these two considerations gives the origin of the trade in Canadian square timber and, in large part, of the general lumber industry. Just as Great Britain is nowadays dependent on the outside world for food, so during the eighteenth and early nineteenth centuries, she was dependent upon it for wood – then, on account of the needs of a wooden navy, as important as wheat today. Her first sharp realization of her dependence came during the American Revolution, when the supply of pine masts from New England, carefully fostered for a generation or two by bounties and other expedients, came suddenly to an end. As a result, efforts – successful after the occasion for them had passed – were made to develop a reliable supply of masts from the pineries of New Brunswick,[1] the timber industry of which province, in consequence, dates from about 1784.

Within a generation came a second and still sharper experience, this time at the hands of Napoleon, who by 1808 had by his so-called "continental system," succeeded in closing to British trade the Baltic, the traditional region of supply for all ordinary types of timber and boards. As an impending result, Great Britain saw her navy languishing and the war lost.

Once more she turned to her North American colonies. By the imposition of heavy duties on Baltic timber, masts, and deals, and by direct encouragement to British merchants to bring these articles from Canada, she found her salvation in the Canadian forest. Thenceforth there was no more scarcity

[1] See R. G. Albion, *Forests and seapower* (Cambridge, 1926), ch. vii.

of ship-timber or timber for any one of the other innumerable needs of war.

The differential duties, as they came to be called, accorded a preference to colonial timber that really was a preference. Duties were imposed on foreign timber which finally mounted to over one hundred per cent, while colonial timber went into British ports free. Once imposed, these duties on timber proved as hard to take off as any other duties, with the result that the people of Great Britain had for many years to pay fantastic prices for their wood, prices from which the chief people to benefit were the vested interests involved – in this case, the British merchants who conducted the trade, and the British shipowners who carried the cargoes.

Diagrams 2 and 3 illustrate the imposition of the duties and their abolition, as also their effects on the trade in timber. After reaching their maximum during the wars, the duties remained almost intact for a generation or until 1842, the first year of Sir Robert Peel's ministry. During the course of that ministry they

Diagram No. 2 — Imports of Square Timber into Great Britain from British North America and from the Baltic Countries during the existence of the Differential Duties and for a few years before and after.

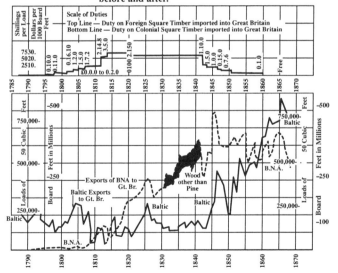

Diagram No. 3
Imports of Deals into Great Britain from
British North America and from the
Baltic Countries during the existence
of the Differential Duties and for a
few years before and after.

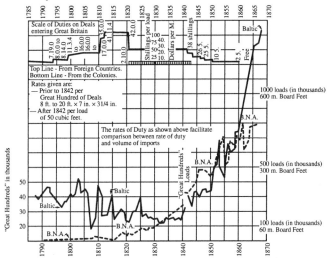

were cut down to minor proportions. Peel, Conservative though he was, thus by his abolition of the duties on timber and on sugar, and of the corn laws, effectively destroyed the old ideal of a self-contained empire, which by 1846 had become a mere excuse for the greed of certain strongly entrenched vested interests.

The diagrams indicate by year and amount each increase or decrease of duty on foreign timber. Even before the stoppage of supplies in 1808 – the stoppage is clearly reflected in the line in each graph representing imports of Baltic timber into Great Britain – there was a strong tendency to increase imperial preference in order to secure independence of the foreigner, but after that occurrence, the policy of reliance on colonial supplies was very obviously reflected in the duties, which were repeatedly increased before the wars ended.[2] The protectionist mania survived the causes which had produced it and not until some years after the peace did a measure of fiscal sanity return,

[2] Note the especially drastic increase made in 1811.

and then only under the stimulus of profound industrial stagnation. The reasons for the maintenance of the duties from 1821 to 1842 at a very high level lie beyond the confines of this article, but it may be said in passing that they were bound up with the prevailing mercantilism of the day and the strength of the vested interests concerned.

The effect of each increase of protection in increasing exports from British North America and decreasing those from the Baltic is also readily discernible from the diagrams. After 1821, when twenty years elapsed before a single change was made in the preference and when the situation must have reached a certain state of equilibrium, the Canadian trade passed from the category of a "hot-house" war industry, perfected its organization, and, still under the stimulus of very high protection, enjoyed a large expansion in the rapidly increasing British market. The Baltic timber trade, despite good organization, good material, and proximity, either actually decreased or barely held its own.

However great the artificial stimulus, the ordinary ups and down of trade cannot be eliminated, may, indeed, be increased by the stimulus. The diagrams show the fluctuations in the Canadian timber trade during the period of unchanging duties. The ups and downs were naturally accentuated once the established pattern of the duties on timber was disturbed, that is from 1842 to 1851 (the fiscal changes after this latter date are not very important, as the diagrams indicate). What seems to have happened in these years is that rumour of a coming reduction in the preference would give rise to a rush to get timber in before the reduction actually took place and that this oversupply in turn would glut the market so that when the preference really was cut down, the reduction would naturally coincide with a fall in prices and a consequent sharp decrease in imports into Great Britain. Then with the new tariff accepted, trade would apparently pick up again and shortly surpass its old levels, only once more to be cut down at the prospect of the next reduction. The decreases in protection do not seem to have affected the power of Canadian timber to compete with Baltic, despite the differences in distance and it was only at a comparatively late date when other factors had entered, such as steamship transport, that Canadian totals began to show to disadvantage. Even then, owing to the general growth of the world's economic structure, they were very much higher than they had been under protection.

The manufacture of "deals" (that is, softwood planks two or three inches thick) grew up as a result of the protective duties in much the same way as the square timber industry, but since the process called for more technical skill, larger supplies of capital, greater uniformity in the product, and for high and uniform quality, the Baltic countries were able to retain their priority longer, until about 1835. However, they had to yield at last and only succeeded in recapturing the lion's share of the British markets some years after the abolition of high protection. Diagram number 3, which illustrates the same set of facts for deals as number 2 does for square timber, leaves little doubt that a stiff enough dose of protection can overcome the natural advantages of geography, but at a great cost to the consumer. It may also furnish support for the "infant industry" argument for protection, since without the period of high preference, the deal industry might not have been able to develop to the point where, within fifty years, it apparently could do well without preference of any kind. Certainly the two diagrams show very clearly that Canadian exports of wood to Great Britain continued to increase despite the abolition of the preference. An industry which had begun under very artificial conditions, continued under conditions of free competition, and prospered under them, something to be accounted for, presumably, by the natural advantages which Canada possessed. Had the wood trade not been founded in the nature of the country, it doubtless would have collapsed as soon as the support was withdrawn. As it was, withdrawal of protection made it obvious that the chief beneficiaries had been the vested interests involved. After withdrawal, the spread between prices in Canada and those in Great Britain decreased, that is, the vested interests had to take smaller profits.

Diagram number 4, in addition to throwing some light on the course of prices in Canada during the period from 1785 to 1870, illustrates the above statement. Compared with the huge increase in the price of Canadian white pine in England during the Napoleonic Wars, there was a very moderate increase in Canada. Then, until the preference began to disappear, the price in Canada, with the exception of fluctuations during the crises, remained rather steady, while that in England tended to in-

Diagram No. 4

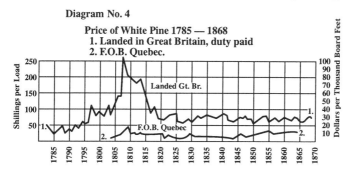

Price of White Pine 1785 — 1868
1. Landed in Great Britain, duty paid
2. F.O.B. Quebec.

crease. After the abolition of the preference, the reverse tended to be the case, That is the loss of the preference did not greatly cheapen timber to the English buyer but rather enabled the Canadian producer to get more for his timber. The port-buyers had to offer him more and owing to Baltic competition had to pay the shippers smaller freight rates. In the thirty years from 1820 to 1850 freights fell by about twenty shillings a ton, or by about $8.00 per thousand board feet, this amount representing about 35 per cent of the figure at which they stood in 1920.[3] In the same way the price of timber from the Baltic came down after the repeal to the Canadian level, but in the Baltic ports it rose, the producer of the timber presumably getting the difference.[4] There is no doubt that while the duties lasted it was a golden age for the English middleman and the English shipowner.

III. THE TIMBER MERCHANTS

Of the vested interests, while the British shipowners probably constituted the most numerous and the most powerful group, the British timber-houses which conducted the business have the greater pertinence to the subject of this paper. A study of them throws interesting light on the general commercial system of Britain in the eighteenth and nineteenth centuries.

[3] Approximately 55 shillings a ton or $22.00 per M.

[4] Some idea of the *ad valorem* rates of duty on foreign timber can be obtained by comparing the line in diagram number 4 for prices of white pine landed in Great Britain, which is approximately the same as prices of Baltic timber of equivalent grade, with the rates of duty given in diagram number 2.

British timber firms had been established in Baltic ports, such as Memel and Danzig, for generations. One of these, the house of Thomson, Bonar and Company, founded early in the eighteenth century, is of interest from the fact that one of its cadets, C. Poulett Thomson, became the first governor general of United Canada.

When the cutting off of the Baltic supplies in 1808 caused the Canadian trade to be opened up, some of these houses, on the encouragement of government, transferred their operations to British North America and there set up the type of organization with which they were already familiar.

The earliest pioneer of whom there is record was Henry Usborne who came out privately to Quebec in 1801. He was the first of a long line which extends to the present day and which includes many names still well known in the city of Quebec, such as the Prices, the Sharples, the Gilmours, the Burstalls, and the Dobells. These men did not for the most part set up independent houses but merely opened branches of the parent house of London or Liverpool. They were "factors." Their business was purely that of middlemen: they bought the timber which was brought down to the ports, loaded it, and consigned it to their English houses. In Canada they were concentrated in one city, Quebec, the only port of shipment, and in the Maritimes also mainly, though not exclusively, in one, Saint John.

The English house financed the transaction and in those days when communications were rudimentary, this problem of financing was a great one, especially as the industry became more complicated. Almost at once the Quebec house had to begin financing the man who got the timber out of the woods and that meant that the money which was put out one summer remained locked up over the winter, over the next summer, and probably over most of the next winter also, when the timber was being sold in England, that is, for a year or a year and a half. During all this long period, there would be the thousand ordinary hazards of the trade, the prospects of over-production or under-production in the two winters concerned – wide oscillations of supply were the bane of the trade – the uncertainty induced by Baltic competition in England, the extreme variability of freight rates, the possibilities of loss from dry rot, shipwreck, fire, etc., and the ordinary ups and downs in England affecting general prices. Add to these the necessity for each side of the Atlantic acting on its own best judgment in such matters as the amount of stock to be purchased or held, owing to the length of time required to get word across and back, and it becomes obvious that the trade in timber was one of the most uncertain trades in which it was possible to engage. Fatalities were numerous among timber firms. The business was, many of its enemies declared, essentially speculative, a gambling trade. In the circumstances it is a marvel that so many of the firms have had such long and honourable records. The present company of Price Brothers, for example, goes back to about 1817, and there are others which have been in business for over a century: rather a remarkable record for a country which is supposed to be characterized by unceasing and rapid change.

Most of the timber firms were family affairs, sons and cousins being utilized for the conduct of the colonial branch houses. As time went on and children were born into the colonial establishments, it was inevitable that some degree of naturalization should take place; the Canadian branch would tend to lose organic unity with the English and to have merely friendly relationships with it. Yet a considerable degree of contact was always maintained. For example, the Canadian partners were in the habit of paying annual visits to England to keep in touch with business there, and they invariably sent their sons to England for their education. Quebec lumber circles have, until recent years, represented a little England overseas.

Some of the firms have had interesting evolutions. The Gilmours began in Glasgow as Baltic timber merchants in the eighteenth century. In the early nineteenth they migrated to Liverpool and sent out branches to America: Quebec, Saint John, the Miramichi, and New Orleans. They extended up country and became producers, entering the sawmill industry. Their mills migrated towards the shifting sources of supply and finally extended over most of Ontario, Quebec, and New Brunswick. They owned their own fleet of ships and when the trade in square timber declined, the English branch continued on in shipping. It is still established at Liverpool but now as a steamship firm pure and simple. The Canadian branch survived until a few years ago in the shape of an ordinary lumber company but this business has now passed into other hands. Besides several men prominent in Canada, the family has contributed to public life the present (1932) British minister of agriculture. The firm began as Pollok, Gilmour and Company but a century and a half witnessed many changes: Gilmour, Rankin and Company; Rankin, Gilmour and Company, etc.; the varying titles reflecting the succession of the generations. It illustrates very nicely the general evolutionary trend of these timber-houses.

The Gilmour firm owned their own fleet of timber-ships. Most houses did not, but depended upon the arrival in Quebec of ships looking for a cargo, "seekers" as they were called. Naturally a rough cargo like timber would attract the poorest class of ships. The result was that the harbour of Quebec was filled with the queerest collection of shipping, old barques and brigantines, ships "swifted" with chains passed round their hulls to hold them together, full-rigged ships that perhaps had once been East Indiamen, even the occasional old man-of-war, much degraded and disguised, turned into a sort of cart-horse of the seas.

The timber merchants changed Quebec from the sleepy old town of French colonial days to a lively port and gave to it a character as distinctive as it had under Frontenac or Bigot. Their days passed and now little visible evidence of their age remains except the ruins of their wharves and offices lining the shore up as far as the present bridge. The timber port they created has given place to still another Quebec.

IV. THE TIMBER INDUSTRY

British necessities in timber had come providentially for Canada. Prior to the year 1800, the province had little to depend on but furs for securing its necessary imports and it needs no demonstration that no community that amounted to much could have been erected on furs alone. Moreover, Upper Canada had just received its Loyalist settlers, and it was essential if they were not to stagnate and live merely the self-contained lives of a peasantry, that some sort of outlet for their products should be obtained. The necessities of war provided this outlet. When the first British timber-factors came over, they came with ad-miralty contracts in their pockets and their idea was to hire men to cut timber wherever it could be found on the waste lands of the crown. They soon found that it would serve their purpose

Map One
The Square Timber Industry; "Laurentia" or The St. Lawrence Region

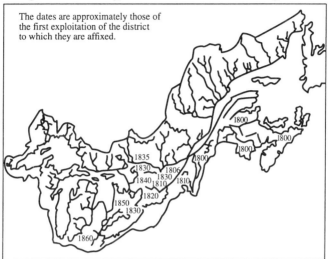

The dates are approximately those of
the first exploitation of the district
to which they are affixed.

better not to hire timber-cutters but merely to buy timber. Consequently, as the demands became known, the natives of the country began to bring down rafts of timber to Quebec to dispose of them there for cash to the contractors in an open market.

This market for timber and these rafts were instrumental in opening a channel of trade for the Upper Canadian settlements. Men who were clearing their lands could cut and haul pine-timber to the water's edge, form it into rafts, load upon these rafts whatever produce they could scrape together – a barrel of ashes, some pork or wheat – and launch forth upon the voyage down river to Quebec. In this humble way the St. Lawrence timber trade began to grow and by 1805 the complete river technique, the construction of rafts and the knowledge of the river's channels, including the channels through the rapids, appeared to have been mastered.[5]

Within fifty years after these humble beginnings, the industry which was to mean so much for Canada had spread throughout

[5] As the French for many years had been accustomed to bring down small amounts of timber, much of this had already been available.

the length and breadth of the St. Lawrence system with the exceptions of Lake Superior, the north shore of Lake Huron, and the extreme headwaters of the Ottawa. Just as the great river had from the first beckoned explorers and missionaries inland, so now it was to lure the timber-maker into the wilderness.

Maps 1 and 2 illustrate the extension of the industry. Map 1 conveniently represents the extent of the St. Lawrence watershed and its outlying districts. Until the Canadian Pacific Railway was built, within this region there lay, for all practical

Map Two   Ranges of the Red and White Pine in Eastern North America purposes, the whole of Canada. Map 2 illustrates how large was the extent of the country the industry could draw on for its raw material, the red and white pines. With the exception of the long tongue which the white pine sends down the Appalachian Mountains, the range of these trees is approximately coincident with the St. Lawrence watershed and the fact that much of that watershed lies in the United States affects the situation less than might be expected for the purposes of the square timber industry. American territory on the St. Lawrence and New Brunswick watersheds was tributary to such ports as Quebec and Saint John in much the same way as was Canadian. The red and white pine are essentially the trees of what might be called "Laurentia" and in the period with which this article deals, their exploitation was its dominating activity.

As the needs of war increased the importance of the Quebec market, timber-makers operated further and further up the river. Not only did increasing demand require larger and larger areas of supply but the nature of the industry itself caused a rapid migration from one district to another. Square timber was a wasteful and extravagant form of exploiting the forest. Only the choicest and largest trees could be taken. They had to be large, straight, and sound; the slightest rot at the heart disqualified them and so many trees on being cut, having rot at the centre, were left lying where they fell. Squaring (with the broad axe) took off four huge slabs of the best wood in the tree, well over a third of the whole log. The enormous amount of inflammable litter thus produced gave rise to innumerable fires. Hence the square timber industry necessarily had to keep on the move and thus each year saw timber-cutters further upstream. Therefore, while the first contracts appear to have been cut on the Richelieu, it was not long until the best of the timber was gone from that region. By 1820, timber was coming from as far up as eastern Lake Ontario, and when steamships came into use on the lakes, rafts were made further up still and towed across the lakes. When the Welland Canal was opened in the early thirties, timber began to come through it and by 1850, Lake Erie had been traversed and the southern parts of Lake Huron were being drawn upon.

But great as was the production of the St. Lawrence itself and vital as it was to Canadian pioneers, there was another region which was destined to surpass it, the St. Lawrence's great tributary, the Ottawa. The Ottawa valley has an area of some eighty thousand square miles, most of which is land which cannot be used for agriculture. Consequently, lumbering finds there a natural home.

Very fortunately there is a good record of the initial attempt to exploit its resources. The first pioneer above the Carillon Rapids, forty miles above the confluence, just at the beginning of the century, was Philemon Wright from Massachusetts, who, having found good land, made a settlement which he called Hull at the foot of the cataract known as the Chaudière, just opposite the modern national capital. Here he spent five years clearing and building. Being then at the end of his resources he realized that if he was to have anything more than a mere existence he must find some saleable commodity, and he decided to try to get some timber down to Quebec on the chance of selling it there. Consequently, in 1806, after some exploration of the river, he built a raft and set out for Quebec. He was an amateur and he had to keep his raft off shoals and rocks, run the Carillon Rapids, find a new channel behind Montreal, and get across Lake St. Peter, all without guidance. But after weeks on the way, he got to his destination and, after waiting further weeks in Quebec, he managed to find a purchaser and returned home with ready money in his pocket. He did not know that he had begun a trade which was to be as picturesque in its day as the fur trade before it or as vital as the wheat trade after it.

Wright's pioneering raft was soon followed by others and within a few years pine-timber was being cut far above the Chaudière. There is some reason to believe that as early as 1835 a point as high up as Lake Temiscaming, some four hundred miles above the confluence, had been reached. This great distance, with its succession of falls and rapids, could not have been overcome without the aid of the various technical improvements which followed rapidly in the wake of increasing demand.

V. THE TECHNIQUE OF THE INDUSTRY

Completely different methods of handling the timber were evolved on the two principal rivers: there was a St. Lawrence technique and an Ottawa technique. As an interesting description of the St. Lawrence technique is readily available,[6] it need not be referred to at length here. Briefly, it was based upon what was called the "dram," a float of timber made within a frame, with each individual stick bound to the members of the frame by withes (saplings) of birch or hazel. To withstand the stresses of the St. Lawrence Rapids, drams had to be put together very securely and they were consequently expensive to construct. Hence, on the St. Lawrence the tendency was for the industry to pass into larger and larger hands, a development which was hastened when the steam-tug came in and timber began to be brought across the lakes. Rafting became in itself more and more of a business and there was eventually almost a complete divorce between the producer of timber and the man who took took it to market.

A raft of timber consisted of several drams and the whole structure might cover a large area. In its construction, at least in the early days and probably down to the end, not a piece of iron was used; the withes were crushed and twisted, making unbreakable cables, and they were looped about the timbers so skilfully that even the force of the St. Lawrence Rapids was unable to break them. The frame was put together with wooden pins, with an appropriate assemblage of crosspieces (*traverses*). A second layer of timbers filled in the spaces between the *traverses* and on top of this was often a third layer. When oak was rafted, it had to be inserted skilfully, a stick here and there, so that it might be floated by the buoyancy of the pine.

The only way of getting down river before the days of steam was by taking advantage of the wind and current. During a head wind the raft remained at anchor. In no wind it drifted and in a fair wind great primitive square sails were hoisted.

When the rapids approached it was "all hands to the oars," a row of which was mounted fore and aft, to enable the dram to be swung at the pilot's word. Iroquois Indians were the best rapids-men, French Canadians next, other Canadians last. Passing the rapids on a heavy mass of timber has been described as one of the most exhilarating of experiences, with the surge and roll of the waves, the grinding and bumping of the timbers, the perfect skill of the crew, the rocks missed by a hair's breadth,

[6] D. D. Calvin, "Rafting on the St. Lawrence" (*Canadian Geographical Journal*, October, 1931). See also G. S. Thompson, *Up to Date or the Life of a Lumberman* (Toronto, 1895), *passim*.

the terrific speed, and everywhere the consciousness of being in the grip of elemental forces.

On the Ottawa, the unit employed was known as the "crib." A crib was a small raft composed of a score or so timbers laid parallel to each other in a frame consisting of two outside round logs and *traverses* fastened to them by wooden pins, the whole kept together by the friction of the buoyant pine against the *traverses* above. A second layer of "loading timber" laid over the layer which formed the foundation increased the friction and the security of the timber. It was thus much smaller than a dram and handier in tributary streams and in the small channels into which the Ottawa divides itself in places.

Crossing the lake expansions of the Ottawa or in the long stretches of the river, the separate cribs were made up into rafts by the simple expedient of putting a plank with two augur holes in it over two stakes, one on one crib, one on the next. Any desired number could thus be put together. Lakes, in the early days before steam-tugs, could be crossed only by sailing or, more commonly, by kedging along with an anchor laid out ahead of the raft and the raft worked up to it by capstan and windlass.

The utility of the crib system was revealed when the rafts approached a rapid, for it was then broken up into its cribs and these were run through one by one. If there were falls, the cribs had to be broken up, too, and the pine-timbers sent through separately, all the oak being carted round, a most expensive proceeding. But about 1828, a means was devised of obviating this – the timber-slide, the invention of Mr. Ruggles Wright, son of Philemon. The timber-slides revolutionized the industry, making it a capitalistic pursuit conducted in a big way and enabling all the upper reaches of the valley to be tapped. The timber-slide was simply an inclined plane of timber built round the falls. Coming through the slides on a crib was a sensation equal to the joys of a toboggan-slide.

It was lumbering which built the city of Ottawa and it was the timber-slide which gave the city something of a unique character. To the Ottawa of two generations ago, the timber-slide was what its ski-runs and ski-runners are today, both of them lending the city a distinctive air.

VI. THE ENTREPRENEUR

The timber industry naturally called forth not only its own distinctive technique but also its own class of entrepreneurs or producers. In the earliest days when British merchants sat in their counting houses at Quebec and bought the timber that happened to come down, most of the timber producers were small men, of little or no financial standing, many of them farmers, others fly-by-night characters of various types, and all of them very much in the hands of the merchants who bought their timber and financed their efforts. They had not a good name; the trade was too precarious and if prices were much against them, they were apt to yield to the temptation to abandon their raft, leave their men unpaid and the merchants' advances unpaid, and then seek pastures new, probably in the western states.

Timber-making in those days was not a "large-scale" undertaking, not in the least like lumbering today. All that was necessary was a "gang" of about six men, consisting of a scorer, hewer, liner, trail-maker, and a boy for a cook, broad and narrow axes, enough pork and beans for the winter and not much more. Consequently hundreds of people tried their luck. It seemed so easy for the pioneer farmer, at the end of his harvest, to go into the woods – the crown lands, defended by regulations on paper only, in reality open to everyone – with his sons or neighbours and "make" a little timber. The raw material cost him nothing and he probably had a good deal of equipment. A timber-making expedition would seem like not much more than a winter's adventure with the prospect of some ready money into the bargain.

But the farmer found that getting his raft down to the port in the spring was not the simple matter that it seemed. There were the thousand and one uncertainties of the water: too early a spring, too quick a run-off, river-bars, shoals, jams, headwinds, and so on. If he arrived late, the market might be flooded and his timber not bring him in enough to pay his winter's work. Again, he might have to wait for some weeks before he sold. That meant that all the spring's work on his farm went undone or half done, that his harvest was poor, and that he ultimately lost his farm. The two occupations, in truth, were incompatible, as many a man found to his cost, but the facility with which the farmer could turn to timber-making and the prospect of cash money – it was something like mining placer-gold in that respect – ruined thousands of good pioneers and held up the process of taming the wilderness for many years, especially in New Brunswick and along the Ottawa.

It was towards the middle of the century before this hap-hazard organization of production began to disappear: by 1850 farmers no longer to any extent went into the woods as entre-preneurs; in fact, the crown lands were no longer open to all comers, but the system of timber limits had arrived. The operators were for the most part substantial men, managing many camps and bringing down many rafts. They could talk to the Quebec merchant on equal terms and they were much more conversant with conditions of the market than a small amateur could be. Consequently there was much more regu-larity, much less hazard about timber-making than before, though by no means all of it was eliminated.

VII. DECLINE OF THE INDUSTRY

The square timber industry had hardly got into larger hands before it began to decline. It had weathered the storm involved in the removal of the preferential duties only to encounter a number of other adverse factors which in the end proved its undoing. The western part of the province was turning to sawn lumber, much less wasteful and readily marketable in the United States. The best of the white pine was being rapidly cut or destroyed or burnt. Every year the timber-maker had to go further afield, and thus his costs became higher. Again, efforts were being made to induce the British importer to take his wood in the form of boards. Here a tremendous revolution was necessary. To the British importer, wood meant square timber, which he could have cut up in England. Moreover, wood was not wood unless it was hand hewn. It mattered not to the importer that the best of the tree was left in the forest to rot. He had always used heart timber and he would always use it. Yet slowly and in great part, it is said, by the efforts of one exporter – R. M. Cox, "Ready Money Cox," as he was known, from his exemplary practice of always paying in cash – a market was found in Great Britain for sawn lumber and as it extended year by year, the export of square timber fell off. A mortal blow was struck in the 1880's when steamships were introduced into the trade, with the consequences that they began to come up to Montreal and load lumber brought to that port by rail. Each year fewer and fewer sailing ships sought the St. Lawrence, firm after firm went out of business, and finally the industry ceased to exist. The last crib went through the slides at Ottawa in 1908.

Diagram number 5 illustrates the rise and fall of the industry. A century of Canadian economic history is compressed into this diagram and every major economic movement of the whole period is reflected in it. Here reference can be made but to a few salient things, and these only by way of recapitulation. The rise at the beginning is coincident with the application of the heavy war duty on Baltic timber. Then there appears the recession caused by the War of 1812 and the further recessions during the depressions of 1821 and of 1826-27. Next the disturbed political period in the 1830's causes Quebec exports to mark time. The industry no sooner gets on its feet again than it encounters the British tariff preference and has wide fluctuations in consequence, though with a general tendency upward despite the loss. Next, the Crimean War, with the usual accompaniment of boom and depression, is clearly mirrored in the line. Lastly, after 1863, decline sets in and thereafter with the factors discussed above making themselves more and more strongly felt, the trend is steadily downward. In the new century the line tails away and disappears.

Diagram No. 5
The Rise and Fall
of the
Square Timber Trade
The Exports of a Century
1810 — 1910

Top Line — Exports of all British North America
1810-1841 — Pine
1842-　　　— All timber
Bottom Line — Exports from Quebec
1810-1849 — "Pine"
1850-1910 — White Pine

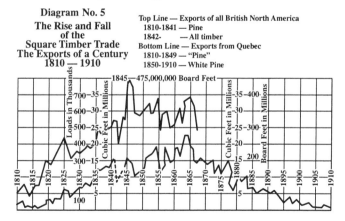

The trade in square timber has gone. But in its day it provided this country with what was in many respects a satisfactory staple, a commodity of unlimited supply, of fairly uniform quality, and for which there was a ready market, a staple, therefore, on which a solid and fair-sized community could be erected. Quebec, Saint John, Ottawa are its monuments, and the modern pulp and paper towns are its heirs. It was an industry which, on the one hand, founded many a large Canadian fortune and which, on the other, ruined its thousands. It was an occupation which was picturesque and romantic in itself and which gave to this country a technique of broad-axe and raft that has permanently enriched its cultural heritage.

A Staple Theory of Economic Growth

M. H. WATKINS

The staple approach to the study of economic history is primarily a Canadian innovation; indeed, it is Canada's most distinctive contribution to political economy. It is undeveloped in any explicit form in most countries where the export sector of the economy is or was dominant.[1] The specific terminology – staple or staples approach, or theory, or thesis – is Canadian, and the persistence with which the theory has been applied by Canadian social scientists and historians is unique.

The leading innovator was the late Harold Innis in his brilliant pioneering historical studies, notably of the cod fisheries and the fur trade;[2] others tilled the same vineyard[3] but it is his work

Source: M. H. Watkins "A Staple Theory of Economic Growth," *Canadian Journal of Economics and Political Science*, Vol. XXIX, no. 2, May 1963, pp. 141-158. Reprinted by permission of the publisher.

Financial assistance for the summer of 1961 is gratefully acknowledged from the Ford Foundation. For helpful comments on earlier drafts of this paper, I am indebted to J. H. Dales, W. T. Easterbrook, J. I. McDonald, A. Rotstein, and S. G. Triantis of the University of Toronto and C. P. Kindleberger of the Massachusetts Institute of Technology.

[1] The American economic historian, Guy S. Callender, however, devoted considerable attention to the importance of international and interregional trade in staples in the United States, an aspect of American growth which has been much neglected but has recently been revived by Douglass C. North. See Callender, *Selections from the Economic History of the United States, 1765-1860* (Boston, 1909), and North, *The Economic Growth of the United States, 1790-1860* (Englewood Cliffs, N.J., 1961).

[2] See his *The Fur Trade in Canada: An Introduction to Canadian Economic History* (Toronto, 1930; 2nd ed., 1956); *The Cod Fisheries: The History of an International Economy* (Toronto, 1940; 2nd ed., 1954). For a collection of his writings in the Canadian field, see *Essays in Canadian Economic History* (Toronto, 1957). For a complete bibliography of his writings, see Jane Ward, *Canadian Journal of Economics and Political Science*, XIX, May, 1953, pp. 236-44.

[3] W. A. Mackintosh is sometimes given credit as a co-founder of the staple theory; see his "Economic Factors in Canadian History," *Canadian Historical Review*, IV, March, 1923, 12-25, and "Some Aspects of a Pioneer Economy," *Canadian Journal of Economics and Political Science*, II, Nov., 1936, pp. 457-63.

that has stamped the "school." His concern was with the general impact on the economy and society of staple production. His method was to cast the net widely. The staple approach became a unifying theme of diffuse application rather than an analytic tool fashioned for specific uses. There was little attempt to limit its application by the use of an explicit framework.[4] Methodologically, Innis' staple approach was more technological history writ large than a theory of economic growth in the conventional sense.[5]

Once solidly entrenched in Canadian studies, the staple approach has now fallen on more uncertain days as its relevance has come to be questioned by Canadian economic historians.[6] The strongest attack has come from Kenneth Buckley who maintains that it is "practical and efficacious" as a theory of economic growth to 1820, but that thereafter "other sources of national economic growth and change" are impossible to ignore; he concludes that Canadian economic historians should "replace the notion of an opportunity structure determined by geography and natural resources with a general concept of economic opportunity without specifying determinants."[7] Vernon C. Fowke's emphasis on agriculture serving the domestic market as an impetus to investment and hence to economic growth in central Canada prior to Confederation involves a devaluation of the role of staple exports.[8] W. T. Easterbrook has argued, after extensive review of the literature, that the staple theory no longer constitutes – and apparently ought not to – an adequate

---

[4] This point has often been noted; see, for example, Richard E. Caves and Richard H. Holton, *The Canadian Economy: Prospect and Retrospect* (Cambridge, Mass., 1959), p. 30; and W. T. Easterbrook, "Problems in the Relationship of Communication and Economic History," *Journal of Economic History*, XX, Dec., 1960, p. 563.

[5] Kenneth Buckley makes this point strongly; see his "The Role of Staple Industries in Canada's Economic Development," *Journal of Economic History*, XVIII, Dec., 1958, p. 442.

[6] For its use in communications study – where, following the later Innis, the media become the resource or staple – see Marshall McLuhan, "Effects of the Improvements of Communication Media," *Journal of Economic History*, XX, Dec., 1960, pp. 566-75; and *The Gutenberg Galaxy* (Toronto, 1962), particularly pp. 164-6.

[7] "The Role of Staple Industries," pp. 444, 445.

[8] Fowke, *The National Policy and the Wheat Economy* (Toronto, 1957), chap. 2.

unifying theme for the study of Canadian development.[9] On the other hand, Hugh G. J. Aitken has remained satisfied with the approach. His own recent writings have been focused on the new resource industries of the twentieth century;[10] in commenting on Buckley's paper he suggested that the staple approach was relevant at least to 1914,[11] and he has subsequently maintained that "it is still true that the pace of development in Canada is determined fundamentally by the exports that enable Canada to pay its way in the world."[12]

The sample is small, but so too is the number of practising Canadian economic historians. There would appear to be declining confidence in the relevance of the staple approach, especially if consideration is given to what has been said as well as what has been written. But, curiously, the decline has been paralleled by rising interest among non-Canadians who may or may not refer to Innis and Canada. The leading advocate of the staple approach today is Douglass C. North, whose work may well have set the stage for a reconsideration of the causes of American economic growth from the American Revolution to the Civil War.[13] Two American economists, Richard E. Caves and Richard H. Holton, have critically re-examined the staple approach from the viewpoint of modern economic theory as a prelude to forecasting the state of the Canadian economy in 1970, and have given it a surprisingly clean bill of health.[14]

[9] Easterbrook, "Trends in Canadian Economic Thought," *South Atlantic Quarterly*, LVIII, Winter, 1959, pp. 91-107; and "Recent Contributions to Economic History: Canada," *Journal of Economic History*, XIX, March, 1959, pp. 76-102 and reprinted in this volume on p. 259.

[10] Aitken, "The Changing Structure of the Canadian Economy" in Aitken et al., *The American Economic Impact on Canada* (Durham, N.C., 1959), and *American Capital and Canadian Resources* (Cambridge, Mass., 1961).

[11] "Discussion," *Journal of Economic History*, XVIII, Dec., 1958, p. 451.

[12] *American Capital and Canadian Resources*, p. 74.

[13] North, "Location Theory and Regional Economic Growth," *Journal of Political Economy*, LXII, June, 1955, pp. 243-58; "International Capital Flows and the Development of the American West," *Journal of Economic History*, XVI, Dec., 1956, pp. 493-505; "A Note on Professor Rostow's 'Take-off' into Self-sustained Growth," *Manchester School of Economic and Social Studies*, XXVI, Jan., 1958, pp. 68-75; "Agriculture and Regional Economic Growth," *Journal of Farm Economics*, XLI, Dec., 1959, pp. 943-51; *The Economic Growth of the United States, 1790-1860*.

[14] Caves and Holton, *The Canadian Economy*, Part I.

R. E. Baldwin has provided a brilliant theoretical article on the impact of staple production on an economy, and both North and Caves and Holton have acknowledged their indebtedness to him.[15] Mention must also be made of the analytical approach used by Jonathan V. Levin in his study of the role of primary product exports in Peru and Burma,[16] of the implications for the staple approach of the application of modern income and growth theory to the classic problem of the transfer mechanism for capital imports in the Canadian balance of payments, particularly in the great boom before the First World War,[17] and of the distinction made by Harvey S. Perloff and Lowdon Wingo, Jr., between "good" and "bad" resource exports in the context of American regional growth.[18]

The simultaneous waning of the reputation of the staple approach among Canadians and its rise elsewhere has created a gap in the literature which this paper will attempt to bridge. It will argue that the staple theory can fruitfully be limited to a distinct type of economic growth; restate a staple theory so constrained in more rigorous form, primarily by drawing on the literature cited in the paragraph above; contrast this staple theory with other models of economic development; and finally, consider again the relevance of a staple approach to the Canadian case.

I

The linking of economic history and the theory of economic growth is a prerequisite to further advance in both fields. One obvious link lies in the development of theories appropriate to

[15] Baldwin, "Patterns of Development in Newly Settled Regions," *Manchester School of Economic and Social Studies*, XXIV, May, 1956, pp. 161-79.

[16] Levin, *The Export Economies: Their Pattern of Development in Historical Perspective* (Cambridge, Mass., 1960).

[17] G. M. Meier, "Economic Development and the Transfer Mechanism: Canada, 1895-1913," C.J.E.P.S., XIX Feb., 1953, pp. 1-19; J. C. Ingram, "Growth and Canada's Balance of Payments," *American Economic Review*, XLVII, March, 1957, pp. 93-104; John A. Stovel, *Canada in the World Economy* (Cambridge, Mass., 1959).

[18] Perloff and Wingo, "Natural Resource Endowment and Regional Economic Growth" in Joseph J. Spengler, ed., *Natural Resources and Economic Growth* (Washington, 1961), pp. 191-212; this article draws on Harvey S. Perloff, Edgar S. Dunn Jr., Eric E. Lampard, and Richard F. Muth, *Regions, Resources and Economic Growth* (Baltimore, 1960).

particular types of economic growth. The staple theory is presented here not as a general theory of economic growth, nor even a general theory about the growth of export-oriented economies, but rather as applicable to the atypical case of the new country.

The phenomenon of the new country, of the "empty" land or region overrun by the white man in the past four centuries, is, of course, well known. The leading examples are the United States and the British dominions. These countries had two distinctive characteristics as they began their economic growth: a favourable man/land ratio and an absence of inhibiting traditions.[19] From these initial features flow some highly probable consequences for the growth process, at least in the early phase: staple exports are the leading sector, setting the pace for economic growth and leaving their peculiar imprint on economy and society; the importation of scarce factors of production is essential; and growth, if it is to be sustained, requires an ability to shift resources that may be hindered by excessive reliance on exports in general, and, in particular, on a small number of staple exports. These conditions and consequences are not customarily identified with underdeveloped countries, and hence are not the typical building blocks of a theory of economic growth. Rather, the theory derived from them is limited, but consciously so in order to cast light on a special type of economic growth. Because of the key role of staple exports it can be called a staple theory of economic growth.

II

The fundamental assumption of the staple theory is that staple exports are the leading sector of the economy and set the pace for economic growth. The limited — at first possibly nonexistent — domestic market, and the factor proportions — an abundance of land relative to labour and capital — create a comparative advantage in resource-intensive exports, or staples. Economic development will be a process of diversification around an export base. The central concept of a staple theory,

[19] Both features are recognized by W. W. Rostow in *The United States in the World Arena* (New York, 1960), p. 6; the first is also cited by Bert F. Hoselitz, "Patterns of Economic Growth," c.j.e.p.s., XXI, Nov., 1955, pp. 416-31.

therefore, is the spread effects of the export sector, that is, the impact of export activity on domestic economy and society. To construct a staple theory, then, it is necessary to classify these spread effects and indicate their determinants.

Let us begin with the determinants. Assume to be given the resource base of the new country and the rest-of-the-world environment – the international demand for the supply of goods and factors, the international transportation and communication networks, the international power structure. The sole remaining determinant can then be isolated, namely, the character of the particular staple or staples being exported.

A focus on the character of the staple distinguished Innis' work. C. R. Fay expressed the point most succinctly: ". . . the emphasis is on the commodity itself: its significance for policy; the tying in of one activity with another; the way in which a basic commodity sets the general pace, creates new activities and is itself strengthened or perhaps dethroned, by its own creation."[20] The essence of the technique has been thrown into sharp relief by Baldwin. Using the method of ideal types, he contrasts the implications of reliance on a plantation crop and a family farm crop respectively for the economic development of an area exporting primary products. The important determinant is the technology of the industry, that is, the production function, which defines the degree of factor substitutability and the nature of returns to scale. With the production function specified and the necessary *ceteris paribus* assumptions – including the demand for goods and the supply of factors – a number of things follow: demand for factors; demand for intermediate inputs; possibility of further processing; and the distribution of income.

These determine the range of investment opportunities in domestic markets, or the extent of diversification around the export base. If the demand for the export staple increases, the quantity supplied by the new country will increase. This export expansion means a rise in income in the export sector. The spending of this income generates investment opportunities in other sectors, both at home and abroad. By classifying these income flows, we can state the staple theory in the form of a

[20] Fay, "The Toronto School of Economic History," *Economic History*, III, Jan., 1934, pp. 168-71. See also Easterbrook, "Problems in the Relationship of Communication and Economic History," p. 563.

disaggregated multiplier-accelerator mechanism. In Hirschman's terms, the inducement to domestic investment resulting from the increased activity of the export sector can be broken down into three linkage effects: backward linkage, forward linkage, and what we shall call final demand linkage.[21] The staple theory then becomes a theory of capital formation; the suggestion has been made but not yet elaborated that it is such.

Backward linkage is a measure of the inducement to invest in the home-production of inputs, including capital goods, for the expanding export sector. The export good's production function and the relative prices of inputs will determine the types and quantities of inputs required. Diversification will be the greatest where the input requirements involve resources and technologies which permit of home-production. The emphasis usually placed in studies of economic development on barriers to entry into machinery production suggests a high import content for capital-intensive staples, and hence a small backward linkage effect. Caves and Holton, however, emphasize the importance of capital-intensive agriculture in supplying linkage to domestic agricultural machinery production. Theory and history suggest that the most important example of backward linkage is the building of transport systems for collection of the staple, for that can have further and powerful spread effects.

Forward linkage is a measure of the inducement to invest in industries using the output of the export industry as an input. The most obvious, and typically most important, example is the increasing value added in the export sector; the economic possibilities of further processing and the nature of foreign tariffs will be the prime determinants.

Final demand linkage is a measure of the inducement to invest in domestic industries producing consumer goods for factors in the export sector. Its prime determinant is the size of the domestic market, which is in turn dependent on the level of income – aggregate and average – and its distribution.

The size of the aggregate income will vary directly with the absolute size of the export sector. But a portion of the income may be received by what Levin has called "foreign factors" – factors which remit their income abroad – rather than "domestic factors." To the extent that income received by foreign factors

[21] Albert O. Hirschman, *The Strategy of Economic Development* (New Haven, 1958), chap. 6.

is not taxed away domestically, final demand linkage will be lessened. The servicing of capital imports is a case in point. Primary producers are notoriously susceptible to indebtedness, and the burden will be greater the more capital-intensive the staple. Leakage can also result from wages paid to migratory labour and from immigrants' remittances.

The average level of income, that is, the per capita income of the domestic factors, depends on the productivity of "land" or the resource content of the staple export, for other factors are importable. The distribution of income, on present assumptions, is determined by the nature of the production function of the staple, in Baldwin's models being relatively unequal for the plantation crop and relatively equal for the family farm crop.

The impact of these two market dimensions on final demand linkage can be seen by classifying consumer spending in two ways. Firstly, consumer spending may be either on home-produced goods or on imports, and the higher the marginal propensity to import the lower the final demand linkage. Secondly, it may be either on subsistence goods and luxuries, or on a broad range of goods and services; the latter are more likely to lend themselves to those economies of mass production which lie at the heart of on-going industrialization, while luxury spending – other than for labour-intensive services – is likely, given the tendency to ape the tastes of more advanced countries, to be directed towards imported goods, that is, to create in Levin's terminology "luxury importers."

Final demand linkage will tend to be higher, the higher the average level of income and the more equal its distribution. At a higher level of income, consumers are likely to be able to buy a range of goods and services which lend themselves to domestic production by advanced industrial techniques. Where the distribution is relatively unequal, the demand will be for subsistence goods at the lower end of the income scales and for luxuries at the upper end. The more equal the distribution the less likelihood of opulent luxury importers and the greater the likelihood of a broadly based market for mass-produced goods.

The discussion of the linkages so far has assumed that investment is induced solely by demand factors. But on the supply side the expansion of the export sector creates opportunities for domestic investment which may or may not be exploited. Consideration must be given to the relationship between staple production and the supply of entrepreneurship and complementary inputs, including technology.

The key factor is entrepreneurship, the ability to perceive and exploit market opportunities. Entrepreneurial functions can be fulfilled by foreigners, and to the extent that this makes available technical and marketing skills the result can be advantageous to the new country. But the literature on economic development, and particularly on the dual economy, raises many doubts as to the adequacy of foreign entrepreneurship. It may flow freely into the export and import trades, but fail to exploit domestic opportunities. Exports may be regarded as safer, in part because they earn directly the foreign exchange necessary to reimburse foreign factors, but largely because export markets are better organized and better known than domestic markets. Foreign domination of entrepreneurship may militate against its general diffusion.

An adequate supply of domestic entrepreneurship, both private and governmental, is crucial. Its existence depends on the institutions and values of society, about which the economist generalizes at his peril. But the character of the staple is clearly relevant. Consider, for example, Baldwin's polar cases. In the plantation case, the dominant group with its rentier mentality on the one hand, and the mass of slaves who are prevented from bettering themselves on the other, can produce a set of institutions as inimical to entrepreneurial activity as is to be found in any tradition-ridden society. Business pursuits may be castigated as "money grubbing"; education – which, as North has emphasized, is very important – is likely to be confined to the élite and to slight the development of technical and business skills; political activity tends to be devoted to the defence of the *status quo*. On the other hand, in the family-farm case, as in wheat areas, the more equal distribution of income can result in attitudes towards social mobility, business activities, education, and the role of government which are more favourable to diversified domestic growth. These are gross differences; the more subtle ones could be worked out for specific staples.

Even where domestic entrepreneurship is forthcoming, its effectiveness rests on the availability of labour and capital, both foreign and domestic. The "push" from the old countries has in the past created a highly elastic supply of labour, although not, as the slave trade attests, without some resort to the use of force.

But the individual receiving country has to create conditions sufficiently favourable to the inflow of labour to compete with other receiving countries. The original staple may create a social structure which is unattractive to the immigrant with skills suitable for the development of domestic economic activity. Where the staple is land-intensive, as is fur, the staple producers may find it in their own self-interest to discourage immigration and settlement. The transport technologies associated with particular staples provide varying passenger fares and hence differential stimuli to immigration. The availability of labour domestically will depend on the competing attractions of staple production and the quality of the labour force that has resulted from the exploitation of the particular staple. The staple activity may attract excess labour through non-pecuniary advantages: the romantic life of the fur trader and the aristocratic life of the planter are frequently alleged to have had detrimental consequences for other sectors of the economy. The quality of the labour force is significantly related to education.

Foreign capital, both in substance and in preference for foreign trade over domestic industry, is difficult to distinguish from foreign entrepreneurship, which we have already discussed. The availability of capital domestically will depend on the extent of domestic saving and the biases of the savers in placing their funds. The amount of saving will be determined by the production function for the staple. For example, Baldwin argues that savings will be higher with the skewed income distribution of the plantation crop than with the equal distribution of the family-farm crop. This would be the conventional view, although the opposite would be true if it were assumed that saving was encouraged by greater investment opportunities at home or discouraged by a greater concern with consumption for status in a more hierarchical society. But the amount of saving may not matter greatly. For domestic savers, like foreign capitalists, may be biased against domestic activities; they may prefer to expand the export industry further or to invest in the import trade. They may also prefer to invest abroad, for in an open economy capital can flow out as well as in. It is only when there are abundant opportunities in domestic markets waiting to be exploited that the amount of domestic saving will significantly determine the rate of investment.

The technology applied in domestic sectors is likely, to the extent that it is up to date, to be substantially borrowed from abroad. The newness of the country will minimize the difficulties of adapting borrowed technology and create a potential minimum growth rate not significantly lower than that achieved by advanced economies. The inflow of foreign technology will be facilitated by the inflow of foreign entrepreneurship and capital. To the extent that innovation is necessary and possible in the export sector, confidence may be gained by domestic entrepreneurs which will facilitate creative responses in domestic sectors. As domestic entrepreneurship emerges, innovations should become more appropriate to domestic factor proportions and the requirements of the domestic market.

A historically relevant theory must allow not only for the differing character of particular staples but also for the impact of the resource base of the new country and the international environment. For any particular new country the initial conditions can vary, and these conditions can change over time, both autonomously and as a result of the actions of the new country consequent on its success in exploiting its particular staple or staples.

Although these points are important, it is difficult to say much in general about them. For any given inducement to invest offered by the market, an appropriate resource base is necessary; the best of all possible staples will do little to encourage development if the resource base is sufficiently bad, and the impact of a particular staple can vary widely depending on the resource base of the particular country.[22] The resource base itself can change through discovery, and success in staple production, at least for some staples, may expedite the process.[23]

So too the international environment can vary in its suitability for the development of new countries. Staple producers begin as colonial outposts of old countries and differences among the latter, in their markets for staples, their supplies of factors for export, their institutions and values, and their colonial policies,

[22] North's book is weakened by his failure adequately to appreciate the importance of the resource base. He applies Baldwin's polar cases to the American South and West in the period prior to the Civil War, but has very probably exaggerated their efficacy in explaining rates and types of development by understating differences in the general resource base which favoured the West.

[23] Note the Canadian mineral discoveries consequent on railway building and hence linked ultimately to the development of the western wheat economy.

will affect growth prospects. Change can take place in any of these dimensions: in foreign demand and foreign supply, which can destroy old staples and create new ones; in transport facilities, which can cheapen internationally traded goods; in the "push" of factors from the old countries and the "pull" from other new countries; in colonial policy and in the frequency of wars which can either encourage or discourage growth. And the new country, to the extent that it is successful, may gain power to mould the environment to suit its needs. It can develop a transport system adequate for both domestic and export requirements; it can pursue a commercial policy by which it can cause further processing of its exports and promote import-competing industry without unduly interfering with the optimal allocation of its resources.

What is the likely growth path of a staple economy? Growth is initiated by an increase in demand for a staple export. If the spread effects are potent, as the export sector grows so too will the domestic sectors. The result will be increasing demand for factors. Domestic slack, if it exists at all, will be quickly absorbed, and the continuation of growth will depend on the ability to import scarce factors. If the supply of foreign factors is elastic, the customary tendency for the expansion of one sector – in this case exports – to affect domestic sectors adversely by driving up factor prices is mitigated. This explains the very strong booms that are a feature of growth in staple economies.[24]

But what of the nature of growth in the long run? In a staple economy, as in any other, sustained growth requires an ability to shift resources at the dictates of the market – what C. P. Kindleberger calls "a capacity to transform." Particular export lines can create prosperity, but typically only for a short time. Over the longer pull they cease to be profitable either because of diminishing returns on the supply side, or adverse shifts in demand consequent on competition from cheaper sources of supply or from synthetics, or because of the income-inelasticity of foreign demand, or simply because of changes of taste. This tendency can be slowed up by attempts to improve marketing and by seeking out cost-reducing innovations. The possibility

[24] On external diseconomies generated by an expanding sector when factor supplies are inelastic, see Marcus Fleming, "External Economies and the Doctrine of Balanced Growth," *Economic Journal*, LXV, June, 1955, pp. 241-56. On the character of export-led booms in Canada, see the literature cited in n. 17.

of the latter depends on the character of the staple; for example, because of the physical properties of the plants, cotton production was historically much more resistant to mechanization than wheat-growing. But the law of diminishing returns cannot be checked indefinitely. Sustained growth, then, requires resource flexibility and innovation sufficient to permit shifts into new export lines or into production for the domestic market.

The probability of long-run success for the staple economy is significantly increased by its two distinctive initial features: a favourable man/land ratio and an absence of inhibiting traditions. The first implies a relatively high standard of living which facilitates expanding domestic markets and substantial factor mobility. The fact that new countries do not start their development with population pressing against scarce resources gives them an enormous advantage over the typical underdeveloped country. Specifically, they have neither a large subsistence agricultural sector severely limiting markets for domestic industry, nor a pool of cheap labour permitting industrialization to proceed with only limited impact on the incomes of much of the population. Subsequent population growth, in part by immigration, means that the size of population is closely related to economic opportunity at a relatively high standard of living. The second feature, the lack of traditions, means that institutions and values must be formed anew, and although there will be a substantial carry-over from the old world, the process will be selective and those transferred are likely to take a form more favourable to economic growth.

These are substantial advantages, and go far to explain the extraordinary success of some new countries. But even for the staple economy, historians have insisted that the process of growth is not without pitfalls. It is frequently alleged, at least implicitly, that the achievement of a high level of national income masks deficiencies in the structural balance of the economy. W. W. Rostow charges that the high levels of welfare achieved in new countries by exploiting land and natural resources will delay their reaching the "take-off" stage.[25] If the concept of take-off is interpreted as meaning simply the growth and diversification of the manufacturing sector, this argument runs counter to the staple theory. Rostow's claim, however, is no more than an untested hypothesis. He has not outlined the

[25] Rostow, *The Stages of Economic Growth* (Cambridge, 1960), p. 36.

specific mechanism by which primary exports delay industrialization. It is not clear that he is saying anything more than that if a country has a comparative advantage in primary exports it will perforce have a comparative disadvantage in manufactures. This static view communicates nothing about the process of growth in a world where factor supply can be highly elastic and the composition of imports can shift radically over time. The first peril, then, is illusory.[26]

A more real difficulty is that the staple exporters – specifically, those exercising political control – will develop an inhibiting "export mentality," resulting in an overconcentration of resources in the export sector and a reluctance to promote domestic development. Our previous comments on the social and political structure associated with particular staples are relevant here, but the literature on economic development in general is replete with other hypotheses and examples. Easterbrook, developing a theme of Innis', has commented that bureaucratic institutions concerned with "playing it safe" tend to emerge in the face of the initial uncertainties of a marginal status, and then to persist.[27] In the Cuban case, H. C. Wallich emphasizes the importance of the "sugar mentality" which "gives sugar an economic and political dominance even greater than its true weight in the economy."[28] H. W. Singer has pointed out that, when export earnings are high, the country is able to finance development but lacks the incentive to do so; when the earnings are low, the incentive exists but the means are lacking.[29] In Canada, there is evidence of a boom-and-bust psychology; excessive optimism causes booms to proceed beyond their proper limits,[30] while depressions are met by resort to tariffs

[26] North, after appeal to the American case, reaches a similar conclusion.

[27] See his "The Climate of Enterprise," *American Economic Review*, XXXIX, May, 1949, pp. 322-35; "Uncertainty and Economic Change," *Journal of Economic History*, XIV, Autumn, 1954, pp. 346-60; "Long Period Comparative Study: Some Historical Cases," *Journal of Economic History*, XVII, Dec., 1957, pp. 571-95.

[28] Wallich, *Monetary Problems of an Export Economy* (Cambridge, Mass., 1960), p. 12.

[29] Singer. "The Distribution of Gains between Investing and Borrowing Countries," *American Economic Review*, XL, May, 1950, p. 482.

[30] The classic example is the building of two additional transcontinental railways during the wheat boom, 1896-1913. The general phenomenon is noted by A. F. W. Plumptre, "The Nature of Economic Development in the British Dominions," c.j.e.p.s., III, Nov., 1937, pp. 489-507.

which are "second best" in the short run and probably inappropriate in the long run and which persist once introduced.[31] One is led to conclude that staple economies are often believed to be much more at the mercy of destiny than they actually are. As Levin has demonstrated in his study of Burma, planning can alter income flows, thereby strengthening linkages and increasing domestic investment.

The serious pitfall is that the economy may get caught in a "staple trap." Sustained growth requires the capacity to shift attention to new foreign or domestic markets. The former requires a favourable combination of external demand and available resources. The latter requires a population base and level of per capita income that permit taking advantage of the economies of scale in modern industrialism. Both require institutions and values consistent with transformation, and *that* requires the good fortune of having avoided specialization in the wrong kind of staple, such as Baldwin's plantation crop. If the staple is unfavourable or if stagnation persists for any extended period because of a weak resource base, the staple economy can take on the character of the traditional underdeveloped country in both respects stressed by Rostow. Firstly, institutions and values can emerge which are inimical to sustained growth, and the process of remoulding will be difficult. Secondly, a population problem can be encountered as the population initially established through immigration continues to expand through natural increase. Persistent unemployment and underemployment will become characteristic of the economy. Immigration may be replaced by emigration, as resort is had to the Irish solution. In the absence of alternative opportunities, factors will tend to accumulate excessively in the export sector or in subsistence agriculture. In the former case, growth may become "immiserized" as the terms of trade turn against the country.[32] In the latter, the economy will face a problem common to most underdeveloped countries: develop-

---

[31] The high correlation between depressions and tariff increases is noted by John H. Young, *Canadian Commercial Policy*, A study done for the Royal Commission on Canada's Economic Prospects (Ottawa, 1957).

[32] For a formal presentation of the theory of immiserizing growth, see J. Bhagwati, "Immiserizing Growth: A Geometric Note," *Review of Economic Studies*, XXV, June, 1958, pp. 201-5, and "International Trade and Economic Expansion," *American Economic Review*, XLVIII, Dec., 1958, pp. 941-53.

ment will depend on the interdependent growth of agriculture and industry. In any event, the initial opportunities for easy growth will no longer exist.

If the pitfalls are avoided – if the staple or staples generate strong linkage effects which are adequately exploited – then eventually the economy will grow and diversify to the point where the appelation "staple economy" will no longer suffice. Population growth will come to result more from natural increase than from immigration. Per capita income will rise beyond the level consistent with any customary definition of underdevelopment. With the gaining of enterpreneurial confidence and the expanding opportunities of domestic markets, domestic entrepreneurs will persistently usurp markets from foreign suppliers.[33] A well-developed secondary manufacturing sector serving domestic markets and possibly even foreign markets will emerge. Staple exports and imports of manufactured goods may fall as a percent of national income. If "land" remains relatively abundant, this may not happen; that should not be taken as proof of backwardness, however, for it may be no more than the momentary outcome of the operation of the law of comparative advantage.

III

We have taken pains throughout to emphasize the special character of the staple theory. Consideration of the range of relationships possible between foreign trade and economic development will underline the point. In a recent synthesis of the literature, Kindleberger has put forth three models relating foreign trade and economic development; these cover cases where foreign trade is, respectively, a leading, a lagging, and a balancing sector of the economy.[34] In the model in which it leads, autonomous foreign demand, typically accompanied by technological change in the developing country, sets the pace, and economic development is a process of diversification around an export base. The staple economy is clearly a special case of this model.

In the model in which foreign trade lags, domestic investment

---

[33] This mechanism has recently been emphasized by Hirschman, *The Strategy of Economic Development*, p. 120 *ff*.

[34] C. P. Kindleberger, *Economic Development* (New York, Toronto, London, 1958), chap. 14.

leads, tending to create pressure on the balance of payments which is met by import-substitution. A large number of under-developed countries believe that this is the relevant model. The restrictive nature of the commercial policy of developed coun-tries, combined with the tendency for import demand to expand more rapidly than income in the early stages of development – chiefly because of the need to import capital goods and possibly also industrial raw materials and food – lend credence to this belief. The contrast between the leading and lagging models is that between development based on trade-expansion and devel-opment based on trade-contraction.

The model in which foreign trade is the balancing sector covers the case of trade-expansion which is not demand-led, but rather based on autonomous supply pushes in the export sector. It applies to the case where domestic investment leads, creating balance of payments difficulties which are met by pushing exports rather than by limiting imports. A trade pattern based on exporting manufactures, in order to import food and take the strain off domestic agriculture, has been espoused by both W. Arthur Lewis and the late Ragnar Nurske, and is a particular version of the balancing case.[35]

Kindleberger's classification applies to countries already in the process of development. The limitations of the staple theory emerge most clearly when we consider the case where export production is superimposed on a pre-existing subsistence eco-nomy. For the staple economy, the export sector can be an engine of growth; for the subsistence economy, the consensus appears to be that the export sector will have either limited or adverse effects on the economy. The linkage effects are likely to be slight, regardless of the character of the export good, because of the internal structure of the underdeveloped country, including the existence of non-competing groups in the domestic and foreign sectors.[36] Even where groups are competing, if there is disguised unemployment in the subsistence sector, increases in productivity in the export industry will not bring increases in real wages; these depend on raising productivity in the subsist-

[35] Lewis, *The Theory of Economic Growth* (Homewood, Ill., 1955); Nurkse, *Patterns of Trade and Development*, Wicksell Lectures, 1959 (Stockholm, 1959).

[36] H. Myint, "The Gains from International Trade and the Backward Countries," *Review of Economic Studies*, XXII, 1954-55, pp. 129-42.

ence sector and to this exports make little or no contribution.[37] The country might have been better off if it had never exported in the first place. Growth may have become immiserized, as was previously noted. Domestic factors may have been drawn into export production when they could have been more productively applied to domestic manufacture.[38] Investments made complementary to the export sector may generate pecuniary external economies which excessively encourage primary export production.[39] Imports which flood in as a result of exporting may destroy existing handicraft production, and if the export sector does not absorb the labour which is displaced, the gains from trade may be negative.[40] If exports and domestic investment compete for available saving, then a rise in the export volume can directly reduce the rate of growth of income.[41]

IV

The closeness of the link between the staple approach and Canadian historical research makes it unlikely that the application of a more explicit theory will add much to our understanding of Canadian economic development. Nevertheless, a few comments are in order, both to clear up some specific ambiguities and to resolve the issue of the relevance of the staple theory to Canada's economic development, past and present.

1. The cod fisheries and the fur trade were clearly the leading sectors of the early period. Neither staple required much permanent settlement, although as the fur trade came to rely less on the Indian and penetrated further west and as the cod fisheries shifted from the green cure to the dry cure – an example of forward linkage – the impetus to settlement increased. In New France the distribution of income consequent on the fur trade may have been such as to lower final demand linkage –

[37] W. Arthur Lewis, "Economic Development with Unlimited Supplies of Labour," *Manchester School*, XXII, May, 1954, pp. 139-41.
[38] Singer, "The Distribution of Gains."
[39] Lewis, *The Theory of Economic Growth*, p. 348.
[40] G. Haberler provides a geometric demonstration of a case where free trade is harmful, given rigid factor prices. "Some Problems in the Pure Theory of International Trade," *Economic Journal*, LX, June, 1950, pp. 223-40. The argument is extended in Steffan Burenstam Linder, *An Essay on Trade and Transformation* (New York, Stockholm, 1961), chap. 2.
[41] R. J. Ball, "Capital Imports and Economic Development: Paradoxy or Orthodoxy," *Kyklos*, XV, 1962, fasc. 3, pp. 610-23.

although it would hardly bear comparison with that resulting from a plantation crop – and the aristocracy may have been as much feudal as *bourgeois* in its attitudes, although the drive of men such as Jean Talon should not be forgotten. But neither the character of the staple nor the Frenchness of the colony explain the slow growth relative to the American colonies. Rather, what is fundamental was poor location compared with New England for supplying the West Indies market. This limited the diversity of exports and thus retarded the development of commercial agriculture, lumbering, and above all the carrying trade and shipbuilding which were then the keys to development. A small population base, established more for reasons of imperial design than of economics *per se*, grew rapidly by natural increase. In the face of limited economic opportunities, labour accumulated in subsistence agriculture and New France came to approximate the dual economy, with a compact agricultural community of habitants and the moving frontier of the fur traders, which had only limited contacts one with another.[42] By the time of the Conquest the colony had clearly taken on some of the coloration of an "old" society and was partly ensnared in the staple trap.

In the Atlantic colonies, New England's success in developing an aggressive commercial economy around the fisheries shows that the character of cod as a staple can hardly explain the slow growth of Nova Scotia and Newfoundland. Rather, proximity to the markets of the West Indies and southern mainland colonies and, to a lesser extent, good agricultural land and the possibility of a winter fishery, were the prerequisites that were lacking. The effects of a poor location and a weak resource base – the latter being particularly applicable to Newfoundland – were intensified by the frequency of imperial conflict and the commercial and military aggressiveness of New England. The result militated against either England or France taking the effort that was necessary to create an environment favourable to further development. The area was not so much trapped as buffeted about and ignored.

Absence of economic opportunity because of geographic factors was the crucial constraint on both continental and maritime developments. Innis' method has obscured this point

[42] Dietrich Gerhard, "The Frontier in Comparative View," *Comparative Studies in History and Society*, I, March, 1959, pp. 205-29.

and has led to exaggerated emphasis on the character of the staples, particularly of fur. But if the nature of the staples is insufficient to explain the absence of rapid growth, lack of diversified development imprints more clearly the character of those staples around which some success is found and increases the probability that their peculiar biases will persist in institutions and values. Thus, with fur came the life of the habitant and the vision of a centralized transcontinental economy; with cod, parochialism and a commitment to the sea.

2. Fowke has argued that commercial agriculture in Upper Canada rose above the subsistence level prior to the 1840's in the absence of substantial external demand. Although allowance must be made for "shanty demand" linked to timber exports, the point is conceded, and with it the implication that some growth is possible without exports as the leading sector. But the quality of the growth that took place was unimpressive. The census of 1851 shows industrial development to be confined to flourmills and sawmills, both of which were on an export basis, and to the small-scale production of the simpler types of manufacture for the local market.[43] The population and income levels that had been attained were not sufficient to sustain a large or technologically sophisticated manufacturing sector. Buckley rightly insists that the economy became more complex after 1820 and that the range of economic opportunity widened, but this does not mean that staple exports ceased to be of critical importance.

3. One of Buckley's criticisms of the staple approach is its tendency "to ignore any section once the staple which created or supported it is no longer expanding," and he cites as an example the slighting of Quebec's economic development since the decline of the fur trade.[44] His point has some validity, at least so far as Quebec is concerned, but the neglect is not inherent in a properly stated staple theory of economic growth. As the new country (or region) ages, whether it be successful or unsuccessful, it takes on the character of an old country and becomes amenable to analysis as such. In Quebec in the nineteenth century, it is clear that the expansion of timber and ships

[43] O. J. Firestone, "Development of Canada's Economy, 1850-1890" in *Trends in the American Economy in the Nineteenth Century* (Princeton, 1960), pp. 217-52.
[44] "The Role of Staple Industries," p. 447.

as staple exports, the entrepreneurial drive and accumulated capital of the English commercial class carried over from the fur trade, and emigration which relieved the pressure of population on scarce resources combined to lessen the probability that the region would become too deeply enmeshed in the staple trap. Nevertheless, it is the interrelationship between agriculture and industry in the context of a rapidly growing population that should be made the focus of study, as one would expect to be done for any presently underdeveloped country. Statistics on the relative rates of growth of Ontario and Quebec indicate, incidentally, that if one gives credence to the alleged anti-commercial attitudes of the French Canadian, then, given the less favourable man/land ratio Quebec inherited from New France, what needs to be explained is the remarkable success of Quebec.

4. The period of Canadian economic history on which most controversy has focused recently has been the "Great Depression" of 1873-96. So long as it could be properly regarded as a great depression, it was amenable to the staple approach. Its bad reputation was based on the slow growth of population and persistent emigration, and this could be linked to the failure of the western wheat economy to expand in a sustained fashion in the face of a trend decline in the world price of wheat. The absence of rapid extensive growth made it possible for the period to be passed over quickly in the history books, and to be remembered more for the attempts that were made to promote development than for the actual growth achieved. Recent research, however, particularly the statistical work of Firestone, McDougall, Hartland, and Bertram, [45] makes it impossible to continue to regard these years as a great depression; they witnessed, in fact, an impressive increase in real per capita income, comparable to that in the United States, considerable industrial expansion, and substantial capital inflow.

[45] O. J. Firestone, *Canada's Economic Development, 1867-1953* (London, 1958), and "Development of Canada's Economy, 1850-1900"; Duncan M. McDougall, "Immigration into Canada, 1851-1920," C.J.E.P.S., XXVII, May, 1961, pp. 162-75; Penelope Hartland, "Canadian Balance of Payments since 1868" in *Trends in the American Economy in the Nineteenth Century*, pp. 717-55; Gordon W. Bertram, "Historical Statistics on Growth and Structure of Manufacturing in Canada, 1870-1957," Canadian Political Science Association Conference on Statistics, June 10-11, 1962.

The growth in real income can be attributed partly to the export sector. Exports did fall as a percentage of national income. Nevertheless, the real value of exports grew absolutely; there were important shifts in the composition of exports which generated new investment, from wood products to agriculture, and within the latter, from grain to animal products, with cattle and cheese emerging as the new staples; probably exports became more highly manufactured – the growth of cheese factories is striking – and more capital-intensive; railway building provided an important stimulus to growth and its *primum causum* was the expectation of large exports of western grain.

Exports, then, continued to play their conventional role as a leading sector. They can hardly be given full credit, however, for the increase in real income of this period. Factor increments shifted from export markets to domestic markets with a success inconsistent with a markedly backward economy. Yet the extent to which the adaptation was made to a declining stimulus from the export sector should not be exaggerated. The decade rates of growth of manufacturing after 1870 are not comparable to those of the first decade of the twentieth century when exports were expanding rapidly, and at the end of the century Canadian industry was still backward relative to that of such countries as Britain, the United States, and Germany. There was substantial net emigration in every decade from 1861 to 1901. The Canadian economy was not growing fast enough to generate employment opportunities for increments to the labour force by natural increase; while this may be no cause for concern from an international perspective, contemporary political debate and newspaper comment leaves no doubt that Canadians regarded this steady outflow of population as evidence of an unsatisfactory performance by the economy.

5. A restatement of the staple theory might be expected to cast new light on the hoary issue of the long-run impact of the Canadian tariff. A conventional argument has been that the tariff permanently increases population because export industries are less labour-intensive than import-competing industries.[46] Young would appear to have effectively disposed of this line

[46] W. A. Mackintosh, *The Economic Background of Dominion-Provincial Relations, A Study Prepared for the Royal Commission on Dominion-Provincial Relations* (Ottawa, 1939); reprinted in the Carleton Library, 1964, pp. 140 *ff*; and Clarence L. Barber, "Canadian Tariff Policy," C.J.E.P.S., XXI, Nov., 1955, pp. 513-30.

of reasoning,[47] but there may be some validity to the population-sustaining argument for a tariff if one looks at its effect in a boom period, such as 1896 to 1913. It is clear that, by reducing the marginal propensity to import, the tariff increases employment in import-competing industries. At the same time, the fact that factors are in highly elastic supply limits the extent to which costs rise for the export industries, while the sheer strength of the boom, which is being further increased by investment in import-competing industries, keeps imports high in spite of the tariff, thus tending to eliminate foreign repercussion. The tariff would appear to increase employment opportunities, and thereby the population-sustaining capacity of the economy. If, as is probable, the infant industry argument is not valid, however, then the real income has been lowered. We return to the customary view that the Canadian tariff has increased population while lowering real income. But there is an important qualification, as a result of which population may not be increased in the long-run. The tariff will tend to strengthen a boom which is already excessive and thus to increase the problems of readjustment that have to be faced eventually. To the extent that these problems are not otherwise solved, emigration to the United States with its higher wages is likely to be greater than it would have been in the absence of the tariff.

6. The period 1896 to 1913 was undeniably an example of a classic staple boom. But the industrial development which was achieved in its wake so increased the complexity of the Canadian economy as to make it impossible to continue to use staple industries as the unifying theme of economic growth, or so the implicit reasoning seems to run in the best of the textbooks.[48] The notion of a discontinuity in Canadian economic development in the early twentieth century, though superficially attractive, is difficult to maintain, as Caves and Holton have demonstrated. The manufacturing sector appears to have been filling in slowly over a long period of time, without passing through any critical stage of economic maturity. Patterns of short-run change consistent with the staple theory are to be found in all three periods of rapid growth in this century, 1900-1913, 1920-1929, and 1946-1956: the rate of investment closely reflects the

[47] Young, *Canadian Commercial Policy*, pp. 89 *ff*.
[48] W. T. Easterbrook and H. G. J. Aitken, *Canadian Economic History* (Toronto, 1956).

demand for exports, current and prospective; production for
domestic markets expands around the export-base, replacing
imports; excessive optimism leads to over-expansion in the
export sector and complicates the subsequent problems of readjustment; and the quantity of saving adjusts itself to investment demand, in part by inducing capital imports.

Is the staple theory, then, relevant to Canada today, or has
it been long irrelevant? Does the evidence adduced by Caves
and Holton on the common character of growth patterns in the
twentieth century, which could be extended to include the boom
of the 1850's, reflect historical necessity or historical accident?
Is Canada unable to grow at a satisfactory rate unless exports
lead, or able to do so but relieved of the necessity until now by
good luck? There is no doubt that luck is a neglected factor in
Canadian economic history. Nevertheless, the fundamental fact
is the pervasive interdependence with the North Atlantic community, and particularly with the United States. Canada is a
small and open economy, a marginal area responding to the
exogenous impact of the international economy. The basic
determinants of Canadian growth are the volume and character
of her staple exports and the ability to borrow, adapt, and
marginally supplement foreign technology. These guarantee for
Canada a minimum rate of growth that cannot diverge too
widely from that achieved elsewhere, particularly in the United
States. They create no assurance, however, of a rate of growth
sufficient to maintain full employment, even if the expansion of
the labour force be limited to natural increase. The probability
that borrowed technology and staple exports will provide a
sufficient impetus to the economy has diminished as staples have
become more capital-intensive.

That expanding exports and satisfactory economic growth
have been correlated in the past is clear. How this is interpreted
depends on a judgment as to the freedom of action that Canada
possesses. The emphasis increasingly placed by economists on
the link between the inefficiency of Canadian secondary manufacturing industry and the Canadian tariff[49] suggests that the

[49] See H. E. English, "The Role of International Trade in Canadian
Economic Development since the 1920's," unpublished Ph.D. thesis,
University of California, 1957; S. Stykolt and H. C. Eastman, "A
Model for the Study of Protected Oligopolies," *Economic Journal*,
LXX, June, 1960, pp. 336-47; Roger Dehem, "The Economics of
Stunted Growth," c.j.e.p.s., XXVIII, Nov., 1962, pp. 502-10.

major difficulty is an inhibiting export mentality, the elimination of which lies within Canadian control. From this point of view, economic institutions and political values, an inefficient structure of industry combined with an unwillingness to do anything about it, have in the past prevented Canada from growing at a satisfactory rate in the absence of a strong lead from primary exports, but this need not be true for the indefinite future.

Economic Growth in Canadian Industry, 1870-1915: The Staple Model

G. W. BERTRAM

I. THE STAPLE MODEL OF ECONOMIC GROWTH

The paths of economic development of countries of recent settlement may be significantly different from those of many European and Asiatic societies, particularly with reference to their abundant supplies of natural resources and scarcity of population and capital. The countries of recent settlement developed within the "benign" atmosphere of the nineteenth century, often finding their place in an existing international economy through eventual establishment of a comparative advantage in agricultural extractive industries as successive shifts in demand and technology made these resources economic. A. J. Youngson's observation about American economic history may apply to Canada as well: ". . . the political and economic conditions of the nineteenth century enabled her development to be geared to largely complementary developments in western Europe in an unprecedented and probably for the most part unrepeatable fashion.[1]

While the characteristics of staple production have changed somewhat in recent decades there is still much to recommend the staple theory as a conceptual framework useful in explaining the operation of long-run growth factors in the Canadian eco-

Source: Gordon W. Bertram, "Economic Growth and Canadian Industry, 1870-1915: The Staple Model and the Take-off Hypothesis," *Canadian Journal of Economics and Political Science*, Vol. XXIX, no. 2, May 1963, pp. 162-184. Reprinted by permission of the author and publishers. Deletions have been made in preparing this text for the Carleton Library.

The author wishes to express his appreciation to the Institute of Economic Research, Queen's University, Kingston, for financial and research assistance during the summer of 1960.

[1] Youngson, *Possibilities of Economic Progress* (Cambridge, 1959) p. 269.

nomy. Canadian economists have long been familiar with the extensive staple theory literature which developed in Canada, particularly the insights of W. A. Mackintosh and Harold A. Innis.[2] The staple model is essentially a theory of regional growth within the framework of an international economy. Export staples can be identified as industries based on agricultural and extractive resources, not requiring elaborate processing and finding a large portion of their market in international trade. They may range from standardized agricultural commodities involving mainly storage and transport facilities to industries we have classified here as primary manufacturing industries. The term, which was introduced by the recent Royal Commission on Canada's Economic Prospects, covers in the main manufacturing industries supplied by staple extractive industries.

The basic factors determining economic growth in expanding economies such as Canada's have been the success of export staples, the structural characteristics of the export industries, and the disposition of income received by the export sector. The staple theory requires that, in an open economy such as Canada's, development can only proceed if it is related to the special characteristics of the Atlantic and international economy. From the viewpoint of the staple-producing country or region, demand for the staple export was largely an exogenous factor and the

[2] Although an American economist, G. S. Callender, made one of the earliest statements of the staple approach (*Selections from the Economic History of the United States, 1765-1860* [Boston, 1909]), it has only been in recent years that American economic historians have apparently discovered the Canadian literature, rediscovered Callender, and begun some fruitful applications – particularly with respect to the American period 1790-1860. See particularly D. C. North, "A Note on Professor Rostow's 'Take-Off' Into Self-Sustained Growth," *Manchester School of Economic and Social Studies*, Jan., 1958, pp. 68-75. In this critical review of Rostow's article, North advocated a staple model interpretation of economic growth. He suggested that for the United States and Canada ". . . one could advance a hypothesis which is the reverse of Rostow's, namely, that the opening up and development of new areas capable of producing primary goods in demand in existing markets induced the growth of industrialization." See also North, "Location Theory and Regional Economic Growth," *Journal of Political Economy*, June, 1955, pp. 243-58, and *The Economic Growth of the United States, 1790-1860* (Englewood Cliffs, N.J., 1961). In a later statement Youngson, in *Possibilities of Economic Progress*, p. 284, also noted in his discussion of case studies of economic progress in Sweden, 1850-80, and Denmark, 1865-1900, the tendency in economic history to neglect the interdependence between industry and agriculture.

expansion of income in the Atlantic economy in the nineteenth and twentieth centuries provided Canada with the essential background for growth. Land and natural resources in various regions, changing over time and climaxing in the opening of the West, played a fundamental role. Given the natural resources, there existed a series of production possibilities which were to develop with technological change (another exogenous factor for the economy) and with further settlement in a rich resource base under the guidance of public policy. The success of the export sector depended upon the degree of comparative advantage the product possessed, and this in turn depended upon the resource endowment, international commodity prices, transportation costs, and relationships with established trading systems.

Throughout Canadian economic history the familiar succession of export staples initiated increases in productivity and income expansion. The export staple was the base for whatever commercialization existed in the developing economy. As the market sector widened with international trade, economic functions became more rationalized, resources shifted to more productive employment, and economies of scale were realized, so that productivity advanced. The success of staples as a growth-inducing factor was also dependent in a large measure on their respective production functions and the resulting distribution of income – a basic point made by Innis, developed more recently by R. E. Baldwin, and given a central position in D. C. North's analysis of economic growth in the United States from 1790 to 1860.[3] With regard to inputs, some export staples like the fur trade were not conducive to inflows of labour and consequent settlement; other staples such as timber and wheat had more favourable effects in encouraging labour inflow. Shifts in export staples meant new requirements in associated intermediate goods and social overhead capital. In important cases, social overhead came as a result of government action, prior to the export staple's complete appearance.

In Canada, as in the American "Old Northwest" of the 1820-1850's, the production of such agricultural products as wheat for export provided a pattern of income distribution in sharp contrast to, say, plantation export staples. The expansion of the domestic market was significantly influenced by the more widely distributed incomes of a commercially-oriented proprietor-farmer economy. The growth-inducing income distribution resulting from certain staple industries operated through the consequent increase in consumption and through further effects on investment in local residential construction. In addition, as Duesenberry has shown, a powerful stimulus to growth was provided through the multiplier-accelerator processes set in motion from the additions to income resulting from the geographic shifts involved in western wheat production.[4] The continually increasing increments in Midwestern income from wheat had multiplier-accelerator effects as income was partly spent on locally produced goods and services, and rising demand induced investment in producers' facilities (warehousing, processing facilities for agricultural goods), residential construction, and public services that could not be imported. Income in the older region might also rise as it supplied investment and consumer goods to the new region. Although there were important differences, the Canadian western frontier experience associated with wheat after the 1890's was undoubtedly analogous to that of the American Midwest in releasing a similar multiplier-accelerator process which influenced income in a number of regions.[5] The rise of communities serving an agricultural hinterland was evidence of the operation of this type of income-generation process in the expanding agricultural frontiers of Ontario in an earlier period.

A model for Canadian historical economic development would then place the export staple, within the context of the Atlantic economy and an expanding geographic frontier, at the centre of the analysis. A prominent position must also be given to large-scale investment promoted by government. After 1867, a major or even dominating purpose of federal government was the achievement of a development plan for Canadian

---

[4] James S. Duesenberry, "Some Aspects of the Theory of Economic Development," *Explorations in Entrepreneurial History*, Dec. 15, 1950, pp. 96-102.

[5] The broad production possibilities of the new resources in the United States may have made the American frontier process unique. See George G. S. Murphy and Arnold Zellner, "Sequential Growth, the Labor Safety Valve Doctrine, and the Development of American Unionism," *Journal of Economic History*, Sept., 1959, pp. 402-3; and Benjamin Higgins, *Economic Development* (New York, 1959), p. 192.

economic expansion. Success or potential success in the export sector induced capital inflows of sizable amounts per capita in the 1840's and 1850's, important inflows in the decades after Confederation, and extremely large amounts in the early twentieth century.

A final factor in the development model which was fundamental to export staples and to growing urbanization and industrialization was the change in technology propagated throughout the Atlantic economy. A very important role must be given to Canada's proximity to the United States, where many innovations were made and tested. In one sense the whole formula for Canadian development which gradually took shape with Confederation might be regarded as an attempt to duplicate the American pattern of frontier expansion, free land, and railroad construction.

II. THE RISE OF SUBSTANTIAL MANUFACTURING SECTORS

The last three decades of the nineteenth century in Canada have been regarded by some economic historians as a period of secular depression,[6] while 1896-1914 has been regarded as the decisive period of successful Canadian industrialization. The study of manufacturing presented here indicates that the last three decades of the nineteenth century was a period of substantial growth, increasing localization of industry and increasing specialization of the production of firms. Part of this growth may be attributed to the influence of staple industries analysed here, while a further significant portion may be attributed to the intensive development of secondary manufacturing within the region of Central Canada.[7]

The main effort of this paper has been the construction of a revised series of manufacturing statistics for Canada and its provinces giving gross value of output and value added for selected years 1870-1957. The original series gathered by the Census of Manufactures was for the decennial years 1870-1910, the intercensal years of 1905 and 1915, and all years

[6] See for a summary of some of the issues G. W. Bertram, "Historical Statistics on Growth and Structure of Manufacturing in Canada, 1870-1957," Canadian Political Science Association, Conference on Statistics, June, 1962.

[7] See E. J. Chambers and G. W. Bertram, "Urbanization and Manufacturing in Central Canada, 1870-1890." Canadian Political Science Association, Conference on Statistics, June, 1964.

since 1919. The new series was necessary in order to overcome the shortcomings of the official census tabulations and permit comparability with more recent classification systems. The revision consisted of three steps. First, the original decennial census data for the decades 1870-1910 and the Postal Census of 1915 were reclassified on the basis of the Standard Industrial Classification of 1948. Second, the data were further reclassified on the basis of primary manufacturing and secondary manufacturing industries. The meaning and usefulness of this analytical tool are noted below. Third, since Census of Manufacturing data were not reported on a full-coverage basis for the years 1900, 1910, and 1915, methods were developed to provide estimates of full coverage. The three techniques were applied to the Canada totals and the first two techniques to the provincial totals to provide a conceptually consistent and fairly reliable manufacturing series.[8] These revisions permitted linkage with a manufacturing series for selected years 1926-53 prepared by the Dominion Bureau of Statistics for the Royal Commission on Canada's Economic Prospects. The Royal Commission's series are classified according to the Standard Industrial Classification of 1948 and also make the distinction of primary and secondary manufacturing industries.

It is necessary before examining the revised series of manufacturing statistics to indicate the meaning of primary manufacturing and secondary manufacturing. Primary manufacturing involves operations where relatively minor processing of domestic resources is required and production is from natural resource materials for sale mainly in export markets. Usually these products have competitive advantages and easy access to world markets. Primary manufacturing industries can be regarded as absorbing the outputs of staple industries or simply as the final step in staple production. Secondary manufacturing industries are characterized by a higher degree of processing, greater dependence upon domestic markets, and reliance on

---

[8] Acknowledgment is gratefully made here to the Dominion Bureau of Statistics and particularly to Mr. T. K. Rymes and the Central Research and Development staff for their assistance in the preparation of this manufacturing series. For a detailed report of the revised manufacturing series, a discussion of methods, and an appraisal of the reliability of the series, see G. W. Bertram, "Historical Statistics on Growth and Structure of Manufacturing in Canada, 1870-1957," *op. cit.*

both foreign and domestic inputs. Generally, secondary manufacturing industries have no pronounced natural cost advantages in international trade.[9]

Table I presents a summary of the gross value of output of primary, secondary, and total manufacturing for selected years

[9] The distinction of primary and secondary manufacturing industries originated in the studies of the Royal Commission on Canada's Economic Prospects. D. H. Fullerton and H. A. Hampson in their Royal Commission study, *Canadian Secondary Manufacturing* (Ottawa, 1957), pp. 3-4, give the following characteristics of primary and secondary manufacturing. Primary manufacturing is distinguished by: 1) "operations which involve either relatively minor processing of domestic resources, i.e., in which the value added by manufactures is relatively low. [2] . . . those highly capital-intensive and often extremely complex industries which produce industrial materials from our basic natural resources for sale mainly in export markets. Flour milling, cheese factories and saw and planing mills are examples of the first type, while pulp and paper production (excluding finished paper goods) and smelting and refining are examples of the second. [3] . . . the primary industries . . . start out with resource, technical and other competitive advantages and generally have easy access to world markets; with few exceptions they have little or no tariff protection and their prosperity depends primarily on the strength of international demand for their products." Secondary manufacturing is distinguished by: 1) "a rather higher degree of processing and by a much greater dependence on the domestic market. They tend to be located close to the centre of the market, while the primary industries are usually found at or near the resource on which they are based. [2] . . . generally produce end products rather than industrial materials. They draw on both foreign and domestic suppliers for raw materials and components and tend to be more labour-intensive than the basic resource industries. Examples of secondary manufacturing are textiles, clothing, transportation equipment and electrical apparatus and supplies. [3] [These industries] generally have no pronounced natural cost advantages and frequently are at a positive disadvantage relative to their main competitors; their main sales outlet is the comparatively small and scattered, although rapidly growing, domestic market in which they are confronted with considerable import competition." The definitions of primary and secondary manufacturing have certain arbitrary properties which follow from the rather broad characterizations listed for the two industries. J. H. Dales has recently suggested a definition of primary industries which appears more precise, and future work in this area might profitably gain from this definition. See J. H. Dales, "A Suggested Definition of Primary Manufacturing," a note appended to his paper, "A Classification of Canadian Manufacturing Statistics, 1870-1915," Canadian Political Science Association, Conference on Statistics, June, 1962. It would appear that Dales's definition would not change the conclusions reached here representing the role of staple industries, but might indicate that the proportion of primary manufacturing industries to total manufacturing had fallen to a lower level by 1957 than to the 30 per cent proportion noted here.

TABLE I

GROSS VALUE OF PRODUCTION, PRIMARY, SECONDARY AND TOTAL MANUFACTURING INDUSTRIES
STANDARD INDUSTRIAL CLASSIFICATION OF 1948
SELECTED YEARS 1870-1957[1]—(in 1000's of dollars)

	Primary		Secondary		Total		Index[2] 1935-39 =100
	Current	Constant	Current	Constant	Current	Constant	
1870 Includes estimate for P.E. Island	81,691	102,370	137,534	172,348	219,225	274,718	79.8
1880	102,993	143,444	200,497	279,244	303,490	422,688	71.8
1890	156,529	233,277	296,054	441,213	452,583	674,490	67.1
1900 All Firms Adjusted plus correction factor	199,300	319,380	335,300	537,320	534,600	856,700	62.4
1910 All Firms Adjusted plus correction factor	429,170	546,700	769,630	980,400	1,198,800	1,527,100	78.5
1915 Firms of over $2500 plus correction factor	494,000	538,130	851,700	927,770	1,345,700	1,465,900	91.8
1919[3]	879,195	503,260	2,283,376	1,307,027	3,162,571	1,810,287	174.7
1926[4]	1,070,680	821,704	2,038,036	1,564,111	3,108,716	2,385,815	130.3
1929	1,202,276	964,909	2,676,589	2,148,145	3,878,864	3,113,054	124.6
1933	627,638	718,121	1,325,266	1,516,322	1,952,904	2,234,443	87.4
1939	1,192,048	1,201,661	2,280,780	2,299,173	3,472,828	3,500,834	99.2
1946	2,773,121	1,996,487	5,259,977	3,785,880	8,033,099	5,783,367	138.9
1957[5] Excludes Newfoundland	6,572,205	2,890,152	15,397,048	6,770,909	21,969,253	9,661,061	227.4

[1] Years 1870-1915 computed for this study. For methods of computation see G. W. Bertram, "Historical Statistics on Growth and Structure of Manufacturing in Canada, 1870-1957," Canadian Political Science Association, Conference on Statistics, 1962, Table I.

[2] Dominion Bureau of Statistics, *Prices and Price Indexes*, 1949-52 and 1958. Wholesale price index.

[3] Special study of Dominion Bureau of Statistics, preliminary, 1960. Data arranged according to Standard Industrial Classification of 1948. Division between primary and secondary industries estimated on basis of 1915 proportions.

[4] Data for years 1926-46 from worksheets of the staff of the Royal Commission in Canada's Economic Prospects, supplied by the D.B.S. Value added is net of cost of fuel and electricity.

[5] Data refer to selling value of factory shipments. Computed from DBS, *"The Manufacturing Industries of Canada, Summary for Canada, 1957."*

1870-1957 in current and constant dollars. The detailed tables on which Table I is based and an evaluation of the problems involved in using decennial census data for the years 1870-1900 are available in the author's paper, "Historical Statistics on Growth and Structure of Manufacturing in Canada, 1870-1957."[10] One conclusion reached in that study was that no serious error involving decade comparisons in different phases of the business cycle arises from using single year estimates since each of the years 1870, 1880, 1890, and 1900 appear to occur in a prosperity phase of the cycle.

TABLE II

GROWTH RATES OF GROSS VALUE OF MANUFACTURING OUTPUT
IN CONSTANT 1935-39 DOLLARS
TOTAL, PRIMARY AND SECONDARY MANUFACTURING
SELECTED YEARS, 1870-1957

Period	Compound Rate of Growth Per Year	Total manufac- turing	Primary manufac- turing	Secondary manufac- turing
1870-1880		4.4	3.6	5.0
1880-1890		4.8	4.9	4.7
1890-1900	All firms adjusted plus correction factor	2.4	3.4	2.0
1900-1910	All firms adjusted plus correction factor	6.0	5.0	6.2
1910-1919		1.9	2.7	2.2
1919-1926		4.0	3.2	4.5
1926-1929		9.3	5.5	1.2
1929-1939		1.2	1.5	.7
1939-1946		7.4	7.5	7.4
1946-1957	Excludes Newfoundland	4.8	3.4	5.4
1870-1890		4.6	4.2	4.8
1870-1910		4.4	4.3	4.5
1870-1946		4.2	4.0	4.2
1870-1957		4.2	3.9	4.3
1919-1929		5.6	3.8	6.5

Source: Table I.

An examination of Table II showing compound rates of growth per year for various periods and the semi-logarithmic output graphs of Chart 1 indicate that the total manufacturing sector has shown a fairly steady and rapid rate of growth over the 87-year period 1870-1957. On the basis of actual values in

[10] See n. 6.

constant dollars, the annual average rate of growth, 1870-1957, was 4.2 per cent compounded. Particularly interesting is the almost constant rate of growth over the period. This is indicated by the logarithmic transformation of the growth function of real manufacturing output (fitted by least squares) for certain decades and selected years 1870-1957 taken from Table I. The logarithmic equation log y = 2.28 + .168x gives a good representation of the trend of this series, even without omitting the depression year 1933. The exponential trend equation y = 189.5 (1.472)^x of the above logarithmic equation has a constant compound interest rate of 47.2 per cent per decade or an average of approximately four per cent compounded per year over the period 1870-1957. Real manufacturing output in this series does not display any visible discontinuities over the 87-year period.

A second significant observation is the early and high rate of growth of manufacturing (in constant 1935-39 dollars) indicated for the decades 1870-90 (Table II). The average annual rate of 4.6 per cent for the decades 1870-90 is above the 87-year annual average rate and almost as high as the buoyant period of 1946-57. It appears that the decade 1890-1900 was a period of only modest manufacturing growth, just slightly greater than one-half of the previous decade. The period 1900-1910 records a rate of growth at 6.0 per cent per year. After a substantial growth at 4.6 per cent per year in the two decades 1870-90 and a decline to 2.4 per cent in 1890-1900, the manufacturing sector apparently experienced a rapid surge forward that would double real output approximately every twelve years instead of approximately every sixteen years as in the period 1870-90. The early period 1870-90 appears to have been one of vigorous expansion in manufacturing output. As indicated later, there is also considerable evidence of specialization among firms in size and function and increasing geographical specialization in manufacturing output in this period. The surge forward, at the turn of the century, discussed below, was a response to a confluence of various exogenous factors of a type which have frequently determined Canadian long-run economic growth. . . .

We will review below the evidence of later nineteenth-century economic growth and retardation. It should be noted, however, that a number of economic historians have accepted the view that there was a sharp break in Canadian economic development around 1896 associated with western wheat. The famous statement of O. D. Skelton that in 1896 "at last Canada's hour had struck[11] has made a deep impression. For example, various reports of the Royal Commission on Dominion-Provincial Relations reflect this view and Kenneth Buckley in his *Capital Formation in Canada, 1896-1930*, has described the period 1870-95 as one of secular depression.[12] The western wheat boom was unquestionably a highly significant event in the development of the Canadian economy. However, one can suspect that the dramatic quality of the event and the considerable scholarly attention devoted to it have obscured the significant industrial growth that had already occurred in eastern Canada.

Growth in Primary and Secondary Manufacturing

The division of Canadian manufacturing into primary and secondary industries portrays the behaviour of two fairly distinctive aggregates and appears to be useful for economies with

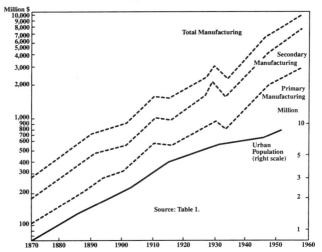

Chart 1. Growth of Gross Value of Production for Primary, Secondary, and Total Manufacturing, 1870-1957, in Constant 1935-39 Dollars.

[11] O. D. Skelton, "General Economic History, 1867-1912," in A. Shortt and A. G. Doughty, eds., Canada and Its Provinces, IX (Toronto, 1914), 191.

[12] (Toronto, 1955), pp. 4,5, and reprinted in this volume, pp. 171-73.

important agricultural and extractive resources heavily involved in international trade and with smaller domestic markets. Examination of growth in the primary and secondary divisions of manufacturing in Table I and Chart 1 indicates a fairly close movement in the rates of change of real output over most of the period 1870-1957 with a long-run decline in primary manufacturing output from 37 per cent in 1870 to 30 per cent in 1957. Primary manufacturing has continued to be an important source of Canadian economic growth. It would appear that the increase in the proportion of secondary manufacturing is associated with periods of prosperity, to judge by its higher growth rates in 1900-10, 1926-29, and 1945-57 (Table II).

Major Industry Groups in Primary Manufacturing

Continuing the method of successive disaggregation, an examination is made of the historical changes in real output in the major industry groups classified here as primary and secondary manufacturing. Reclassification of the various censuses of manufacturing on the basis of the Standard Industrial Classification of 1948 resulted in seventeen major industry groups. The use of the concepts of primary manufacturing and secondary manufacturing yields twenty-three major industry groups from the original seventeen, of which six are primary and seventeen are secondary manufacturing. Space does not permit the reproduction of the tables of output by major industry group in current and constant dollars for selected years 1870-1957. The semi-logarithmic Charts 2 and 3 summarize the history of output in the main primary and secondary major industry groups.[13]

From the staples of fish and furs, the nineteenth-century

[13] The paper indicated in n. 6 provides in Table III current dollar values of gross value of output for the twenty-three major industry groups. The constant dollar output plotted in Charts 2 and 3 was obtained by deflating these current values by DBS component price indexes. The 1913 = 100 index was mechanically linked to the 1935-39 = 100 index. The particular component indexes used to deflate a major industry group referred to the same group of commodities in most cases. However, in the absence of component indexes for transportation equipment and electrical products, the iron and steel products component index was used for deflating these series. The current value series for the food and beverage products major industry group were deflated by a weighted average of the vegetable component index and the animal products component index from weights in the 1913 = 100 wholesale price index.

TABLE III

VALUE ADDED AS A PERCENTAGE OF TOTAL MANUFACTURING VALUE ADDED
AND RANK OF INDUSTRY OF TWENTY-THREE INDUSTRY GROUPS
SELECTED YEARS 1870-1957
CURRENT DOLLARS

	1870 %	Rank	1880 %	Rank	1890 %	Rank	1900 %	Rank	1910 %	Rank
1. Food & beverages										
Primary	8.7	4	8.7	5	9.6	4	9.6	4	9.2	3
Secondary	7.6	5	6.3	6	6.6	6	7.8	6	7.9	5
2. Tobacco products										
Secondary	1.3	15	1.2	16	1.6	14	3.4	11	2.4	15
3. Rubber products										
Secondary	.2	19	.2	18	.3	20	.3	22	.6	22
4. Leather products										
Secondary	14.0	3	11.6	3	7.9	5	8.1	5	5.3	7
5. Textiles										
(except clothing)										
Secondary	3.7	9	5.0	8	6.0	8	5.9	7	4.1	8
6. Clothing										
(textile and fur)										
Secondary	6.8	7	8.9	4	10.4	3	10.2	3	8.6	4
7. Wood Products										
Primary	16.6	2	16.6	1	15.8	2	14.3	1	13.2	2
Secondary	4.3	8	4.5	9	4.3	9	4.5	9	3.2	11
8. Paper products										
Primary	.6	17	.9	17	.9	16	2.0	14	2.3	16
Secondary	.3	18	.2	19	.5	18	.8	19	.9	20
9. Printing, publishing										
& allied industries										
Secondary	2.8	11	3.3	10	3.2	11	4.2	10	3.4	9
10. Iron and steel										
products										
Secondary	16.8	1	15.6	2	15.9	1	12.1	2	14.0	1
11. Transportation										
equipment										
Secondary	6.9	6	6.2	7	6.3	7	5.8	8	7.4	6
12. Non-ferrous metal										
products										
Primary	.0	21	.0	22	.8	17	1.1	17	3.1	12
Secondary	1.0	16	1.8	14	1.2	15	1.3	16	2.9	13
13. Electrical Apparatus										
and-supplies										
Secondary	.0	21	.0	22	.3	21	.8	18	1.6	18
14. Non-metallic										
minerals										
Primary	.1	20	.1	20	.1	22	.3	23	1.0	19
Secondary	3.1	10	3.3	11	4.2	10	2.7	12	3.4	10
15. Petroleum & coal										
products										
Secondary	1.8	13	1.4	15	.3	19	.6	20	.8	21
16. Chemical products										
Primary	.0	21	.0	21	.0	23	.0	21	.1	23
Secondary	2.1	12	2.3	12	2.1	12	2.3	13	2.9	14
17. Miscellaneous										
Secondary	1.4	14	1.9	13	1.6	13	1.9	15	1.8	17
Percentage of total										
for top 7	77.4%		73.9%		72.5%		68.0%		65.6%	

1915 %	Rank	1926 %	Rank	1929 %	Rank	1933 %	Rank	1939 %	Rank	1946 %	Rank	1957 %	Rank
10.5	2	8.3	4	7.3	4	10.2	2	9.0	3	7.9	4	6.2	5
9.8	3	9.4	2	10.5	2	12.0	1	10.9	2	9.6	2	8.4	3
2.3	3	3.3	11	3.4	12	2.2	17	1.8	18	1.2	22	.9	22
1.3	19	2.7	14	3.0	14	3.0	12	2.6	14	2.7	12	1.8	18
4.6	8	2.7	15	2.1	18	2.9	13	2.2	16	2.4	14	1.2	21
4.0	11	6.4	6	5.8	7	9.3	3	7.5	4	6.7	6	4.3	11
7.8	5	5.4	9	5.0	8	5.6	8	5.0	9	6.0	7	3.6	13
8.1	4	5.8	7	5.0	9	2.5	14	3.8	11	5.2	8	3.9	12
2.9	13	2.7	13	2.7	15	2.3	16	2.3	15	2.5	13	2.1	16
3.5	12	8.4	3	6.9	5	6.2	6	6.7	5	7.5	5	6.9	4
1.2	20	1.3	21	1.3	21	1.8	18	1.7	20	2.2	17	1.8	17
4.3	10	5.8	8	5.8	6	7.4	5	5.5	7	4.5	9	4.9	8
13.5	1	12.3	1	13.5	1	7.7	4	11.7	1	13.4	1	15.1	1
7.3	6	7.4	5	7.9	3	4.3	10	6.4	6	8.0	3	9.8	2
4.9	7	2.1	18	3.5	11	5.9	7	5.2	8	2.0	18	4.6	10
1.7	16	1.5	20	1.4	19	1.3	20	1.8	19	2.3	16	1.6	19
1.6	17	3.0	12	3.6	10	2.4	15	3.2	12	3.8	11	5.8	6
.7	22	.7	23	1.2	22	.6	23	.8	23	.8	23	.9	23
2.6	14	2.4	17	2.4	16	1.6	19	1.9	17	1.9	19	2.6	14
1.1	21	2.5	16	2.1	17	3.5	11	2.9	13	2.3	15	5.5	7
.1	23	1.2	22	1.1	23	1.1	22	1.2	21	1.8	20	1.4	20
4.5	9	3.4	10	3.4	13	5.0	9	4.7	10	4.2	10	4.8	9
1.5	18	1.5	19	1.3	20	1.2	21	1.2	22	1.4	21	2.1	15
61.9%		58.0%		57.7%		58.7%		57.7%		59.1%		57.7%	

Canadian economy shifted to a significant reliance on the timber trade and lumber industry with the agricultural staple products of wheat, cheese, and meat playing an important but lesser role. Each of these commodities had large export markets.[14] As the market sector expanded through the direct and indirect influence of the export sector, productivity advanced as economic functions became more rationalized, resources shifted into higher productivity employment, and economies of scale were gained which in turn had favourable effects on other industries. With later staples, such as lumber after the 1840's and particularly western wheat in the 1890's, their production functions required a large investment in transport facilities which had significant secondary effects on urbanization and internal industrialization.

Charts 2 and 3 portray the statistical evidence regarding changes in real output in primary and secondary manufacturing industries for selected years 1870-1957. The process of manufacturing growth consists in part of an acceleration and retardation of output among various industry groups in response to shifts in supply and demand conditions. Chart 2, indicating the growth rates of the real output of five primary manufacturing major industry groups and the production of wheat, displays much greater variation in growth rates than is the case for the major industry groups in secondary manufacturing shown in Chart 3. Growth proceeded in the secondary industries at a much more stable pace and tended to approximate the growth rate of the total manufacturing sector.

[14] In estimating the total export importance of all primary manufacturing, the industry major groups cannot be conveniently related to exports, item for item in some cases, but a substantial part of export commodities can be identified from K. W. Taylor's export series as of either primary or secondary origin. It would appear by conservative computation, without allowance for items which are classified so as to include both primary and secondary items, that some 30 per cent of exports in 1870 and some 40 per cent in the remaining period through 1915 were products of primary manufacturing. In 1910 and 1915 the proportion of exports from manufacturing production would probably be well above 40 per cent if account could be taken of other items where classification is unclear. In some cases exports were in excess of 50 per cent of total production, i.e., cheese production and paper and pulp in 1910 and 1915. Lumber exports were from about 50 per cent of the production of sawmills in 1870 and around 40 per cent in the remaining decades through 1900. See K. W. Taylor, "Statistics of Foreign Trade," in Taylor and H. Michell, eds., *Statistical Contributions to Canadian Economic History*, I (Toronto, 1931), 12.

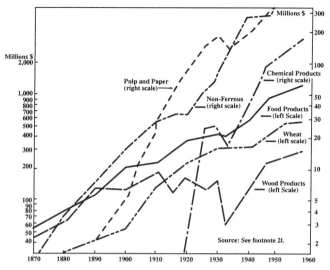

Chart 2. Growth Rates of Gross Value of Production for Major Industry Groups in Primary Manufacturing, 1870-1957, in Constant 1935-39 Dollars, and Wheat Production, 1870-1957, in Bushels.

In the early period 1870-90, the two most significant staples in rate of growth (Chart 2) and magnitude of value added in manufacturing (Table III) were primary wood products and primary food products. Judged by its more rapid expansion and size of value added, it would appear that the lumber trade continued during 1870-90 to be the dominant nineteenth-century staple. The linkages and secondary income effects of lumber are considered below. Chart 2 shows that after two decades of rapid expansion at an annual average rate of 5.7 per cent compounded, primary wood products by 1890 were the largest major group in manufacturing industry in constant dollars of gross value of production. In value added, primary wood products ranked second in 1890 among all manufacturing industries. An inspection of output over the whole period 1870-1957 in Chart 2 indicates that primary wood's great expansion came to an end before the turn of the century. Table III indicates the decline of this important industry in value added as a proportion of total manufacturing value added. The proportion of exports of wood, wood products, and paper had in the fiscal year 1871 been approximately 38 per cent of total exports, but by the fiscal year 1911 this proportion had fallen to 17 per cent.[15]

Primary food products, largest in constant dollars of gross value of production in 1870 and 1880 (Chart 2), fell below primary wood products in 1890 but surpassed them again in 1900.[16] Throughout the nineteenth century and into the first half of the twentieth, primary food production has occupied a significant place in the form of a group of staple commodities (Table III). The fortunate timing of the rise of wheat (reflecting favourable changes in price and transport costs) with the decline in the growth of primary wood products is evident from Chart 2. Wheat production, measured in bushels rather than in constant dollars, was a fairly important though not very rapidly growing industry in the period 1870-1890. Wheat had already been an important cash crop in eastern Canada and served an export market. Production of wheat rose rapidly at the rate of 9.4 per cent per year compounded from 55.6 million bushels in 1900 to 132.1 million bushels in 1910 and exports more than quadrupled.[17]

Chart 2 also indicates that in the early period 1870-90 the new primary manufacturing industries of pulp and paper and non-ferrous metals were just beginning to come into production. These two major industry groups showed spectacular rates of growth in the twentieth century, eventually reaching the position of large primary manufacturing sectors and significant staple products. The extremely rapid acceleration of output (Chart 2) of pulp and paper in the period 1910-1926 of 11.8 per cent per annum compounded brought this major industry group from sixteenth place in value added in 1910 to third place in 1926 (Table III). This brief examination of the statistical record indicates that a number of new staple industries emerged in the period after 1915 resulting in a more diversified economy.

[15] Ibid.
[16] Cheese, meat products, wheat flour, and canned or cured fish were all important production items with significant export markets. Flour and grist mill domestic production accounted for about one-third of primary food products in 1900, rose to 43 per cent in 1910 and continued near 40 per cent in 1915.
[17] Canada Year Book (Ottawa, 1960), pp. 1262 and 1268.

Leading Sectors, Linkages and Income Effects

In the Canadian case, the statistical growth record of the output in certain primary manufacturing and agricultural industries (identified as staple export industries) and an analysis of their input-output linkages and income effects indicate that the concept of staple export industries is somewhat similar to the Rostow concept of leading sectors[18] and is useful in interpreting Canadian economic history. However, there are important differences. First, the influence of these staple industries did not commence with the specific period of 1896-1914 which Rostow considered to be the Canadian take-off period. They have been important contributors to economic progress from the beginning of Canadian economic history. Second, staple industries are not confined to the manufacturing sector as are Rostow's leading sectors. In the critical take-off period chosen for Canada, 1896-1914, the sector which filled most adequately all the dimensions of a leading sector, i.e., rapid growth, linkages, and income effects, was western wheat, rather than some manufacturing industry. Previously the main staple industry had been timber, and later pulp and paper and non-ferrous metals added further to the expansion. Third, the export connection of the staple in the staple model of economic growth is fundamental, while in the leading sector concept, although it may be present, it is given less significance.

The concept of leading sectors perhaps derives from an implication of Schumpeter's analysis that certain sectors are key propulsive sectors with different rates of growth in different periods.[19] Cairncross has suggested that in discussion of economic growth attention should be focused on factors operating over a long period with cumulative force rather than on events in a specific period, and if certain events are to be singled out then "The 'march of compound interest' was far more the march of mechanical power and the engines that supplied it than any individual industry or 'leading sector.' "[20] While this view seems

[18] W. W. Rostow, "The 'Take-Off' Into Self-Sustained Growth," *Economic Journal*, March, 1956, pp. 25-47, and *The Stages of Economic Growth* (Cambridge, 1960).

[19] See G. M. Meier and R. E. Baldwin, *Economic Development* (New York, 1959), p. 224.

[20] A. K. Cairncross, "Review of The Stages of Economic Growth," *Economic History Review*, Second Series, XIII, 1960-61, 457-8.

relevant to the British case that Cairncross apparently had in mind, in the peripheral economies of countries such as Canada (and the United States in an earlier period) the achievement of a market economy was dependent upon the economic success abroad of a limited number of commodities. Economic progress in Canada without timber, wheat, and pulp and paper (and in United States without cotton and wheat) would have been far less assured. Consequently, analysis of particular leading sectors may be useful without underemphasizing that changes in technology frequently provided the opportunity for these industries.

In view of its growth, linkages, and income effects, the propulsive sector in the period 1896-1914 appears to have been wheat and the lines of causation were the reverse of Rostow's. The backward linkages of the western wheat industry are determined by the production function of wheat and its rapid growth meant an expanding demand for the inputs of labour, capital, and other supplying organizations and agencies. In respect to labour inputs, western wheat production techniques required and attracted large numbers of both migrant and immigrant settlers. The production function of wheat also determined a form of farm organization of single proprietorships using relatively little wage labour. This type of economic unit had considerable significance for the pattern of income distribution and the consequent secondary effects on other industries.

The very large railway transportation requirements for Canadian wheat are well known. These requirements created external economies for other manufacturing industries, linked together a larger domestic market, and contributed to further localization of manufacturing. Industries supplying capital goods, such as agricultural implements and rolling stock equipment, expanded very rapidly. Real output in the iron and steel products industry group and the transportation equipment industry group both expanded at the exceedingly high average rate of 12.4 per cent per year compounded in the period 1900-10, higher even than the rate of 9.4 per cent per year for wheat production. Secondary industry expansion had of course its own linkages with the rest of the economy as its costs fell and its demand increased, but the initial impetus is regarded as coming from the expansion in demand for wheat.

The income effects of wheat production had a particularly

important influence on the whole economy. J. S. Duesenberry's analysis, noted earlier, demonstrated the multiplier-accelerator effects of the increases in income from wheat production in the Midwest region of the United States in the 1820's to 1850's, while D. C. North has convincingly demonstrated the significance of the follow-up process of income expansion from cotton production through to the Civil War.[21] The growth of Canadian western wheat released a similar multiplier-accelerator process which influenced income in the prairies, the Pacific coast, and eastern manufacturing regions. As an international good, wheat also helped to secure an income effect from the increase in exports and at the same time was one factor in the attraction of capital imports, which, while accompanied by a current account deficit, induced complementary domestic investment by Canadians.

The timber and later the lumber trade, which we have identified as primary wood products, also had a number of linkages and income effects. In the second half of the nineteenth century the urbanization accompanying industrialization in the United States shifted Canadian exports from timber to sawn lumber for the rapidly expanding American cities of the Midwest and the Atlantic. With the canals built on the Great Lakes–St. Lawrence system, and the advent of steam tugs and railways, the accessible regions for lumber operations and the extent of the market to the south increased. Immigration in the Great Lakes watershed tended to precede timber operations and part of the labour force required was already established in agriculture. Owing to their reverse seasonality, farming and logging were often combined. In Ontario this situation provided ready markets for agricultural products, assisted in the development of lumber port centres and towns, and required an extensive organization of specialists in transportation, marketing, and financing. The lumber industry gradually became more capital-intensive and the average firm doubled in size in the period 1870-90 as steam-powered sawmills replaced water-driven mills. New demands for inputs from the iron and steel products and the transportation equipment industries were made as the lumber trade continued its expansion in north-south trade and in a growing domestic

[21] North, *The Economic Growth of the United States, 1790-1860.*

market.[22] Like the wheat industry which followed, the lumber industry developed in a complementary environment as an export staple supplying the needs of more advanced economies, assisting in financing imports, and attracting some foreign investment.

Secondary Manufacturing

The changes which have occurred in the secondary manufacturing sector during the period 1870-1957 are summarized in Chart 3, showing the rate of growth of selected secondary major industry groups, and Table III, where the twenty-three industry groups have been ranked in order of value added. There is evidence in the secondary manufacturing sector of the relative rise and decline of various major industry groups similar to that noted in the primary manufacturing sector, although the secondary industry groups generally experienced a much steadier expansion in the period 1870-1957 than the primary industry groups.[23] However, in the period 1900-10 the two major groups of iron and steel products and transportation equipment both display (in constant 1935-39 dollars) the very high average annual rates of 12.4 per cent compounded, a departure from the average growth rate of total secondary manufacturing, and in excess of the growth of 9.4 per cent for wheat production. This rapid expansion of real output for these two industry groups should be viewed beside their considerable, but lesser, annual

[22] The average size of Canadian sawmills measured in constant 1935-39 dollars of gross value of output was $7,200 in 1870 and $17,000 in 1890. Approximately half the production of sawmills was located in Ontario in the years 1870-90 and during this period their gross value of real output in this province increased about two and one-half times. Some of the growth of Ontario's large iron and steel products industry by 1890 can be traced to the expansion of the lumber industry directly and indirectly. In 1890, the gross value of output for several related industries in current dollars was as follows: saw and file cutting, $456,000; boilers and engines, $2,085,000; foundry and machine shops, $8,460,000.

[23] The electrical products and petroleum products industry groups showed great advances in growth rates comparable to a number of industry groups in the primary manufacturing sector, particularly after 1915. The expansion in electrical products could be considered an example of industrial growth dependent mainly upon major technological innovation rather than an industry responding to linkages with a primary industry involved in export activity. The classification of petroleum and coal products as a secondary industry was made by the Royal Commission only after some hesitation.

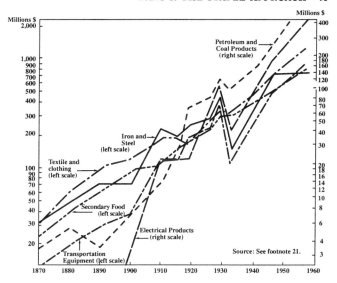

Chart 3. Growth Rates of Gross Value of Production for Selected Major Industry Groups in Secondary Manufacturing, 1870-1957, in Constant 1935-39 Dollars.

growth in the period 1870-90 of 4.1 per cent compounded for iron and steel products and 3.8 per cent for transportation equipment.

The staple model of growth would consider the expansion of secondary manufacturing industries generally as responses to staple expansion. These responses were further secured by such devices as the national policy on transportation and tariffs. The expansion of transportation equipment production during the period 1870-90 was probably linked not only to existing export staple production, but to the staple export production which the federal government had expected. Government participation in railroad financing in this period could be regarded as an important exogenous variable.

Even in 1870 the iron and steel products industry group held first place among the twenty-three industry groups in magnitude of value added and continued throughout the period through 1957 to hold first place, except in 1880 and 1900 when primary wood products were first, and in 1933 when it ranked fourth. The early emergence of this industry to a position of prominence appears to indicate an economy experiencing industrial development, even though the heavy industrial complex of coal and iron inputs associated with the iron and steel production was largely missing. The census records reveal diversified products and large firms in the 1870-90 period with inputs supplied from imported blooms, pigs, billets, and rolling mill products.[24] Export staples and the proximity of the United States provided the basis for the necessary iron and steel inputs which continued to be missing throughout most of Canadian industrial expansion. During the process of economic growth, the transformation or redistribution of inputs among industries may be quite different for open economies such as Canada where primary products were exchanged for other resources.

Changes in Industry Structure

The revised censuses of manufacturing for Canada and the provinces yield considerable evidence that during the early period 1870-1900 increasing specialization in production at the level of the firm and in localization of industry occurred, both in urban areas and in particular provinces. These tendencies, which continued throughout the period 1870-1957, indicate that industrial differentiation proceeded from an early date in Canadian manufacturing. Only a brief note concerning these changes can be made here.[25]

The average value of output of all manufacturing firms

[24] In the three periods 1870-79, 1880-89, and 1890-99, respective average annual imports in constant dollars of pig iron, billets, and blooms were $.4 million, $1.3 million and $1.5 million. Imports of rolling mill products in the same periods in constant dollars average respectively, $1.6 million, $4.6 million, and $5.0 million per year. See Taylor, "Statistics of Foreign Trade," pp. 22-27. In 1870, six firms (five in Quebec and one in Nova Scotia) were operating iron-smelting furnaces and making steel with a total value of output of $.3 million, and the five rolling mills reported an output of $1.7 million. In 1880, thirteen iron-smelting and steel-making firms (three now in Ontario) produced an output of $1.2 million, while in 1890 rolling mills had an output of $3.2 million. Foundry and machine shop output rose from $8.9 million in 1880 to $17.2 million in 1890. The diversity and growth of iron and steel products output is illustrated by the fact that agricultural implements, boilers and engines, cutting and edge tools, pumps and windmills, sewing machines and wire were all important industries ranging in 1870 from $.2 million (pumps) to $2.7 million (agricultural implements). By 1890 the range of output for this group of industries was $.6 million for pumps to $7.5 million for agricultural implements.

[25] See n. 6.

increased from $7,100 in 1870 to $9,600 in 1890 in constant 1935-39 dollars and in the same period the number of establishments increased from 38,402 to 70,123. While these large increases in the number of firms indicated expanding business opportunities, part of the increase in numbers was a result of firms concentrating more completely on a limited phase of production. This vertical disintegration yielded increasing returns. The increase in average size of manufacturing firms in the period is obscured by the exceptionally large increases in the number of firms in certain industries. Further disaggregation discloses that particular manufacturing industries had firms of considerable and growing size in the period 1870-90.[26] Preliminary investigation indicates that in the last three decades of the nineteenth century there was a definite tendency towards greater localization of production in larger urban centres. While urban population increased by 38 per cent in the period 1881-91, total population increased by only 11.7 per cent. In the calendar years 1880-90, the gross value of urban manufacturing output increased by 58 per cent and the greatest manufacturing growth was in the larger cities and towns.[27]

An index expressing the per capita output of provincial manufacturing as a percentage of Canadian per capita output provides a revealing indication of the regional specialization which had already occurred in the period 1870-1900. Total manufacturing output in Ontario, for example, moved from an index of 112 per cent in 1870 to 123 in 1900, while Quebec tended to remain nearer the national average. Particular industry groups display even more striking evidence of regional specialization. The index for the iron and steel products group increased in each decade in Ontario from 128 in 1870 to 148 by 1900, while in other provinces the index declined. In Quebec the textile index showed a rapid upward climb from 75 in 1870 to 133 in 1900. These and other examples indicate that a process

[26] Some examples of large and growing manufacturing firms in the period 1870-90 are the following. Rolling mills: 1870, five firms, average size $336,000; 1890, six firms, average size $527,000. Railroad rolling stock: 1870, five firms, average size of firm $102,000; 1890, nineteen firms, average size $498,000. Cotton factories: 1870, eight firms, average size of firms $98,000; 1890, twenty firms, average size of firm $384,000.

[27] See Department of Agriculture, Bulletin no. 12, *Census of Canada* (Ottawa, 1892), pp. 4 and 20-24.

of expansion and regional specialization was occurring in the early period of Canadian industrialization which is hardly consistent with the view of secular depression in the period or a sudden leap forward at the turn of the century. The Canadian economy appears to have been moving steadily at the close of the nineteenth century towards a more efficient resource allocation as transfer costs fell and comparative advantages developed.

CONCLUSION

. . . Industrialization in Canada appears to have been a gradual process associated with the general expansion of the nineteenth-century Atlantic community. Manufacturing in 1870 was dominated by agricultural and commercial activity, but the movement towards a more industrialized economy came very steadily. The development of an economy in connection with international trade opportunities for export staples appears to be fairly common, and the leading sectors are often export industries resting upon an extractive or agricultural base. The history of economic growth in some countries can be most usefully approached in one phase of its growth from an export staple approach, and in a later phase from some other conceptual framework. The United States would appear to be a notable example of the usefulness of the export staple approach in the period 1790-1860, but this approach is less revealing in the later period.

The export staple model continues to be a useful approach in the Canadian economy, and with allowances for differences in production functions, may also be a useful analytical tool in determining economic policy in certain underdeveloped countries where the export sector may continue to be regarded through colonial eyes.

PART TWO

LAND POLICY AND AGRICULTURE

Administration of Land Policy and the Growth of Corporate Economic Organization in Lower Canada, 1791-1809

G. F. McGUIGAN

It is no revelation to Canadian historians to hear that there are large areas where basic research is required either to fill out patterns of historical development already outlined or in other cases to explore areas where little or nothing has been done. Perhaps economic history suffers more from this lack of basic research than any other branch of Canadian history. Tenuous lines of development have been traced out by studies in the fur trade by Innis and in the timber trade by Lower. While these and other works which deal with such aspects of economic development as canal building, railroads and commerce are an indispensable base for explaining the process of development and for establishing some of the relationships between the economic and the political in the period before 1867, they are by no means sufficient for a clear and complete picture of the period. Knowledge of those areas where research has been

Source: G. F. McGuigan, "Administration of Land Policy and the Growth of Corporate Economic Organization in Lower Canada 1791-1809," The Canadian Historical Association, *Report, 1963, of the Annual Meeting held at Quebec June 5-8 of this year with Historical Papers*, edited by John P. Hersler and Fernand Ouellet. Reprinted by permission of the Canadian Historical Association. Minor revisions have been made by the author.

lacking has been left mostly to our imaginations or to what can be drawn by inference. Relatively little is known, for example, about manufacturing in the period 1790-1867 or the business organization and investment connected with it. Perhaps the most neglected area has been the history of land policy and the distribution and ownership of land during the period 1790-1867 and its relation to economic and political development. Some work has been done on the seigniorial system and the land companies. However, these works, while helpful, have tended to be incomplete and not related to the context of contemporary economic and political development.

The present paper is the product of recent work done on the development of land policy and methods of alienation and distribution of land in Lower Canada from 1763 to 1809.[1] This research, carried on over a period of the past six years, has dealt with land granted under the tenure of free and common socage in that area which now comprises the Eastern Townships of Quebec. The present paper does not make a full report of the work done, but concentrates only on one small aspect of the development of land policy and land tenure – that of the relationship between the emergence of indigenous corporate forms of economic activity in Lower Canada and land tenure, with its attendant rules and regulations as an implementation of land policy. In this paper I would like to show: (1) that there were economic organizations in the sphere of land exploitation during the period 1791-1809, which although not corporations in the legal sense did display most of the rudimentary characteristics of corporate activity; and (2) that there were two distinct but related causes of the emergence of these corporate forms. In order to do this I would like first to indicate briefly the nature of the leader and associate systems as found in Lower Canada in the period 1792-1809, and, secondly, to discuss two related lines of development which begin in the early colonial period and form the background for the adoption of the leader and associates system in Lower Canada. These two developments help to

---

[1] The complete results of this study were presented at the University of Laval in September 1962, in a dissertation entitled "Land Policy and Land Disposal under Tenure of free and common socage, Quebec and Lower Canada 1763-1809." A summary of this work may be found in G. F. McGuigan, "La Concession des Terres dans les Cantons de l'Est du Bas Canada, 1763-1809," *Recherches Sociographiques*, Vol. 4, Jan-Avril, 1963, pp. 71-89.

explain how the leader and associates group assumed the characteristics of crude corporations. The first development deals with the change in British colonial land policy during this period and the contrasts in colonial land policy before and after 1763. The second line of development traces the corresponding changes in the method of administering land policy during the same period.

The tendency for some leader and associates groups to develop along corporate lines, can be explained, I will suggest, by the existence of the tradition of corporate organization in the New England townships which was the sufficient cause of the emergence of corporate organization in the Eastern Townships. However, the efficacious cause of the development was the atmosphere of uncertainty generated by the clash between the internal administrative logic necessary to administer the new policy of grants and distribution of land in severalty which was developed after 1763 in Quebec, and the internal logic of the leader and associates system which had a background of corporate organization in the New England colonies before 1763.

One might ask why 1809 was chosen as the terminal date of this study. The reason is that this date marks the end of the leader and associates system in Lower Canada. This system was the method of colonizing chosen for the Eastern Townships after 1791 in response to the flow of immigrants to Quebec, many of whom came from the New England states.

The leader and associates system was a method of colonizing which originated in the thirteen colonies. It was adapted to Canadian use during the period 1791-1809 in Lower Canada. In broad outline the system was based upon the principle of giving large tracts of land, whole townships in some cases, to groups of settlers who operated under the guidance of a leader. The land was given to the group with the knowledge that each individual would retain only a portion of the land granted to him under the patent. The portion retained by each associate was usually two hundred acres out of a possible twelve hundred acres granted to him in the patent. The surplus one thousand acres went to the leader for his expenses and trouble in organizing, petitioning and surveying the land for occupancy by the group of associates and other settlers who would buy the surplus land from the leader.

In the original thirteen colonies there had been two principal methods for settling colonists on the land.[2] Both systems were employed from the beginning of colonization. The two methods adopted were the headright system and the township system. The headright system[3] was used at one time or another in almost all of the original thirteen colonies, with the exception of the New England colonies where the township system, which was based upon the leader and associates group, was adopted. In both systems the crown chose to delegate the practical aspects of settlement to officials of the chartered colony. For this reason the original charters did not indicate by name the individual settlers and the particular plot of land allocated to him, but indicated only the area to be granted. It was assumed that the grantees – and this was an essential part of the monopoly agreement under the charter system – would further grant the land to the settlers. In the colonies then, the original charter group ordinarily received the land in title held of the king and were given the privilege of dividing and regranting the land to individual settlers under their own seal.

To all outward appearances it was a modified form of the New England township system which was adopted in the Eastern Townships of Lower Canada after 1791. In Canada, however, the system was developed in a political and administrative context entirely different from that in which the system originated. It is this difference in political and administrative context and the resulting clash between the rationale and logic of the leader and associates system coming from New England and the new land policy originating in 1763 for Quebec which lies at the heart of the problem of explaining the rise of the first indigenous corporate forms of economic activity in Lower Canada.

In its most general terms, the context out of which the corporate form developed was one of conflict between the centralizing tendencies of the new land policy and the decentralizing tendencies of marginal areas in political and fiscal matters.

As a first step towards explaining the emergence of indigenous corporate forms of economic activity in Lower Canada

[2] It is extremely difficult to generalize on methods of land disposal in America because of the great variety of land tenure systems and policies and the changes to which they were subject in the pre-revolutionary period.

[3] Marshall Harris, *Origin of the Land Tenure System in the United States*, (Ames, Iowa, 1953), Chaps. 12 and 13.

after 1791, let me deal briefly with the changing political context of economic action from the founding of chartered colonizing agencies down to 1763 and then discuss the corresponding changes in administrative systems.

In all societies one of the main functions of land tenure has been to define the character and mode of operation of the social unit in its political, social and economic aspects. Under the feudal system of land tenure the political, social and economic units were identical. This identity between economic and political power which was the basis of feudal fiscal organization has persisted as an overt form of organization even down to fairly recent times. What is interesting for our purpose is that this social organization characterized by a unity of political and economic power became obsolete as a unit of the landed economy as decentralized political and economic power were replaced by centralized economic and political control. Nevertheless it was adopted in an analogous form during the seventeenth century as the basic unit in the expanding field of commerce with the creation of chartered companies and colonies as instruments of European sovereigns for the extension of economic and political power to the New World. There was in the sixteenth and seventeenth century chartered organization, as there had been in its feudal counterpart, a close relationship between commerce, political power, control and division of land resources.[4] The precise land tenure systems adopted in America and the colonial land policies that grew out of these systems, varied of course from colony to colony depending upon whether the colonies were chartered as proprietary, corporate or royal.[5] After 1763 with the creation of the royal province of Quebec there was a notable change in British colonial land policy.[6] It

[4] *Ibid.*, chaps. 7 and 16.

[5] *Ibid.*, pp. 74-79. Cf. also *Blackstone's Commentaries*, Sharwood (ed.), Phil., 1859, Vol. 1, Intro., p. 108.

[6] Many authors in writing of land disposal during this period mention the introduction by royal instruction of a uniform system of land sales in 1774 in all American colonies except Quebec. (See for example Additional Instructions to William Tyron, Governor of the Province of New York, Feb. 3, 1774.) Reference is also made to the extensive use of land sales before 1774 as a method of land disposal. However, great caution must be exercised in imposing upon these "sales" the modern contractual notion of sale. Legal procedures at this time and for some time after in the Canadian colonies still gave cognizance to the Statute of Uses and trusts were still used to alienate land. In addition remnants of feudal incidence in the quit rent and the continuence of the fee system made alienation by simple deed impossible.

would appear that the experience of two centuries of close association between political and economic power in the chartered company was foremost in the minds of those laying down the basic framework of land policy for those lands to be granted in free and common socage in the royal province of Quebec. After 1763 colonial authority was equally aware of the seigniorial system which had been established in New France for some two centuries past. In addition to these influences shaping land policy were the possible spread of the spirit of American independence to Canada (a contagion which was bred in the culture of politically autonomous chartered colonies) and the military problem of containment and security posed by the unsettled state of Indian lands.

By the end of the Seven Years' War it would seem that the chartered company as a means of colonization and the extension of European economic and political power to the New World had outlived its usefulness. Not only had the joint stock company as a means of accumulating capital and assisting the government in times of financial crisis come under a cloud in the speculation mania of the first two decades of eighteenth-century England but also the commercial corporate colonies, particuparly those in New England, were becoming increasingly independent, politically and fiscally.

Thus even before the Revolution of 1776, the experiment (unsuccessful in the eyes of the British), of colonizing by commercial companies was abandoned as disruptive of the purpose of the British Empire. The crown was fearful of the delegation of political power and possible losses of revenue derived from import and export duties and quit rents.[7] Law too, had set itself firmly against what it thought to be the irresponsibility of the process of accumulating capital by means of the joint stock company.

Thus in contrast with what it had been earlier, the British land policy in Quebec after 1763 appears to have been based upon the principle of retaining in the hands of the king, political power and power over division of land, and over resource alienation and its revenue. To this purpose the older

---

[7] Cf. John Norris, *Shelburn and Reform*, (London, 1963), Chap. 3, "A Policy for America." Cf. also Harris, *Origins*, pp. 324-331, and B. W. Bond Jr., *Quit Rent System in the American Colonies*, (New Haven, 1919).

PART II: LAND POLICY AND AGRICULTURE – 105

system of using chartered companies or colonizing agencies was abandoned and a system of direct grants from the king to the subjects in severalty, without the interposition of any agency holding land in common by charter, was laid down in theory as the basis of the new policy. It would appear that the intention of this policy was first, to prevent the growth of land monopoly, second, to retain the revenues from land in the hands of the king and, third, to discourage in Canada any growth of the revolutionary spirit which had characterized the American corporate colonies.

The second line of development I would like to trace as a basis for understanding the corporate nature of the leader and associates group in Lower Canada is the change in methods of administering the alienation and disposal of land. Generally speaking the administration of land policy under the earlier system of colonization was, in keeping with the decentralized character of the policy itself, one based on delegation of powers over division and alienation to quasi-autonomous bodies which in the course of time assumed many prerogatives of the corporation.[8] Under the new land policy of individual grants in severalty formulated for Quebec after 1763, the administration of land policy and record keeping was centralized.[9]

The clash between the two systems became apparent after 1791. When attempts were made to apply the new policy in Lower Canada, the policy of centralization based upon the individual grant in severalty was shattered upon the reality of the necessity to colonize virgin territory by groups. Under these circumstances the leader and associates system with which the immigrants from the New England states were already familiar was adopted in practice but not as a matter of high policy. The leader and associates system then, as an offshoot of the New England method of corporate colonization, was in Lower Canada grafted on to a bureaucratic structure of quite a different species and inspiration.

The bureaucratic structure of paper work designed to implement the granting of land in severalty directly from the king was in direct opposition to the principles of corporate power

[8] Shaw Livermore, *Early American Land Companies*, (New York, 1939), Intro. and p. 26 *fn.*
[9] Regulations for the Conduct of the Land Board 17th February 1789, P.A.C. RGI, L1, Minute Books, Quebec, Land Book A, pp. 273-282 and pp. 352-357.

and holding land in common. This is most evident when we consider that nowhere in the New England states does one find at present a corpus of government documents dealing with division and distribution of land which corresponds to that found for Lower Canada for the period 1792-1809. In the New England states records dealing with the division and disposal of land for this same period and earlier are ordinarily found even today in the office of the local town clerk and in some cases in the county office. This is what one might expect, since the administration of land in the New England colonies was a local affair designed to accommodate the local autonomous character of the leader and associates group. The paper work in Lower Canada on the contrary was designed to implement a policy of individual grants in severalty and was highly centralized. In the New England system the procedure was for local bodies, having received land in common from the government of the colony, to grant it to individuals and to establish rules of tenure and land transfer or modify existing ones, in so far as they could, to facilitate corporate action. In Lower Canada where individuals received land directly in severalty from the king or his delegate, the grant was recorded and confirmed in a vertical process of responses, confirmations and recommendations to higher and higher authorities until it reached the governor. The approval was then transmitted in the reverse order through the hierarchy to the grantee. In this system individuals were dealt with as individuals. The notion of group representation was completely alien to this system and had no support in common law. At all times even today, except by accident, the bulk of these land papers is located only in the administrative centres of Quebec City and Ottawa.

The immediate consequence of this clash between a centralized administrative process based on individual grants in severalty and the decentralized private system of distribution based upon the group was confusion, delay and uncertainty. The administrators on the one hand attempted to realize the ends of the policy formulated in the period 1763-1791 but on the other they knew that if in practice, colonization was to be undertaken they had to adopt a system which by its nature would weaken if not defeat their intentions. Thus every decision concerning land policy was surrounded with confusion and uncertainty.

Despite the fact that in the first three years of the operation of the leader and associates system in Lower Canada, which began in 1792, the immigrants were issued certificates of pretension to some 10,000,000 acres of land,[10] such vital matters as the amount of land each individual should be given, the fees which would be paid, the responsibility for surveying, the location of clergy and crown reserves, were all left in abeyance and some immigrants were therefore forced to take title by occupancy. Some of the decisions, the matter of fees and the amount of land, for example, were not made until 1797, and the question of surveying not until 1798. Indeed, at one point because of the confusion and disagreement over one requirement of settlement, that of the oath of loyalty, virtually all the pretensions to land held by the American immigrants were declared invalid.[11]

It was precisely this climate of uncertainty and delay caused by the clash of opposing administrative systems which led leader and associate groups to adopt the characteristics and techniques of corporate organization for the purposes of survival.

The detailed financial and administrative records of several leader and associates groups, particularly those of a Samuel Willard, a loyalist from Vermont who was leader in the township of Stukely,[12] show an exact correspondence between the indecision and delay of the government and the adoption of corporate techniques of survival on the part of the leader and associates groups. Among the characteristics of corporate activity thus revealed were (1) the method of land holding by means of the creation of trusts which was distinctly different from that of the simple partnership;[13] (2) the transfer of shares

---

[10] This estimate based on P.A.C., RGI, L1, L.C. Land Book C., Pt. 11, pp. 331-336 and *ibid.*, L3L, Vol. 5, Warrent Book, 1795.

[11] In 1795-96 petitioners holding land in some 70 townships amounting to approximately 3,150,000 acres of land lost their claims. (*Ibid.*, Vol. 1, 37 pp. 34-36 and P.A.C., Collections Brome County Historical Society, IX, Township papers A, Minute Books, Nov. 28, 1797.) By 1809 almost 11 million acres had been promised but by 1815 little more than 2 million acres had been actually granted both in and outside the leader and associates system. (Quebec Provincial Archives, Patents of Land.)

[12] P.A.C., Collections Brome County Historical Society, Samuel Willard Papers 1783-1899.

[13] Lease and Release, Samuel Gale and others to Abraham Cuyler of Lands held in Trust, June 13 and 14, 1799. Deposited P. Lukin, N.P., July 16, 1799, Judicial Archives, Montreal.

and inheritance of shares;[14] (3) the financial support of the associated company by means of investment by persons not engaged in the administration and decision making of the company;[15] (4) the unity of organization obtained by delegation of decision making and authority to agents and attorneys, and (5) the fact that despite the change of personnel in the organization by death and by sales of shares no new agreements were struck.

The adoption of these characteristics of the corporation by leader and associates companies was in 1 sponse to two sets of influences. The combination of delays and confusion concerning regulations and their application created a condition of uncertainty. Logically speaking one could have found many possible solutions to this condition of uncertainty and the threat which it posed to the survival of the leader and associates group. However, in actual fact it was the existing predispositions of the immigrants toward some form of corporate organization which provided a solution and led them in the face of an uncertain future to abandon the partnership form as inadequate and to evolve in the direction of corporate organization.

While the change from the simple partnership type of organization to a more complex form of business organization is evident in a study of the leader and associates groups, the change in form and in quality should not be exaggerated. Of the fifty leader and associates groups actually granted land, out of approximately 157 which had been promised grants in 1792 or 1793,[16] some retained many of the principles of organization of the simple partnership. In addition we find other groups which, while having progressed beyond the partnership form, terminated in a type of organization whose characteristics approximated the syndicate rather than the corporate form. The point to be recognized is that this was a period of crucial change in Canadian economic organization when businessmen were experimenting with new forms of organization. It is to be

[14] P.A.C., Collections, Brome County Historical Society, Samuel Willard Papers, IX, Township Papers by Township, Stukely C., pp. 38-59 and P.A.C. Minutes of Council, June 11, 1798, Land Book D., pp. 179-188, Art. five of the Instructions of 1798.

[15] E.g., Bond for lands in Stukely, Samuel Willard to John Holbrook, June 25, 1801. P.A.C., B.C.H.S., Samuel Willard Papers, B. Land Papers, pp. 86-87.

[16] P.A.C., R.G.I., L3L, Vol. 5, Warrent Book, 1795.

expected that while they displayed some of the techniques of organization which were to emerge in legal form some fifty years later as the non-chartered registered company, nonetheless they retained during the period of change many of the older forms of organization. Had the government accomplished its plan to grant land in severalty in the short time specified in the original regulations, and had there been no clash of administrative systems, it is likely that many of the aspects of corporate activity which characterized the leader and associates groups would not have appeared at all. The simple partnership or joint adventure type of organization would have sufficed.

Although the evidence presented is limited to Lower Canada for the period 1791-1809, it seems reasonable to suggest that further research in the period after 1809, both for Lower and Upper Canada, would show a continuing evolution in the form of corporative structure down to 1850. In tracing the origins of corporate activity in Canada the greatest caution must be exercised in two directions. First, the action of courts and legal precedent do not necessarily reflect the development of the corporation from the point of view of economic causality. Second, evidence seems to indicate that there is no direct line of development between the chartered company and the modern day regulated company. The corporation is not merely a legal creature nor is it some sort of "free floating" economic phenomenon which has come and gone over the past centuries according to the pleasure or displeasure of law. Rather, there is evidence to indicate, at least in its beginnings, that the cloth of corporate organization, whether created within or outside of the law, was part of the very weave of the contemporary social, economic and political fabric. Further this study suggests something of the nature of a "spontaneous generation" of corporate forms.[17] It appears that a variety of unique historical circumstances may give rise to corporate forms of organization, each of which receives the imprint of the system of tenure (as expressed in policy and regulation) out of which it grows.

---

[17] For further discussion of this point see Gerald F. McGuigan, "The Emergence of the Unincorporated Company in Canada," *University of British Columbia Law Review*, Vol. 2, No. 1, April 1964, pp. 31-57.

French-Canadian Agriculture in the
St. Lawrence Valley, 1815-1850

R. L. JONES

Even to the casual observer, the valley of the St. Lawrence
in the first half of the nineteenth century differed in many
respects from Upper Canada, from the northern United States,
and even from the English-speaking parts of Lower Canada. It
had a quaintness which it has not yet lost. The traveller coming
up the St. Lawrence would catch sight of the typical long,
narrow farms along the river front more than a hundred miles
below Quebec. He would soon seen on each bank an endless
row of whitewashed dwellings, with a "close and remarkable"
resemblance to the peasants' cottages of Normandy,[1] and every
few miles, the centre of community life, a parish church with
"its simple spire, distinguished above the surrounding buildings
by its glittering vane and bright roof of tin."[2]

If the traveller left the boat, he could drive by stage through
a countryside "perfectly French in every respect; in the appearance of the cottages; the air, languages and dress of the peasantry; the sign boards on the shops and taverns; and the Virgin's
shrines and crosses by the wayside," and where "nearly every
common labourer and boy, though he had no shoes to his feet,
wore round his waist a sash of some bright colour, generally
red."[3]

Source: R. L. Jones, *Agricultural History*, Volume 16, No. 3, July
1942, pp. 137-148. Reprinted by permission of the Agricultural History Society, Washington, D.C.

[1] [Pierre de Sales Laterrière], *Political and Historical Account of Lower
Canada*, p. 113 (London, 1830).
[2] [Catherine Parr Traill], *The Backwoods of Canada* (London, 1838).
Reprinted in the New Canadian Library, 1966, p. 18.
[3] Charles Dickens, *American Notes*, p. 206 (London and New York,
1908).

It was easy to read romance into the everyday life of the habitants who jingled along the frozen rivers in their red carrioles to chorus the traditional songs of the voyageurs at some festivity;[4] and it was, possibly, equally easy to find in it a realized ideal of peasantry, one which despised all change, "satisfied to live in quiet and simple comfort, without the worry of improvements."[5] But if the traveller were an experienced old-country farmer who could look beyond the picturesque, or if, being less qualified, he consulted the Montreal or Quebec commission merchants, he would have learned, almost any time between the close of the Napoleonic Wars and mid-century, that the French-Canadians of the seigniories were undergoing an adjustment in their economy which was exceedingly painful.

Most of the seigniories occupied by the French Canadians stretched inland from the banks of the St. Lawrence from the border of Upper Canada eastward to the points where the Precambrian Shield on the north shore and the Notre Dame Mountains on the south shore made settlement impossible. Others were situated along the banks of tributaries of the St. Lawrence, especially the Richelieu. On these seigniories the habitants lived from generation to generation, each on his narrow strip, each paying his rent in cash or kind, and each in his lifetime reclaiming a small space from the forest.

In addition to the French Canadians of the seigniories, there were three other groups of agriculturists in Lower Canada. In the vicinity of Montreal and at other places advantageously situated with respect to markets, there were Englishmen and Scotsmen, usually men of some capital, who, as early as 1791, had been impressing travellers with their improved agriculture.[6] "The English farmer," Lord Durham wrote, "carried with him the experience and habits of the most improved agriculture in the world. . . . He often took the very farm which the [French-] Canadian settler had abandoned, and, by superior management, made that a source of profit which had only impoverished his

---

[4] "The Canadian settler scorned the name of peasant, and then, as now, was always called the *habitant*." – Francis Parkman, *The Old Régime in Canada*, p. 303 (rev. ed., Boston, 1895).

[5] E. W. Watkin, *Canada and the United States: Recollections 1851 to 1886*, p. 353 (London, 1887).

[6] P. Campbell, *Travels in the Interior Inhabited Parts of North America in the Years 1791 and 1792*, pp. 117-118 (Toronto, 1937).

predecessor."[7] South of the seigniories, in the Eastern Townships, were pioneers of British or American extraction, who held held their land according to the British system of tenure, and whose agriculture was a reproduction of that of northern New England.[8] Finally, there were some French-Canadian settlements outside the St. Lawrence valley plain which carried on a limited form of agriculture. In the patches of fertile soil along the rocky Gaspé coast, a scattered population farmed as a sideline to fishing. Again, along the south shore below Trois Pistoles, and even along the north shore – where there was no hinterland whatever and no means of land communication – little communities existed by fishing, trapping, cutting timber, and farming.[9] Though the first two of these groups would claim attention in any general history of Lower Canadian agriculture, they are omitted, like the third, from consideration in the following treatment of habitant agriculture.

In 1815, a century and a half after the first occupation of the seigniories, the settlements were never far from the river. In 1813, the country along the St. Lawrence eastward from Quebec "was cleared in a belt ranging from half a mile to three miles in length."[10] About 1816, a traveller reported that "From Quebec to Montreal may be called one long village. On either shore a strip of land, seldom exceeding a mile in breadth, (except near the streams which fall into the St. Lawrence,) bounded by aboriginal forests . . . represents all that is inhabited of Lower Canada."[11]

These limited clearances were evidence that the French Canadians lacked the pushing frontier spirit so characteristic

[7] Sir C. P. Lucas, ed., *Lord Durham's Report on the Affairs of British North America* (Oxford, 1912); Gerald M. Craig, ed., reprinted in the Carleton Library (Toronto, 1963), p. 32.

[8] Joseph Bouchette, *The British Dominions in North America*, I, 309 (London, 1832).

[9] *Ibid.*, I, 327-28; A. R. M. Lower, *Settlement and the Forest Frontier in Eastern Canada*, p. 6 (Toronto, 1936).

[10] New York *Albion*, Nov. 26, 1831, p. 195.

[11] Francis Hall, *Travels in Canada, and the United States, in 1816 and 1817*, p. 124 (London, 1818). Cf. P. Stansbury, *A Pedestrian Tour of Two Thousand Three Hundred Miles in North America*, pp. 159, 208 (New York, 1822); and James Flint, *Letters from America, Containing Observations on the Climate of the Western States, the Manners of the People, the Prospects of Emigrants, etc. etc.*, p. 238 (Cleveland, 1904).

of the Western States, Upper Canada, or the Eastern Townships. The habitants generally, it was remarked, were "far from adventurous; they cling with pertinacity to the spot which gave them birth, and cultivate, with contentedness the little piece of land which, in the division of the family property, has fallen to their share."[12]

In other respects, too, the habitants clung with tenacity to the customs of their ancestors. In nothing was this conservatism more strongly manifested than in their methods of agriculture. The agriculture practised in the seigniories in 1815 was, as it had long been, a type of general farming. The crops chiefly grown were the same as those of the early eighteenth century – wheat, oats, and peas. Other crops, such as barley, rye, and buckwheat, were still comparatively insignificant, although more or less generally grown. Indian corn, a standard pioneer crop elsewhere in North America, was of slight importance in Lower Canada; in fact, among the French Canadians it was seldom used except in the form of roasting ears. Potatoes, which had been scarcely known in New France before the British conquest, were now produced in great quantities.[13] With the exception of wheat, these crops, together with others of less importance such as flax and tobacco, were ordinarily utilized by the habitants on their farms. Wheat alone of their crops could be sold for cash.

To the twentieth-century student, it seems remarkable that wheat could have been regarded as the staple crop of the seigniories, for with its short growing season, the region is better fitted for pasturage. But wheat had been grown extensively during the French period. After the British conquest, and especially during the Revolutionary and Napoleonic wars, the commission merchants of Quebec encouraged an expansion of

[12] Laterrière, *Political and Historical Account of Lower Canada*, p. 120. It was stated in 1826 that, although the population of the seigniories had quadrupled since 1784, the amount of land under cultivation had increased by only one third. – Lucas, *Lord Durham's Report*, II, 293-94.

[13] John Lambert, *Travels Through Lower Canada and the United States of North America in the Years 1806, 1807 and 1808*, I, 98, 136 (London, 1810); William Evans, *A Treatise on the Theory and Practice of Agriculture, Adapted to the Cultivation and Economy of the Animal and Vegetable Productions of Agriculture in Canada*, pp. 42, 183-84, 187-88 (Montreal, 1835).

acreage by sending out agents who circulated among the habitants buying their grain and building warehouses in the villages along the rivers for storing and shipping it.[14] Wartime demand, with only nascent competition from the new lands along the Great Lakes, made wheat a profitable crop, in spite of rather frequent failures of the harvest, and considerable fluctuations in the market.[15] With a cash income, steady or intermittent, the habitants imperceptibly passed from the stage of economic self-sufficiency, which had been so characteristic of the Old Régime along the St. Lawrence, to one wherein they were buying many of the articles they used. About 1830, a writer remarked that the habitant "at one time perhaps entirely produced, whatever he consumed. The introduction of English luxuries, however, has, in some degree, altered this; tea, English broad cloths and calicoes, cutlery &c., now form part of the Canadian's necessaries; though the degree in which he is dependent solely on himself is far greater than that of an English farmer."[16]

The easiest way for the habitants to maintain their new standard of living was to continue to depend on wheat, a choice made inevitable by the fact that the fertile soil of the St. Lawrence and Richelieu valleys had long produced abundantly when the seasons were favourable.[17] By 1815, much of their land had been under cultivation for so many years that it was becoming worn out. Further, the long concentration on wheat had developed certain undesirable concomitant characteristics in the agriculture of the habitants. They had a tendency, like New World farmers in general, to cultivate too much land, and to do it poorly. They gave insufficient emphasis to stock raising, for reasons pointed out later. Above all, they were content with defective methods of tillage; they practised what Lord Durham

---

[14] F. W. Burton, "The Wheat Supply of New France," Royal Society of Canada, *Transactions*, XXX, 141-47 (Ottawa, 1936); Isaac Weld, *Travels through the States of North America and the Provinces of Upper and Lower Canada during the Years 1795, 1796 and 1797*, II, 7-8 (ed. 3, London, 1800); Bouchette, *British Dominions*, II, "St. Denis," "St. Ours."

[15] Lambert, *Travels Through Lower Canada*, I, p. 100.

[16] Laterrière, *Political and Historical Account of Lower Canada*, p. 127.

[17] H. Y. Hind, and others, *Eighty Years' Progress of British North America*, p. 52 (Toronto, 1863).

called "the worst method of small farming."[18]

Essentially, the habitants used a simple two-year rotation. In this "old French system" it was customary to divide the arable portion of the farm into two nearly equal parts, one part to be sown one year, the other the next. The half to be sown was ploughed in the fall if there was time,[19] otherwise in the spring, but usually it was done very badly and harrowed in a slovenly fashion. When it was seeded with wheat (generally a spring variety, as fall wheat in Lower Canada was subject to winter-killing),[20] oats, peas, or perhaps barley, the habitant did not spend his time summer fallowing the idle part of his land, as the advanced British farmer in the Canadas did,[21] but simply left it alone or used it as a pasture. The lack of crop rotation, or even of fallowing, meant that there was no check on the growth of thistles, wild oats, wild mustard, and other weeds. Even as a pasture the idle land was not worth much, for the habitant never sowed either grass or clover seed. In the autumn, it was ploughed, and the next year the other part lay idle. "This alternating system is carried on for an indefinite period," declared William Evans, "and I have no doubt it has in some instances been continued for a century or more."[22]

Occasionally a habitant would put little piles of manure on the idle land in summer, where it would leach till fall before it was ploughed in, but even this practice was certainly far from general. In fact, as late as 1860, the custom of carting manure on to the ice of a neighbouring river to be washed away in the

[18] Lucas, *Lord Durham's Report*, II, 28-29; Carleton Library edition, p. 27. The description which follows is based primarily on the account in *Journal d'Agriculture* (Montreal), août 1850, p. 247-49. It may be confirmed by comparison with Lambert, *Travels*, I, 135; *Journal of the Legislative Assembly of Lower Canada*, 1816, App. E.; *Journal of the Legislative Assembly of Canada, 1850*, App. TT; William Evans, *Review of the Agriculture of Lower Canada with Suggestions for its Amelioration*, p. 28 ff. (Montreal, 1856); *L'Agriculteur* (Montreal), octobre 1859, p. 25.

[19] The habitants seem usually to have ploughed with two yokes of oxen and a horse. — Bouchette, *British Dominions*, I, "Beauharnois." The oxen were yoked by the horns. – Flint, *Letters from America*, p. 331; [B. Silliman], *Remarks Made on a Short Tour Between Hartford and Quebec in the Autumn of 1819*, p. 241-42 (ed. 2, New Haven, 1824).

[20] Evans, *Treatise*, p. 175.

[21] C. F. Grece, *Facts and Observations Respecting Canada and the United States of America*, pp. 95, 101, 106 (London, 1819).

[22] Evans, *Review*, p. 29.

spring, or of removing the barns when the manure accumulated, still prevailed to a considerable extent.[23]

By 1815, the unwelcome results of these farming methods were plainly manifest. From the statistics given by Joseph Bouchette about 1830, it is clear that the amount of wheat grown in all Lower Canada was not greatly in excess of that required for local consumption. The consequence was that the large overseas export of wheat from the Richelieu valley was almost counterbalanced by the importation of cheap flour from Upper Canada, New York, or Ohio for use in Montreal, Quebec, and elsewhere.[24] In regions once spoken of as "the granaries of Lower Canada," the inhabitants were reduced to producing scarcely enough grain for themselves; and in still others, especially along the lower St. Lawrence, the wheat crops failed year after year.[25]

But worse was to come, both in the comparatively progressive parts of the seigniories and in the most backward, from the ravages of the worst pest the wheat growers in the Canadas ever had to contend with — the wheat midge.[26] This insect was first noticed in western Vermont in 1820, probably having been brought to Quebec in its larval state in some unthreshed wheat from Europe, and having spread unnoticed southwards. In 1828, 1829, 1832, and 1833, it caused much loss in large areas of Lower Canada, as well as in the adjacent parts of Vermont, New Hampshire, and New York. In 1834, 1835, 1836, and 1839, it occasioned great havoc, not only in the Richelieu valley, but also "west and northward of Montreal for many miles."[27]

[23] *Journal d'Agriculture*, mars 1850, p. 75; *ibid.*, aôut 1850, p. 247-48; Hind, *Eighty Years' Progress*, p. 34.
[24] Bouchette, *British Dominions*, I, 369; Rochester, N.Y., *Daily Advertiser*, quoted in Montreal *Canadian Courant*, Dec. 24, 1833.
[25] *Neilson's Quebec Gazette*, quoted in *Canadian Courant*, Nov. 23, 1833.
[26] The midge is not to be confused with the Hessian fly, which did much damage in the seigniories between 1805 and 1816, and did not pass away completely till after 1830. - H. Y. Hind, *Essay on the Insects and Diseases Injurious to the Wheat Crops*, pp. 42-43 (Toronto, 1857).
[27] *Ibid.*, pp. 77-78; Montreal *La Minerve*, quoted in Hallowell, Upper Canada, *Free Press*, July 30, 1833; Henry Taylor, *Journal of a Tour Thro' Berthier and Sorel to the Eastern Townships*, pp. 5, 23, 27 (Quebec, 1840). The failure of the wheat crop in the Montreal region and the Richelieu valley undoubtedly had much to do with the unreasoning discontent which prevailed in Lower Canada in the middle

Every conceivable means was resorted to in an effort to check the plague, from sowing lime or a mixture of Scotch snuff and wood ashes broadcast on the standing grain when the dew was heavy to holding religious meetings and processions,[28] but all to no purpose. Apparently nothing could be done to overcome the midge.

As early as 1838, many of the British farmers in the Montreal district were ceasing to grow wheat,[29] but their distress was not to be compared with that which overtook the habitants of the seigniories. Among them, men who once had wheat to sell in large quantities now had to buy flour for their own use. In 1829, crop shortages in Yamaska in the heart of the Richelieu valley resulted in the importation from New York of 4,000 barrels of flour of different kinds, an incident which presented "the novel occurrence of the Inland parishes of Lower Canada being fed by supplies received seaward, from the United States."[30] In 1835, when the wheat crop in Lower Canada was almost a complete failure, and the Upper Canada surplus was marketed in the United States, nearly 500,000 bushels of wheat had to be imported from Europe to feed the population of the province.[31] This importation of breadstuffs for home use continued down to mid-century,[32] though, after 1836, always from the western interior.

Evans, an excellent authority, in 1849 estimated the damage already done by the midge alone in Lower Canada as fully £6,000,000 currency, or about $24,000,000.[33] Added to the

thirties. As it was where the midge was worst that the risings of 1837-1838 took place, something might be made of the contention that it was not without responsibility for them. Cf. the remark in H. A. Innis and A. R. M. Lower, *Select Documents in Canadian Economic History, 1783-1885* (Toronto, 1933): "The editor hazards the suggestion that the Lower Canada crop failure of 1835 was not without its bearing on the political agitation of these years." – p. 256.

[28] Hind, *Essay*, pp. 95-101; Patrick Shirreff, *Tour through North America, Together with a Comprehensive View of the Canadas and the United States as Adapted for Agricultural Emigration*, p. 136 (Edinburgh, 1835); *Canadian Agriculturist* (Toronto), August 1859, p. 180.

[29] *Canadian Quarterly Agricultural and Industrial Magazine*, I, 71 (Montreal, 1838).

[30] Quebec *Mercury*, quoted in Kingston, U.C., *Gazette*, June 5, 1829.

[31] Montreal *Morning Courier*, Dec. 31, 1836.

[32] *British American Cultivator* (Toronto), February 1843, p. 20; *Journal d'Agriculture*, septembre 1849, p. 257.

[33] *Ibid.*, février 1849, p. 33.

problem of the midge was that of wheat rust, which in certain seasons was equally destructive.[34] As a result of the annual devastation by one enemy or the other it was quite clear in the early forties that the habitants had been driven out of wheat, with consequences depicted by Evans in these words: "The loss of wheat to the farmer is most severely felt. It has been the cause of deranging the whole system of agriculture. A large proportion of the arable land of every farm might have been appropriated to the growing of wheat, but since the failure of that crop, all the land is employed in producing crops that can only be consumed in Canada. Hence, the market must be glutted with this description of produce."[35]

Evans here touched on one effect of the failure of wheat – the turning more and more to coarse grains such as oats, peas, and barley.[36] Unfortunately, there was little demand for barley or rye, except at the breweries and distilleries of Montreal and Quebec. Oats could be sold to advantage only to the liveries, draymen, and garrisons of the towns, or at the shanties of the lumbermen operating in the Ottawa valley or towards the Maine frontier.[37] None of these coarse grains would stand the cost of transportation overseas. Under these circumstances, the habitants found little profit in producing them for sale, though some drove into Montreal from distances as great as a hundred miles with loads of oats and barley.[38] The consequence was that the only place most of them could be disposed of was on the farm, if not in oaten or barley bread or in pea soup, then in livestock feed; but, for reasons to be pointed out shortly, livestock raising was not an enterprise on which the habitants could embark with confidence.

At the time the habitants were finding that growing coarse grains for market was not the answer to their problem, they suffered a calamity which was scarcely less devastating than the failure of wheat. In their endeavour to find a substitute for the wheat flour which they would have to purchase, they began to

[34] *British American Cultivator*, October 1842, p. 148; *Canadian Agricultural Journal* (Montreal), Oct. 1, 1844, p. 154.
[35] *British American Cultivator*, August 1842, p. 117.
[36] J. F. W. Johnston, *Notes on North America: Agricultural, Economical and Social*, I, 363 (London, 1851).
[37] Cf. *Report from the Select Committee on the Timber Duties, No. 113*, p. 147 (London, 1836).
[38] *Journal d'Agriculture*, janvier 1850, p. 18.

depend in large part on potatoes for food. Then, in 1843, the potato crop in Lower Canada, as throughout North America in general, was attacked by the "late blight" or "rot." The disease was exceptionally bad in 1844, 1845, and 1846, and by the end of 1847, the crop had to be given up in large sections of Lower Canada.[39] As an acute observer remarked, "in this state of things, when by the previous failure of the wheat, the potato had become doubly precious, it will be understood how the potato disease must have produced a more intense amount of suffering among the Lower Canadians."[40]

In many parts of North America, farmers who have been driven out of wheat growing have turned to livestock husbandry. Eventually, the habitants did find some salvation in this branch of farming, but this was not till after 1850. The delay is to be explained as follows.

The habitants had long raised livestock as part of their general farming. They kept the different animals common in the New World, with this distinction – theirs as a rule were smaller, but hardier, than those kept elsewhere. Their "landshark"-type pigs were inferior even to those of Vermont, but the habitants liked them, because, pea fed, they produced excessively fat pork.[41] Their sheep somewhat resembled Merinos in size, but they had such coarse wool and so little of it, that they were of no commercial significance.[42] Their cattle belonged to a small breed, black or red, closely related to the Jerseys. So inferior was their beef considered that the butchers of Montreal and Quebec raised their own cattle to some extent, instead of buying from the habitants, and the government contractors obtained from Vermont most of what they supplied to the Lower Canada garrisons.[43] Furthermore, although their milk was good, these cattle were not ordinarily used for commercial dairying. In fact, the

[39] *Journal and Transactions of the Board of Agriculture of Upper Canada for 1855-56,* p. 39 (Toronto, 1856); *Canadian Agricultural Journal,* Oct. 1, 1844, p. 154; Oct. 1, 1845, p. 46; *Journal d'Agriculture,* avril 1848, p. 110.

[40] Johnston, *Notes on North America,* I, 363.

[41] Lambert, *Travels,* I, 75, 143; Evans, *Treatise,* p. 187.

[42] Bouchette, *British Dominions,* I, "Beauharnois"; Ezra Carman, E. A. Heath, and John Minto, *Special Report on the History and Present Condition of the Sheep Industry in the United States,* pp. 343-46 (Washington, 1892).

[43] Lambert, *Travels,* I, 82, 142; evidence of Philemon Wright, *Journal of the Legislative Assembly of Lower Canada, 1824,* App. TT.

only cheese manufactured by the habitants was of a kind ungraciously called "stinking cheese," and little of this, or of any other Lower Canadian kind for that matter, reached the market; and only one region, Kamouraska, developed a reputation for butter.[44]

The best animals the habitants had were their horses. They fitted in so well with wheat growing that the habitants had always raised a greater proportion of them than of any other kind of livestock; too many perhaps, for the good of their farms.[45] Though, except in Kamouraska, French-Canadian horses were so small as to be referred to by Europeans as "ponies," they were strong and well-proportioned.[46] On account of these desirable qualities, they had been exported through Connecticut or New York to the West Indies even before the American Revolution. Nor was the trade less active thereafter. In the first half of the nineteenth century, American dealers, as well as some from Upper Canada, were accustomed to visit Montreal and other places in Lower Canada to purchase the best of the French-Canadian horses, bringing with them in trade larger but inferior ones.[47]

The habitants liked to have the "Yankee horse-jockeys" buy their colts, for the income thus provided was often all they had, aside from that brought in by their wheat. And yet the emphasis on horse raising which was thus encouraged was possibly unfortunate, for the horses were pampered, relatively, at the expense of the rest of the livestock. The habitants were notorious for the defective manner in which they fed and sheltered their

[44] Lambert, *Travels*, I, 86, 106; Laterrière, *Political and Historical Account of Lower Canada*, p. 128.

[45] Thus, Kalm wrote in the middle of the eighteenth century: "It is a general complaint that the country people begin to keep too many horses, by which means the cows are kept short of food in winter." Peter Kalm, *Travels into North America* . . . (ed. 2, 1772), as translated in John Pinkerton, *General Collection of the Best and Most Interesting Voyages and Travels in all Parts of the World*, p. 662 (London, 1812).

[46] Campbell, *Travels*, I, 114; Lambert, *Travels*, I, 142.

[47] P. W. Bidwell and J. I. Falconer, *History of Agriculture in the Northern United States 1620-1860*, p. 113 (Washington, 1925); Lambert, *Travels*, I, 143-44; Evans, *Treatise*, p. 119; *Canadian Agricultural Journal*, March 1845, p. 43. So extensive was this trade into the United States that by 1845 there was a noticeable infusion of the blood of the French-Canadian horse in Vermont. – *Cultivator* (Albany, N.Y.), August 1845, p. 256.

cattle, sheep, and pigs. Their pastures were deficient, except for a few valuable ones along the river fronts, and even these were probably entirely composed of wild grasses.[48] Ordinarily, animals nourished themselves as best they might on the weeds of the idle arable land previously referred to, or on the waste or woodland portions of the farm. When winter came, many of them were butchered, to avoid the labour and expense of keeping them over till the next year, as well as to make it possible to feed the horses all the forage cut during the summer.[49] In no respect was there a greater difference between the habitants and the British farmers in Lower Canada than in the care they took of their livestock.[50]

With this heritage, habitants who desired to engage in cattle, hog, or sheep raising were handicapped from the start. Moreover, livestock raising required capital, which, owing to the failure of wheat, they lacked. To be profitable, it also required some assurance of a market, and this too they did not have.

Before 1843, the habitants could not hope to produce butter, cheese, or meat for export overseas, as the British duty was prohibitive;[51] nor did they have a home market for such articles. After 1815, Montreal and Quebec were great exporters of the agricultural surplus of the basin of the Great Lakes. The consequence was that the foodstuffs they consumed were more easily obtained from the westward than from any but the most adjacent parts of Lower Canada. Thus, the lumber shanties of the Ottawa valley came to be supplied through Montreal with Cincinnati pork, the butchers of Montreal and Quebec with Vermont cattle, and the grocers of the towns of Lower Canada with Ohio or Vermont cheese.[52] The British farmers around Montreal did get a share of the local livestock market, and so did the inhabitants of the Eastern Townships,[53] but both of these groups found difficulty in competing with American imports. They therefore campaigned persistently, like their fellows in

[48] George Heriot, *Travels through the Canadas*, p. 58 (London, 1807); Lucas, *Lord Durham's Report*, II, 97.

[49] Weld, *Travels*, I, 395.

[50] Bouchette, *British Dominions*, I, "Beauharnois."

[51] *Canadian Agricultural Journal*, January 1, 1844, p. 8.

[52] Evans, *Treatise*, pp. 43, 116-17, 133; *British American Cultivator*, May 1842, p. 80; February 1843, p. 20; R. L. Jones, "The Canadian Agricultural Tariff of 1843," *Canadian Journal of Economics and Political Science*, VII, 532-33 (Toronto, 1941).

[53] Taylor, *Journal*, p. 39.

Upper Canada, for an agricultural tariff, which they finally achieved in 1843.[54] Nevertheless, even after this act went into operation, complaints continued to be made that the Lower Canada markets were glutted with American produce.[55] Under these circumstances, when the relatively efficient British farmers of Lower Canada could not meet American competition, it would have been unreasonable to expect any appreciable growth in livestock raising among the habitants; and none took place.

Nothing the habitants could do, seemingly, promised economic salvation. By mid-century their situation had become one of chronic distress. Clergy, businessmen, newspaper editors, and politicians continually discussed it. They agreed in their analyses of the more obvious defects of agriculture in the St. Lawrence valley – lack of fertilizing, lack of proper rotation, lack of approved stock-raising methods, lack of improved implements, too much concentration on wheat — but they showed much difference of opinion when they tried to account for these defects.

Some believed that the seigniorial or feudal system of land tenure was responsible for the bad agriculture of the French Canadians. Thus, Lord Durham pointed out that the British purchaser of a seigniory found that the tenure made it difficult for him to improve his land, because, so long as the habitant paid his rent, he could not be removed, nor forced to adopt more advanced farming methods. Moreover, Durham claimed that the French tenure was unpopular even with the habitant.[56] However, it did have certain advantages for the latter, particularly in the pioneering period, for it enabled him to use his limited capital entirely in equipping his holding, instead of in purchasing land. It sometimes happened, therefore, that the habitant settled in an undesirable location in the seigniories in preference to going into the adjacent Eastern Townships.[57] On the whole, it seems that, though the seigniorial tenure had outlived its usefulness, it was not the prime cause of the bad agriculture of the French Canadians. The best informed students of

[54] Cf. Jones, "The Canadian Agricultural Tariff of 1843," p. 534-35.
[55] Journal d'Agriculture, juillet 1848, p. 214.
[56] Lucas, Lord Durham's Report, II, 24-25, 28, 36, 263.
[57] Laterrière, Political and Historical Account of Lower Canada, pp. 168-69, 179-80. On the advantages of the seigniorial system, cf. A. L. Burt, "The Frontier in the History of New France," Canadian Historical Association, Report, 1940, p. 94-95.

Lower Canadian farming, such as William Evans, seldom accorded it more than passing mention.

Others believed that the root of the problem lay in over-population of the seigniories, with the consequent emigration of the French Canadians to the United States, and this opinion has been repeated with much emphasis in a recent book.[58] It is true that, in some of the seigniories, the land had become so excessively subdivided in the course of generations that it was unable to support all its inhabitants by farming, and the young men accordingly often went off to work in the fisheries of the Gulf, in the harvest fields of Upper Canada, in the timber industry of the Ottawa, or, after about 1840, in the factories of New England.[59] Probably this exodus would have been regarded as no more than normal, if it had occurred among any other group than the French Canadians. In any case, no matter how much overpopulation may have aggravated the rural distress of the seigniories, it does not seem to have been the fundamental reason for the defects in agriculture prevailing in them.

Other critics, with more insight, ascribed the bad farming of the French Canadians to the lack of markets. In one sense it could be maintained that the habitants really had no cause for complaint in this regard; as the Select Committee on Lower Canada Agriculture pointed out in 1850, they were much more favourably situated with respect to a market than the farmers near Lake Erie or Lake Huron or Lake Michigan.[60] Of course, this was true only of wheat, which the habitants could not grow; as already indicated, unless they were very near Montreal or Quebec, they could not sell profitably the other products to which they had been forced to turn, owing to the ease with which similar articles could be brought in from outside. The habitants were among the first in the East to suffer from effective western competition; and their agriculture reflected this fact.

Still others who gave thought to the subject felt that the backwardness of the seigniories was to be attributed, in part at least, to the lack of formal instruction in the theory and practice

[58] Marcus L. Hansen and J. B. Brebner, *The Mingling of the Canadian and American Peoples*, pp. 124-25 (New Haven, Toronto and London, 1940).

[59] *Journal of the Legislative Assembly of Canada, 1849*, App. ppppp; *Journal d'Agriculture*, juillet 1850, p. 196-97.

[60] *Journal of the Legislative Assembly of Canada, 1850*, App. TT.

of agriculture. Carrying this idea to an extreme, a writer recently
has claimed that if the British government had provided such a
program, even of the most elementary kind, it would have
aroused a spirit of curiosity and emulation "to which the most
refractory peasant would not have remained indifferent."[61] This
assertion completely disregards the fact that when the British
in Lower Canada tried to change the old ways, officially or
privately, they were rebuffed, or were met with indifference.
The resistance to changes in the seigniorial system is one example. Another might be found in the attempt to eliminate the
nuisance of the cahots, or pitchholes, which made the winter
roads in the seigniories worse than any other roads in North
America where snow fell.[62] Lord Sydenham in 1841 issued a
special ordinance in the hope of eliminating the cahots, but it
could not be enforced against the will of the habitants, and so,
at least as late as the early 1860s, the nuisance still flourished
everywhere in French Canada, except in the immediate vicinity
of Montreal.[63] Still another example might be found in the
unhappy history of the Lower-Canadian agricultural societies.
The British farmers who promoted these societies and their
exhibitions tried to interest the French Canadians. They met
with scant success, for in the societies where the French and
British farmers competed on a basis of equality, the British won
all the prizes, because they had superior farming knowledge,
and the habitants soon withdrew in discouragement; in the other
societies, which had separate classes for the British and French
exhibitors, the directors found they were giving prizes to the
habitants for rubbish.[64] Finally, the habitants failed to benefit
even from observing the practices of the British farmers who

[61] Gérard Parizeau, "Aperçu de la situation économique dans le Bas-
Canada vers 1837," in Canadian Historical Association, *Report*, 1937,
p. 57.

[62] The habitant did not attach the shaft to the sleigh rigidly, but by
means of a chain. Thus, when the tension slackened, the shaft piled
up the snow in little heaps; when it tightened, the runners went over
the heaps, packing them down; and so was created a succession of
cahots. Cahots were not produced when the shaft was rigidly at-
tached, as was the practice in Upper Canada and the Eastern
Townships.

[63] Evans, *Treatise*, pp. 146-47; Hind, *Eighty Years' Progress*, pp. 105-7;
Montreal (biweekly) *Witness*, Mar. 15, 1862.

[64] *Canadian Courant*, Feb. 27, Mar. 6, 1833; letter of William Boa of St.
Laurent, July 12, 1850, in *Journal of the Legislative Assembly of
Canada, 1850*, App. TT.

were settled in their midst.[65] Under these circumstances, the hopelessness of any program of governmental agricultural education which might have been undertaken is understandable.

One other reason for the backwardness of French-Canadian agriculture was commonly given – the ingrained conservatism of the habitants. Few in Lower Canada, among the British at least, would have quarrelled with Lord Durham's assertion that the French Canadians "clung to ancient prejudices, ancient customs and ancient laws, not from any strong sense of their beneficial effects, but with the unreasoning tenacity of an uneducated and unprogressive people."[66] He was right, for the habitants, it must be remembered, had been cut off from association with France since the British conquest, and under the leadership of their clergy they had since developed a spirit of French-Canadian nationalism. Aside from the notaries, the parish priests, and a few others regarded as their leaders, they were illiterate.[67] Dedicated as they were to the preservation of their laws, their language, and their religion, they resisted any change, however small, in their mode of life. It was this aversion to innovation which rendered the distress in the seigniories so acute, and made it so difficult to ameliorate. When we add to the persistence in eighteenth-century, frontier-farming methods the fact of effective western competition, we find it difficult to conceive of a more discouraging outlook than that which confronted the agriculturists of the St. Lawrence valley in 1849.

Conservatism in agricultural methods was characteristic of the habitants for another generation,[68] but fortunately its effects were less disastrous after about 1850. The change was to be ascribed only in part to the termination in 1854 of the seigniorial system, and to the operation, beginning in 1848, of various plans of church-directed "colonization," that is, the removal of the redundant French-Canadian population to new parishes.[69] Fundamentally, it was brought about by the sudden opening in

[65] *Journal d'Agriculture*, février 1850, p. 30; mai 1850, p. 133.

[66] Lucas, *Lord Durham's Report*, II, p. 30; Carleton Library edition, p. 28.

[67] Cf. Durham's structures on French-Canadian education in *ibid.*, pp. 30-34; Carleton Library edition, pp. 28-30.

[68] G. M. Grant, *Picturesque Canada; the Country as it Was and Is*, I, 84 (Toronto, 1882).

[69] On the subject of "colonization," cf. Lower, *Settlement and the Forest Frontier*.

the summer of 1849 of a market in the United States, not only for more horses than ever before, but also for precisely those commodities in which the habitants had hitherto found no profit – oats, barley, poultry, eggs, and butter.[70] The involved story of the origin and development of this trade we hope to deal with in another article. We therefore pass over it for the present, merely stating that the exports across the border continued to grow in importance till the Reciprocity Treaty expired in 1866. The opening of the American market affected the whole province of Canada, but nowhere was it more welcomed than in the St. Lawrence seigniories, where, after their long succession of disappointments, the habitants now enjoyed a relative prosperity.

[70] *Journal d'Agriculture*, novembre 1849, p. 338-39, and later numbers.

PART THREE

BANKING AND CAPITAL FORMATION

Banking in Canada before Confederation, 1792-1867

BRAY HAMMOND

I. THE SITUATION IN THE PROVINCES

These doings in the States that I have been recounting drew
the utmost attention above the border, as American affairs
always did. In 1829 the cashier of the Bank of Montreal told the
legislative committee of Lower Canada that he did not know
anything about the banking practices of the Bank of England,
or any other British banks, but he was able to give very accurate
information about banking in the United States. Such knowledge
of American affairs was not exceptional or peculiar to bankers.
Every Britisher in the provinces shared it in some degree. "The
influence of the United States surrounds him on every side,"
Lord Durham wrote ten years later, "and is for ever present. It
extends itself as population augments and intercourse increases;
it penetrates every portion of the continent into which the restless spirit of American speculation impels the settler or the
trader; it is felt in all the transactions of commerce, from the
important operations of the monetary system down to the minor

Source: Bray Hammond, *Banks and Politics in America from the
Revolution to the Civil War*, Princeton, N.J., 1957, pp. 631-70. Reprinted by permission of Princeton University Press. Copyright ©
1957, by Princeton Universi'y Press.

details of ordinary traffic; it stamps, on all the habits and opinions of the surrounding countries, the common characteristics of the thoughts, feelings, and customs of the American people."[1]

Approached from Europe, the continent of North America above Mexico comprised three zones or regions suitable for quite different economic development. The southern, extending westward beyond the Mississippi and southward to the Gulf of Mexico from the latitude of Delaware Bay – or what became established as Mason and Dixon's line, the border between Maryland and Pennsylvania – has been from the beginning adapted primarily to the production of agricultural staples. The intermediate, likewise extending westward to the Mississippi and beyond, was also in its pristine state adapted mainly to agriculture, but to shipbuilding and commerce too, and this with its possession of great mineral resources, both ores and fuels, led in course of time to its becoming primarily industrial and financial. The northern zone, now Canada, lying about and above the Bay of Fundy and the Great Lakes, has had the disadvantage of its high latitude and the lesser accessibility of its resources, which for technical and geographic reasons could not be reached and developed so readily as the resources of the southerly regions. Though the three zones became peopled by a homogeneous European stock, they sharply diverged in their later courses, economically and politically.

Of the three the southern zone, comprising the British colonies and later the states of the American Union south and west from Maryland, was the first to accumulate wealth from exports, these being in the main tobacco, indigo, and cotton. From the northern zone, now Canada, the exports of furs, fish, and timber were for a long time the outstanding sources of wealth, relatively little of which, however, inured to the region whence it came; shipbuilding and commerce were important in Nova Scotia, but what Nova Scotia had was repeated many times over in the States, save only that the port of Halifax was the one nearest Europe. The middle zone, now the northern part of the American Union, was notable for the diversity of its

[1] Shortt, "Canadian Currency, Banking, and Exchange," *Journal of Canadian Bankers Association*, VIII, 145-46; Durham, *Report on the Affairs of British North America*, II ([ed. Lucas] Oxford, 1912), p. 311; reprinted in the Carleton Library (Toronto, 1963), pp. 161-62.

economic interests and its accumulation of capital. Its wealth was acquired less simply than by the export of staples to waiting markets where they were already in demand. Its wealth grew to a greater extent by ingenuity, enterprise, invention, technology, finance, and the rise of markets for manufactured products. It grew by the same conditions that gradually impaired the monopoly the South had long had for its products. Canada was dependent still more than the northern part of the Union on what the future would do for her. She had to await railways, peopling, and the exploitation of more accessible areas before her western prairies, reaching toward the Arctic Circle, began to yield their wealth. She had to await the exploitation of resources elsewhere and the greater advance of techniques, before her minerals could be drawn forth profitably. And for a long time – even into the twentieth century – a relatively large volume of her savings was invested abroad, rather than at home in a domestic development that would have been premature.

In these circumstances economic dynamism centred during the nineteenth century in the northern zone of the United States. There the prosperity was greatest. There the most money was made. There change was swiftest. There the economy was most complex and contrived. There the distribution of wealth was most general. This rich and powerful community rose in ominous fashion above its neighbours on either side – the states to the south, the provinces to the north – who envied, feared, and resisted her. The South made a suicidal effort to free herself; Canada lived for generations in a fascinated dread. Both, by comparison, were backward, simple, conservative, and agrarian. Both were shackled to their own institutions and their dislike of enterprise. The South, indeed, retrogressed, being worse off in the latter part of the century than in the first. Canada progressed, but slowly, biding her time so to speak. The nature of her population reflected her economic situation and conditioned her politics. When the American states became independent, what is now Canada was far less populous than they were, most of her people were French, and her complete subjection to British rule was very recent. Canada proper, now the province of Quebec, was wholly French. Nova Scotia, which then included what is now the province of New Brunswick, was still a racked and half-formed colony no longer occupied by the

Acadians and not yet more than sparsely settled by the British. Prince Edward Island also was barely a handful. The provinces received their first substantial English-speaking accretions from loyalists who departed from the revolted colonies, where they were known and vilified as tories. Most of these – some 28,000 – populated New Brunswick, which was separated from Nova Scotia in 1784. Some 10,000 others crossed into what was subsequently Upper Canada and is now Ontario.[2]

The loyalists were welcomed, formally, by the British authorities, but they and their claims, though in sentiment a source of pride, were in fact a burden. To the original Canadians, who were French, Catholic, and fixed, the loyalists were still Americans and therefore abominable. And not unreasonably so; for they were Protestant and enterprising. They were also politically restless despite their loyalty to the British crown. The two races were sorely antipathetic and jealous. At the time of the conquest in 1763, the British authorities had committed themselves to lenity and indulgence toward the French, who at first were far more tractable subjects than either the Americans or the British immigrants, both of whom had economic ambitions and political notions of which the simple habitants were innocent. Too soon, however, reacting to the peculiarity of their position, the French also became refractory. There then was something like anarchy, which reached its height about 1837, the French and English bristling at one another and both being froward with the British authorities, who were themselves something less than perfect. In these circumstances political impediments to economic growth combined with geographic. But it was also in these circumstances that the Earl of Durham wrote his brilliant and superb report, which led in particular to the present union of the British North American provinces as Canada and enlightened everywhere the colonial and the imperial policy of Great Britain. The change was marked by recognition of the value of the provinces, which it had been the fashion in some British

[2] The distinction I try to observe between provinces considered severally and the Provinces considered as a whole – that is, as a nation – is marked by the use of the capital letter P. The same is true of states and the States, the latter in my idiom being a short name for the United States. The Provinces and the States are both federal unions, of provinces and of states respectively.

quarters to deny.[3] Indeed, the improved political relations, though followed in turn by improved economic conditions, had been impelled by what the provinces were already doing economically. This, though less spectacular than what was happening in the States, was diverse and substantial. It had given pressure to demands for reform, it then justified the reforms once they were made, and it put the value of the provinces to the Empire beyond question. The benefits of the turn were confirmed by Britain's repeal of the corn laws and enactment of preferential tariffs which improved the market for Canadian grains and other products.

Till 1867 the name Canada belonged only to what are now, roughly speaking, the provinces of Quebec and Ontario; in that year the Dominion of Canada was created by the confederating of three provinces – Nova Scotia, New Brunswick, and old Canada, the latter becoming divided thenceforth into Quebec and Ontario. Four other provinces which later joined the Confederation at first remained outside it – Newfoundland, Prince Edward Island, Manitoba, and British Columbia. By "Canada," therefore, one must mean different things at different times: to Lord Durham, "Canadian" meant French Canadian; it did not include Nova Scotian; and "the Canadas" did not include Newfoundland, New Brunswick, or Prince Edward Island, their sister colonies.

Between the Provinces and the States as two neighbour groups, there were from the outset ties as well as antipathies. Trade was practically free and moved more naturally over the uncertain international boundary than it did over some of the forest and mountain barriers that divided the Provinces and States within themselves. Montreal had long been the port and trading head not only for much of nearby Vermont and New York lying up the Richelieu River, but for the Ohio and Great Lakes regions, and the fur-producing areas of the Mississippi valley. The St. Lawrence and the Ottawa had been the principal means of access to the interior of the continent, and made

---

[3] Lord Brougham, animadverting in 1840 on the current "Canadian policy of liberal governments," ascribed to them the "senseless folly of clinging by colonies wholly useless and merely expensive, which all admit must sooner or later assert their independence and be severed from the mother-country." Henry Lord Brougham, *Statesmen Who Flourished in the Time of George III*, London, 1840, I, 65.

Montreal's economic hinterland extend naturally to the west and southwest; her influence in the interior was only gradually shrinking under the exigency that the lands which drained toward her lay within the spreading political boundaries of the United States and were being occupied by American settlers.[4] Later, with the Erie Canal in 1825 and then with the building of railways, access to Ontario from the sea became readier by way of New York, and the communities separated by the Niagara River were in fact separated by little. The Maritimes – Nova Scotia, Prince Edward Island, and New Brunswick – were remote, in a practical sense, from the Canadas proper, but close to New England and the northern American ports. Though the dominant movement of population was westward and within the territory of the United States, nevertheless migration and occasional travel of all classes – farmers, merchants, and professional people, rich and poor – to and fro between the States and the Provinces was always important. But the States exercised more influence both positive and negative than was exercised upon them.

II. IMPEDIMENTS TO BANKING

Within the scope of these general conditions I have described there had continued from the seventeenth and eighteenth centuries certain more specific deterrents to enterprise and banking in the Provinces than had had to be faced in the States. One was that government in nearly every province tended to be strongly oligarchic. Political power was not so fluid as in the United States, where a swelling and turbulent population produced greater political instability. The strength and conservatism of the oligarchies were intensified first by the rebellion of the States from British rule and then by the French Revolution, the reaction to these two events being strong in both the French and

4 "The physical condition of the interior of the country made it necessary that certain portions of the United States should find an outlet through Canada and some parts of Canada an outlet through the United States. Thus Montreal became the natural port of entry and outlet for Vermont and northeastern New York; and before the opening of the Erie Canal much of the trade of the western portion of New York state and of all trading posts in the territory bordering on the lakes and as far west as the Mississippi River found its natural outlet through the Detroit, Niagara, and Kingston route, finally centering at Montreal." Shortt, "Early History of Canadian Banking," *Journal of the Canadian Bankers Association*, IV (1896), 8.

British parts of the population, though for somewhat different reasons. The provincial governments became more royal than the king, and Westminster repeatedly had to restrain its despotic subordinates.

In Lower Canada (Quebec) power belonged to the Chateau Clique, representing the great feudal seigniories which continued from the mighty days of seventeenth-century France. This aristocratic set was supported by the humble habitants, and the two together constituted an agrarian interest which was by nature centripetal, Catholic, and averse to speculation and enterprise. Agrarianism in French Canada, like its counterpart in the States, had no great hankering for debt and easy money schemes. It was governed by as potent a tradition, and besides that the land resources then accessible were not so rich as were those of the States, being pocketed sparsely in river valleys between the Laurentian Shield and the sea. The men who settled them had a passion to hold fast to what they had rather than grasp with borrowed money for more and newer holdings. When a demand for bank credit did arise, in the first decade of the nineteenth century, the agrarian interest opposed it in a less dramatic way than in the States but with a steady, consistent effectiveness that curbed the number of banks and restricted credit expansion by those that were allowed. As in the western States, when the agrarians permitted banks they maintained a wholesome and conservative discipline over them.

In Upper Canada (Ontario), power belonged to a group known as the Family Compact, in derisive analogy to dynastic arrangements in Europe. The group was not at all an affair of family relationships, but was extremely compact in devotion to its own privileges. Like the Chateau Clique, it was a landed and ecclesiastical interest, but Anglican, not Roman. Its outstanding personality was John Strachan, a clergyman of remarkable character and abilities, like the "combination of Churchman and statesman common in the Middle Ages." He was the most energetic member of the Governor's Council, champion of the clergy reserves, founder of the University of Toronto, and eventually Bishop of Toronto.[5] The Compact, with somewhat

[5] The clergy reserves were large areas of virgin land set aside in 1791 for support of the "Protestant clergy." The uncertainty as to whom a Protestant clergy included, doubt if it deserved such benefits, and the interference of the reserves with settlement and cultivation made them long a major political issue.

the same dislike of free enterprise as the Chateau Clique's in Quebec, wanted to keep banking in its own hands and out of the hands of others.[6]

In the Maritimes, power belonged to less conspicuous oligarchies, whose interests were markedly commercial but who inclined to foster banking only so long as it was done by themselves. The most important of these was the Council of Twelve in Halifax, whose power in business and in local government enabled it to withstand not only the common run of Nova Scotians but even the crown.

Another factor, closely related to the foregoing, was the structure of the provincial governments. The legislatures had limited powers, and the governors could obstruct law-making either by veto or by the time-killing reference of measures to Whitehall for signification of the royal pleasure. Nearly all the first bank charters were pawns in some such game. The typical governors sent out by the crown were military officers with no war to occupy them, or others for whom places had to be found. They usually fell under the congenial influence of the established oligarchic group, took its advice, and became its instrument; or else they were frustrated by it. The governors being typically military and the oligarchies typically landed, except in Nova Scotia, the merchant class had no such weight as in the States and in the colonies that preceded them. Henry Boulton, a lawyer, considered it a merit in the Family Compact's bank, then the only one chartered in Upper Canada, that merchants had little to say in its management. Though Whitehall was friendly to the merchant interest, because it wished to encourage trade, it was too far away for more than occasional appeals to reach it effectively, and its benevolence was complicated by paternalistic notions. The following comment by Professor Adam Shortt shows the nature of Whitehall's interest and its tendency to repeat in its early nineteenth-century dealings with the provinces the same mistakes it had made with the rebellious colonies to the south in the century before, particularly with respect to monetary matters. "Sometimes the tendency of the British authorities to direct or to restrict Canadian legislation on these subjects was very active and persistent, while at other times there was a disposition to allow the colonies to work out their own salvation, or destruction, as the case might be. These variations, however,

[6] Egerton, *History of Canada*, p. 128.

in the paternal mood depended upon the attitude of the British public toward their own monetary affairs, rather than on the danger or safety of the particular colonial measure or practice. Neither the banks nor the colonial governments took very kindly to these evidences of paternal solicitude for their welfare."[7]

Still another factor in provincial banking history was the monetary experience antecedent to banks. This may be said to have begun in 1685 when the French Intendant, having no funds with which to maintain his troops during the winter, when ice in the St. Lawrence prevented the arrival of vessels from France, cut playing cards into four pieces each, gave the pieces various denominations, and on his own responsibility issued them as money. In the spring when ships came with specie, he redeemed the cards. This expedient was reasonably successful, the purpose being merely to finance the government and reflecting no such impulse to augment the money supply for economic reasons as developed in British colonies to the south. Later, a more sophisticated currency was introduced, but it deteriorated with governmental difficulties, and when French rule came to an end, in 1763, it was much depreciated. During the American Revolution, the Canadians got the worst impression from the continental bills of the insurgent colonies. These experiences confirmed a distrust of paper money, especially among the French, who had a peasant aversion to it congenitally, and supported an opposition to banks and bank notes like that in the United States. Meanwhile, however, the Provinces, like the States, were dependent upon the use of foreign coins too numerous in their variety and scanty in their volume. The English pound, shilling, and pence constituted the money of account, though they were a negligible part of the actual circulation. Moreover, conversion rates between the pound and the confusing variety of foreign coins varied in different provinces. In the St. Lawrence valley, New York monetary values were used; in the Maritimes, Massachusetts values, known, however, as "Halifax currency" and not a currency but a money of account or system of conversion values between foreign money and pounds. Counterfeits of provincial money were produced in the

[7] Shortt, *JCBA*, VIII, 4; Ross, Victor, *History of the Canadian Bank of Commerce*, II, (Toronto, 1920-34), 390-91.

United States and of United States money in the provinces.[8]

The weightiest factor in the early development of banking in the provinces was the direct example of banking in the States. Its influence worked in opposite ways, encouraging some people to want banks and others not to. But even the advocates, who tended of course to be the persons who wished to go into banking themselves, shrank from the excesses visible to them from below the border; and while they saw good in the banking function, they discriminated between the good and the equally evident evil. Those merchants who sought to be bankers were the most positive factor of all. They were in the trading centres – Montreal, Quebec, Kingston, York (now Toronto), Halifax, and Saint John – where interest in credit institutions in the early 1800's was like that in Philadelphia, New York, Boston, Baltimore, and Charleston in the late 1700's. But outside the Maritimes, they had not the influential position merchants had had in the States, where commerce had been less monopolistic and yet more powerful in government.

Except for the example of banking in the States, the influences I have recounted were either anterior to the start of banking in the Provinces or contemporary with its early years only, and the governmental reforms instituted in 1841 ended the capricious political impediments to which provincial banking had been subject till then. Thenceforth the influences differentiating the development in the Provinces were more recondite. They are summed up in two general conditions, viz., the less profuse and accessible native resources, which imposed a more modest rate of exploitation, and the greater conservatism of the Canadian character – a conservatism which the environment required and which the people themselves were disposed to cultivate. Otherwise they would have become Americans.

For such reasons, it was harder to get banking started in the Provinces than in the States, and the start came some thirty-five years later: the Bank of North America, Philadelphia, was opened in 1782, the Bank of Montreal in 1817. In time the peculiar obstacles in the way of the first provincial banks disappeared; yet the Canadians did not attempt such numerous

[8] Lester, Richard A., *Monetary Experiments – Early American and Recent Scandinavian* (Princeton, 1939), chap. 2; Ross I, 4, 28-29, 31-32, 37; 25th Congress, 2nd Session, House Document 79, pp. 108, 245; Felt, J. B., *Historical Account of Massachusetts Currency* (Boston, 1839), p. 160.

experiments as the Americans, or manifest such impatience, or fall into such excesses. They took the best of American experience for a pattern, and they stuck to it.

III. THE FIRST EFFORTS AT BANKING, 1792-1808

Although banking in the Provinces made its permanent start with establishment of the Bank of Montreal in 1817, an abortive start had been made long before. In 1792, a year in which eight banks, including the Bank of the United States, were set up in the States, merchants in Montreal and London had formed the Canada Banking Company. An announcement of it, dated in London, 17 March 1792, was published in the Quebec *Gazette*, 9 August 1792, and from time to time thereafter for several months. It was signed by three firms, the first, Phyn, Ellice, and Inglis, domiciled in London, and the other two – Todd, McGill, and Company and Forsyth, Richardson, and Company – in Montreal. Having experienced great inconvenience in Canada from the deficiency and variety of the money then current, they said in language such as American merchants had often used, "and knowing the frequent loss and general difficulty attending receipts and payments," they had resolved to establish a bank in Montreal, to be called the Canada Banking Company. The business of the bank would be that "usually done by similar establishments"; it would be "to receive deposits of cash, to issue notes in exchange for such deposits, to discount bills and notes of hand, and to facilitate business by keeping cash accounts with those who choose to employ the medium of the bank in their receipts and payments."[9]

Save for this brave beginning, there is a strange silence in the records about the Canada Banking Company of 1792. It is said, apparently on no positive evidence, either to have been no more than an "attempt," as implied by Professor Adam Shortt in 1896, or to have been "a private bank only, chiefly of deposit, not of issue," as stated in an account in 1876 by James Stevenson, of the Literary and Historical Society of Quebec.[10] No effort seems to have been made to get a corporate charter. The

---

[9] Shortt, *JCBA*, IV, 238-40.
[10] However a note for five shillings (or "pour 5 chelins"), No. 6803, captioned "Canada Bank," dated 10 August 1792, "for the Canada Banking Company," and signed by John Lilly, Junior, is in the possession of the Canadian Bank of Commerce. Ross I, 7-8.

sponsors, according to their announcement, purposed extending operations to every part of the two Canadas and presumed that the bank would be "particularly beneficial" to Upper Canada; but they had their office in Montreal only. It seems reasonable to think, as Professor Shortt explained, that the ephemeral institution of 1792 was premature. Lower Canada, thanks to its French population, had a fairly adequate accumulation of specie and an agrarian dislike of paper money that as yet was unrelaxed; Upper Canada was still a wilderness with few settlements. The Canadians in these circumstances were not yet ready to sustain an institution specialized in banking but fell back upon the granting of credit by merchants and upon the use, for remittances, of the drafts drawn by them upon the merchants to whom they sent exports for sale.[11]

Locally, according to an account by Professor Shortt in 1897 that pictures a state of trade probably true of many North American frontier towns in the early nineteenth century, "all kinds of goods were supplied by one merchant," and "all kinds of surplus products were purchased and exported by the same merchant." In what is now Ontario, "a typical trading centre consisted of a flour mill, still, sawmill, general store, tavern, and blacksmith shop. In more important places a woollen mill or at least a carding machine was added." Since the settlers needed supplies all the year round but had products to sell mostly in the autumn, "it was customary for the merchants, on the one hand, to give credit for supplies to be paid for in products later on, or on the other hand, in the case of those who brought products in advance, to issue due-bills or *bons*, to be ultimately redeemed in goods or partly in goods and partly in cash." These due-bills "together with ordinary promissory-notes, which enjoyed a considerable local circulation, . . . supplemented the metallic money in the settlements and . . . furnished a fairly effective medium of exchange."[12]

"The merchants, for their part, in obtaining their goods and disposing of their accumulated products usually dealt with a few large importers at such places as Queenstown and Kingston. The merchants in these places also acted as bankers and bill brokers for the local merchants, receiving deposits, obtaining

[11] Literary and Historical Society of Quebec, *Transactions, 1876-77*, pp. 121-22; Ross I, 7-8.
[12] Shortt, *JCBA*, IV, 241-42.

from their customers orders drawn upon various persons, and permitting their customers to draw orders upon them. These wholesale merchants sold as much as possible of the produce sent to them to the Government agents for the supply of the military and Indian posts, exporting the remainder to Montreal and importing from Montreal the supplies with which they furnished the local merchants. As the imports were greater than the exports, the balance was met by bills of exchange on London from the commissariat officers, vouchers for pensions, and other miscellaneous bills coming from all parts of the province.

"The large importers in Montreal acted also as bankers for the wholesale men in the upper province, receiving deposits, making payments to order, and not infrequently advancing loans or credits to be met later on by produce, exchanges, or cash, though we find very little of the latter passing."

This inclusion of the monetary function with that of exchanging goods was proper in a fairly undeveloped economy but inadequate in one more mature. And in March 1807 another attempt at formal banking was made both in Montreal, the commercial capital, and in Quebec, the political one. A petition for establishment of a bank in the two cities was laid before the legislature, but too late to be given attention. A year later, February 1808, a second petition was submitted, the petitioners praying that they might be incorporated as the Bank of Canada in Quebec and Montreal. After consideration of the matter by a committee, a bill of incorporation was introduced and ordered to be printed, but failed to pass. It was contended, as in the States, that the bank "would encourage a spirit of gambling and speculation founded on false capital"; it was also contended, with more originality, that most people were illiterate and could too readily be imposed on by a bank. Whatever was decisive in the matter, no further action seems to have been taken. In 1812, war with the United States began, and it was several years before banking again came before the provincial parliament.[18]

But this rejected bill of 1808 to incorporate the Bank of Canada is of permanent interest because it followed, in the main word for word, the charters of the Bank of the United States and the Bank of New York, prepared by Alexander Hamilton, 1791; and because it was the matrix of all subsequent banking

[18] Shortt, *JCBA*, IV, 248-50; Literary and Historical Society of Quebec, *Transactions, 1876-77*, p. 132.

laws in Canada, being enacted, with appropriate changes, as the charter of one Canadian bank after another. The "Canadian banking system," said Professor Adam Shortt, "is a much more direct and legitimate descendant from the plan drawn up by Hamilton than is the present banking system of the United States."[14]

Though the merchants in Montreal seem to have been discouraged for the time being by the collapse of their efforts in 1808, the merchants up the St. Lawrence at Kingston, in Upper Canada, initiated a like attempt two years later. They were influenced perhaps by their immediate proximity to the state of New York, where there were banks in operation across the river from them, and by the circulation of American bank notes in the province. Before their activities reached the legislative stage, however, the Bank of the United States was let die; this probably dampened their interest, and mounting animosity between the Empire and the United States made progress with their plans impracticable. In Nova Scotia also, efforts to establish banking had aborted. In Halifax in 1801 a bank had been proposed, but the Nova Scotia legislators would not grant a monopoly and the projectors would not go forward without one. Ten years later the effort was repeated, with the same result.[15]

IV. THE WAR OF 1812

The War of 1812 caused a reversal of the economic situation in the Provinces and in the States. The Provinces had shared with Britain the burdens incident to withstanding the long and taxing aggressions of Bonaparte; and yet at the same time, their trade with Britain being impeded by the conflicts in Europe, they had been driven into a one-sided dependence upon the United States, with a balance of payments usually adverse. The Americans, on the other hand, though harassed by both the British and the French, had thriven as neutrals on the wartime needs of both.

But the American embargo of 1807 and the War of 1812, by suffocating the foreign trade of the United States, roughly disturbed American prosperity, threw the economy into confusion, and nearly tore the Union apart. Toward the end of the war, the

[14] Shortt, *JCBA*, IV, 19; Ross II, 389.
[15] Shortt, *JCBA*, IV, 250; Ross I, 37-39.

British invasion precipitated the suspension of specie payments, and the country found itself with an inconvertible and depreciated currency. Meanwhile the Provinces had their turn to thrive. They became bases for the British military, whose needs maintained an immediate market for Canadian products and a uniform and dependable currency in the form of "army bills." The bills were signed by the Commander of the Forces and were payable at the Army Bill Office in Quebec in cash or in drafts on London. They were accepted with surprising readiness, considering the agrarian preference for real money; but there was a need for them, and they were known to be regularly redeemed. The bills themselves were a useful currency, but more important was the prevailing prosperity which the war brought the Canadians. It was the American war hawks – John C. Calhoun, Henry Clay, Felix Grundy, and others, western and southern – who had courted war, with their eyes largely on provincial territory; but the war brought the States reverses with no over-balancing gain, and to the Canadians it was a "veritable godsend."[16] Its stimulus to trade and production was very great. In the States, it diverted energies toward internal trade and production, to the eventual advancement of the country's wealth, but these gains lagged behind current troubles. They were obscured and minimized by the loss of foreign trade, which had long been the country's most prominent and princely business interest. The Canadian gains, on the other hand, were immediate and unqualified – except along the New York border where the housewives suffered some loss of teaspoons and other domestic possessions to the ungentlemanly invader. And besides their economic gains, the Canadians could be thankful for salvation "a second time from the fangs of the neighbouring Republic."[17]

In these circumstances, when the war ended in the winter of 1814-1815, prospects were more favourable for the establishment of banks in the Provinces than they had ever been; for the close of the war meant an end to the army bills, the need of a substitute for them, and an opportunity for banks to provide it. Experience with the bills had diminished agrarian prejudice

[16] Of the Americans it is fair to say that their aim was not land and conquest merely – such projects seldom are. It was "liberation" of the poor Canadians from the yoke of George III.

[17] Literary and Historical Society of Quebec, *Transactions, 1876-77*, p. 122; Shortt, *JCBA*, IV, 344.

against paper money and fostered the belief of others in its benefits. Many persons, indeed, had got an exaggerated and illusory notion of those benefits and attributed Canadian prosperity to the generous supply of army bills rather than to war demands, which had produced both. Yet there were also misgivings based on American experience. The notorious failure of the Farmers Exchange Bank in Rhode Island had occurred in 1809, and the legislative scandals over the Bank of America charter in New York in 1812. The general suspension in the States continued from the late summer of 1814 to the late winter, 1816. The Quebec *Gazette*, 9 November 1815, gave its readers a monitory account of current experiences in the States. "How long the derangement of the American currency will continue is uncertain," it said. "The banking system has long been excessive in that country. It has indeed become a system of swindling and political intrigue. Nothing is more common than to see the directors and stockholders of bankrupt banks rolling in luxury, while thousands have been ruined by their mismanagement or villainy. Still the system has gone on." Such a mixture of plain and embroidered truth could make it appear that the British Provinces were happier without banks, and the longer they could be without them the better.

V. THE FIRST BANKS IN LOWER CANADA

Nevertheless a banking project seems to have been on foot in Lower Canada even before the war ended, for in February 1815 a bill to incorporate a bank was considered by the legislature. It was dropped, but at the next session, February 1816, a bill was again introduced and was being favourably considered when the legislature was abruptly prorogued by the governor, Sir Gordon Drummond, over another question. When the legislature sat again, the same thing happened again: a bill to incorporate a Bank of Lower Canada was introduced a third time and was being discussed, February 1817, when the legislature was suddenly prorogued once more, this time by the new governor, Sir John Sherbrooke. The merchants of Montreal, hopeless about the legislative impasse, decided to proceed anyway. They signed articles of association, 19 May 1817, and in November opened their bank without a corporate charter. This was the Bank of Montreal. The procedure accorded with familiar American precedent, the earliest being that of the Bank of New York, which had opened in 1784 with articles of association prepared by Alexander Hamilton. The Montreal articles of association were derived from him also; they were substantially the same as the rejected bill of 1808 and followed the 1791 charters of the Bank of the United States and the Bank of New York. The bank's notes were issued in dollars. One of its officers was sent from Montreal to get experience in the new Bank of the United States. Another had had banking experience already in the States. The year following, 1818, organization of two other banks was undertaken, the Quebec Bank, in the city of Quebec, and the Bank of Canada, in Montreal. Their articles of association were the same as the Bank of Montreal's. The Bank of Canada was formed with American capital.[18]

Agrarian opposition to these banks, which was mainly French, of course, this being Lower Canada, was passive rather than aggressive – unlike what it was in the United States – and worked to the bank's advantage. For the "country people," according to Professor Shortt, when bank notes came into their hands, obeyed their preference for metallic money and steadily converted the notes "into specie on the first opportunity and thus tended to prevent the banks from overissuing until they had gained experience and corrected their first large ideas about the capacities of paper money. This was an advantage which the first banks in Upper Canada did not enjoy and for lack of which they suffered." The habitants, that is, performed the regulatory function the way the Bank of the United States did. Another advantage of being in the midst of these hard-money folk was that their holdings of specie were substantial and, some of the wealthier being coaxed to become stockholders, their hoards were a principal source of the banks' cash reserves. Thus the French Canadians furnished the Lower Canada banks both discipline and substance.[19]

All three of the banks formed in Lower Canada during 1817 and 1818 asked to be incorporated. An act to that effect for the Bank of Montreal was passed early in 1818 but was reserved for the king's assent and never heard of again. Like measures for the Bank of Quebec failed to pass. While these matters were still pending, the Quebec *Gazette* offered the following wary

[18] Shortt, *JCBA*, IV, 347-51, 354-55; Ross II, 389-90, 393.
[19] Shortt, *JCBA*, IV, 351.

observations, 30 March 1820, taking into account British and American experience: "In England during the late war, the banking system was much overdone and such an immense quantity of notes thrown into circulation by discounting all kinds of accommodation bills, thereby assisting and encouraging wild speculation, immediately ruinous to those embarked and ultimately so much so to the banks that in the years 1815 and 1816 above 240 country banks stopped payment. . . . For the last twelve months there has been very great and very general distress in many parts of the United States arising from the maladministration of their banks. The charters of these banks are in their general provisions good but the direction fraudulently bad. Before any of our banks obtain charters, it is certainly proper to have the subject well canvassed and viewed by the public in every bearing, so as the legislature may have information both as it may operate for and against the country and the banks."[20]

Finally, in 1821, charters were enacted by the legislature at Quebec for each of the three banks in Lower Canada and were given the royal assent the year following. Incorporation of the Bank of Montreal was proclaimed 22 July 1822 and of the Quebec Bank and the Bank of Canada, 30 November 1822. Like the first banks in the States, these Lower Canadian banks were definitely commercial. The Bank of Montreal established offices in Quebec, Kingston, York, and New York – where it dealt largely in foreign exchange. The Bank of Canada, a "direct rival to the Bank of Montreal," had been established by some "speculative Americans, attracted to the country by the prosperity of the war period. . . ." It "was not very firmly rooted in the stable financial interests of the province, depending apparently on the exchange business with the United States." It closed in the "severe depression of the early twenties," and the Bank of Montreal took over its business, with loss to the stockholders but none to the customers.[21]

The Bank of Montreal's charter was to expire in 1831 and its renewal was desired. But awkwardly for the bank, the unfriendliness of merchants and others displeased with her either on principle or because she was an ungenerous lender raised up charges that she was a source of "inconvenience and

[20] Shortt, *JCBA*, IV, 356.
[21] Ross I, 14; Shortt, *JCBA*, IV, 354-56, 360

loss" to the public, maintained an office in Quebec without sanction, monopolized exchange dealings, etc. An investigation of her operations by the Assembly was demanded. The bank wavered before a temptation to resist this outrage to her dignity, and then in a happy access of commonsense turned and welcomed investigation with the expressed hope that she would be exonerated of the charges and her corporate life continued. Her hope was realized, though the charter was extended to 1837 only. About the same time the Bank of Quebec's charter was extended to 1836. The province was in the world-wide state of prosperity that ended in 1837 and new bank charters were sought, but only one – that of the City Bank, Montreal, 1833 – was granted. The jealousy of the banks already corporate and the opposed attitude of the popular Assembly and the executive, with Whitehall an unpredictable third factor, made the path to new corporate charters one of anything but primroses. There were unincorporated or private banking houses, however, and there were offices in Montreal and Quebec of the Bank of British North America, a joint stock bank organized in Great Britain in 1838 and admitted by the individual provinces to operate within their jurisdictions. It brought them fresh capital and a staff trained in banking.[22]

In 1837 the panic embarrassed the banks of the Provinces, but none failed to survive and the suspension of specie payments was shorter and less general than in the States. The panic coincided with the violent outbursts of political disorder which occasioned Lord Durham's mission; and in the midst of this the charters of the banks expired. The Bank of Montreal, for an interval, reverted legally to the status of an unincorporated association, and the other two got their charters extended temporarily by emergency action at Whitehall and Quebec. This was the posture of affairs till the union of the two Canadas in 1841.[23]

VI. THE FIRST BANKS IN UPPER CANADA

Meanwhile in Upper Canada a tangled situation had arisen. The principal commercial town in the province was Kingston,

[22] Shortt, *JCBA*, VIII, 148, 153, 158-59, 161, 163; Ross I, 22; II, 430-31; Breckenridge, Roeliff M., *History of Banking in Canada* (Washington: National Monetary Commission, 1910), pp. 37-38.
[23] Ross I, 17.

but the political capital was York (subsequently renamed Toronto). Early in 1817 some Kingston merchants asked the Upper Canada legislature for a bank charter, mentioning the great number of banks in the United States and the benefit that the Americans derived "from the ready aid afforded by their banks to carry on their establishments and improvements in their western territory, which although of a much more recent date, is in a more flourishing state than any part of this province." In March 1817, complying with the request, the legislature enacted a charter incorporating the Bank of Upper Canada, to be in Kingston. The Family Compact had decided meanwhile that the bank should be theirs and situated at York instead of Kingston; and through the Reverend John Strachan, of the Governor's Council, they had requested a charter of incorporation for a proposed Upper Canada Banking Company. They had not yet got the dominance they later achieved, and their request had been ignored, the Kingston charter being enacted instead, with the provision that the stockholders have till January 1819 to organize their bank. The lieutenant-governor, however, Sir Peregrine Maitland, reserved the charter for the king's approval and sent it to Whitehall, where it lay so long that it expired. The Kingston merchants, having waited a decent interval, followed precedent and organized their bank without a charter, adopting articles of association in July 1818 like those of the Bank of Montreal a year before. They were doubtless impelled to this action by the establishment, meanwhile, of a branch in Kingston by the Bank of Montreal and of another by the Bank of Canada. Their own bank opened in Kingston in April 1819 as the Bank of Upper Canada. Less than a month later, word came that the charter had been given the Royal assent after all, regardless of the fact that it had expired. Whatever the opinion in Whitehall, the opinion in York was that the assent was of no avail, except as evidence of what the king's pleasure would be if a fresh charter to the same purpose were submitted. Yet not quite to the same purpose, as it happened. For the new charter for the Bank of Upper Canada at Kingston had barely been introduced, 12 June 1819, when on the 16th the Family Compact's representatives again requested a charter for their own projected Upper Canada Banking Company. Again the legislature ignored them and enacted the Kingston charter. The Council, where the Compact was stronger, then requested a conference, whom which the Kingston charter emerged with amendments that changed the domicile of the bank from Kingston to the "seat of government," which would be York, and substituted the subscribers at York for those in Kingston. In other words, the charter was taken from the hands of the Kingston merchants and put into those of the Family Compact. This manoeuvre was, of course, to the glory of God and the sanctity of the clergy reserves. The Compact, being fair-minded as well as pious, at the same time transferred to their more worldly rivals down the lake the charter intended originally for themselves at York, altering it appropriately to incorporate the "Bank of Kingston." Both charters were enacted 8 July 1819. An important difference between them was that the original charter – intended for Kingston – was deemed to be already assured of the royal assent and included an authorization for the provincial government, whose funds the Family Compact largely controlled, to take stock in the bank.[24]

But Lieutenant-Governor Maitland disobligingly decided that the bill which the Family Compact had captured for its proposed bank in York was no longer the same as the one which the king had approved for the merchants in Kingston, notwithstanding its subject was still nominally the Bank of Upper Canada; and that the other bill, which incorporated the Bank of Kingston, was really the one for which the royal assent was intended. Accordingly he himself gave assent to the Kingston charter, 12 July 1819, and reserved the one for York. But besides giving their bank a new name, the Kingston charter imposed conditions which the merchants had not the financial resources to meet. So, leaving their new and approved charter in desuetude, they continued the business of their still unincorporated bank under its original name.

Meanwhile, as months passed, while the royal assent to the Compact's Bank of Upper Canada at York was awaited in vain and the unincorporated Bank of Upper Canada at Kingston was unable to meet the conditions of the charter proffered it as the Bank of Kingston, the provinces remained without an incorporated bank. Upper Canada was "over-run with American paper" according to Lieutenant-Governor Maitland in 1819,

[24] Shortt, *JCBA*, 2-3, 8-12.

but it was a nuisance and nowise took the place of a proper
domestic currency, such as every one remembered the army bills
to have been. To meet the need of a medium of exchange, as
had happened earlier in the States, it was proposed that provincial loan offices be set up where bills of credit might be lent on
real estate mortgage security; but this project was adjudged
illegal in 1821 by a legislative committee on the ground that
Parliament's act of 1764 – 4 George III, c. 34 – forbade it. (In
fact, it only forbade making them legal tender.) Yet this
measure, aimed particularly at practices in the colonies which
had since then become independent, had been repealed in substance in 1773 – 13 George III, c. 57...; and apparently under
the sanction of that repeal, or amendment, Nova Scotia had
been issuing similar bills ingenuously and to its advantage since
1812 and was to continue doing so till Confederation in 1867,
calling them Treasury notes.[25] The proposed Upper Canada loan
office issues were also condemned by the 1821 committee for
not being based on specie; and this was probably the real
objection, for a "provincial bank" was proposed in place of the
loan offices, and the legislature promptly adopted the proposal
by authorizing such an institution to be called the Bank of Upper
Canada – a title used a confusing number of times in uncon-
summated measures and already borne by the unincorporated
bank in Kingston. In the minds of its contemporaries this new
charter was based in some way, no longer clear, on the charter
of the Bank of Kingston, already approved by Lieutenant-
Governor Maitland. It received the royal assent, apparently at
the hands of the Lieutenant-Governor himself, 14 April 1821.
But a day or so later there arrived from Whitehall the royal
assent to the earlier charter of the Bank of Upper Canada which
the Family Compact had captured from the Kingston merchants
for its own use in York. It took precedence over the proposed
"provincial bank," because there could not be two Banks of
Upper Canada at York even if two banks by any name. So the
provincial bank was dropped. The Compact promptly organized
the bank that had been approved at Whitehall and opened it for
business July 1822. Its legal name was the Bank of Upper

[25] In 1839 the "Imperial authorities" are said also to have refused to let
Upper Canada issue bills – on what ground I do not know, but I
imagine it was on particular grounds of policy rather than general
grounds of legality. *JCBA*, II, 315-18.

Canada, but it was generally known as the "York Bank," a designation which distinguished it from the unincorporated Bank of Upper Canada at Kingston. The latter now began to be called the Pretended Bank of Upper Canada. It had bad management as well as bad luck and, about the time the bank in York opened, it closed for good. This was Canada's first bank failure. But for years statutes concerned with its prolonged liquidation continued to stigmatize it "The Pretended Bank of Upper Canada," while agents of the government engaged in settling its affairs, Dr. Adam Shortt said, "covered acres of paper with all manner of bewildering calculations, lists of names, claims, and counter claims; carefully rolling up interest against the bankrupt, the vanished, and the dead; fulminating with lawyers' letters; and otherwise living beyond their income."[26]

Meanwhile the "legitimate" Bank of Upper Canada at York had a monopoly in the province, qualified only by the presence of the Bank of Montreal's offices in York and Kingston. It tried to force the latter bank out of Upper Canada by accumulating its notes in large amounts and suddenly presenting them with a demand for immediate payment. The Bank of Montreal retaliated, and neither being able to break the other by these legal and honourable raids, so frequent in the States, they mutually forbore in time. Otherwise the Family Compact was more successful, for, having control of the legislative council, it was able to achieve nearly everything it wanted and to prevent nearly everything it did not. Of the fifteen directors of its bank, nine had important stations in the government, including the Honourable and Reverend Dr. John Strachan. The bank was strong, carefully managed, and prospered in the Lord. Its business was principally the discount of ninety-day promissory notes and the purchase and sale of exchange.[27]

The greater its success, however, the fiercer the opposition to it became. In 1829 it had to frustrate an effort of its enemies to have the Bank of England invited to establish an office in Canada. In 1830 William Lyon Mackenzie, whose comments upon the Jacksonian Democrats during his later sojourn in the States I have mentioned, prepared a bill for the regulation of banking, which would mean regulation of the Compact's bank.

[26] Shortt, *JCBA*, V, 9, 12, 18-20; VIII, 3; Breckenridge, *Canadian Banking System, 1817-90* (New York, 1895), pp. 215-18; Ross II, 397.
[27] Shortt, *JCBA*, VIII, 5, 229.

Mr. Mackenzie was an intelligent man of passionate and reckless sincerity and a skilful writer much given to gross and disgraceful vituperation. He was a member of the Assembly and chairman of the currency committee. The Compact, failing to get his bill thrown out, tried to get him thrown out himself. It failed in its first attempt, but the year following it secured his expulsion by a charge of libel. His constituents elected him again, he was again expelled and again elected. His charges against the bank were not that it exercised a monopolistic restraint upon credit but that it was inflationary and irresponsible, conducting business on the "visionary basis of two shillings in the pound." Had Whitehall approved what the Compact sought, he said, "we should have had nearly four millions of paper money afloat next year in Upper Canada and the farmers, labourers, and mechanics exchanging their wheat, labour, and industry for paper rags. . . ." Mr. Mackenzie spoke for "agriculture, the most innocent, happy, and important of all human pursuits"; and he voiced the traditionary agrarian view, held since the South Sea Bubble, which associated monopoly with speculation and depreciation – not with restraints upon enterprise.[28]

"The American banking system," said the report of a committee in 1830 of which he was chairman, "may be defined to be a paper currency unsupported by an adequate metallic basis – a continuation of the delusive systems adopted in the Thirteen Colonies and France during their revolutionary wars." The Report said it was "a mistaken notion that to increase the number of banks upon the American system and to encourage the unlimited circulation of their notes will enrich the tradesman and the farmer. . . . The prosperity of the farmer does not depend upon the amount of money or bank bills in his possession but upon the quantity of the necessaries and comforts of life which the profits of his farm and labour will procure for himself and family. It is favourable to an industrious people that wages and produce should be at a moderate money price and that money should command abundance of the necessaries and comforts of life." This dear-money orthodoxy, so far from exemplifying an agrarian radicalism, exemplified traditionary

[28] Lindsey, Charles, *William Lyon Mackenzie* (Toronto, 1862), I, 181-82; Shortt, *JCBA*, VIII, 14, 229-41, 306; Mackenzie, William L., *Sketches of Canada and the United States* (London, 1833), pp. 456-58.

agrarian conservatism.[29] It was exactly what the Loco Focos were crying aloud in New York.[30]

The same conservatism had an unexpected display a little later in Mr. Mackenzie's stand against a proposed competitor of the Compact's bank in York, current prosperity having spurred the ambition of rival interests in Kingston to be incorporated as the Commercial Bank of the Midland District. To this the Compact made a stubborn resistance. Mr. Mackenzie, instead of aiding the newcomers against the Compact, fought them with even more energy and determination than did the Compact itself. Indeed, the latter soon found it expedient to acquiesce in the new institution. But Mr. Mackenzie did not. In 1832, when the charter passed the Assembly and was approved by the Lieutenant-Governor, Mr. Mackenzie went to England, as he had threatened to do, and besieged the ministries so effectively that to the astonishment of the provincial authorities it began to look as though the charter might be disallowed – which however it was not. Mr. Mackenzie's intransigent and paradoxical conduct seemed to most people merely crazy. On the contrary, though fanatic, it was entirely consistent with his beliefs and character. He held the venerable opinion that corporate privileges were evil, particularly the exemption of the owners of a corporation from personal liability for the debts of the corporation. For one group to be so favoured was bad enough; for two groups to be so favoured was worse. Like innumerable men of intelligence he could not believe, corporations being privileged, that a multiplication of corporations would destroy privilege. Mr. Mackenzie's views were again those of the contemporary Loco Focos in New York, who made the bitter choice of continuing the monopoly of existing banks rather than have more banks.[31]

[29] In his interesting volume, *The Government of Canada*, page 499, Professor R. M. Dawson says that the Clear Grits of Canada were influenced "by the successors to the Jeffersonians, the Jacksonian Democrats," and like them "favoured soft money." But the Loco Focos and other Jeffersonian and Jacksonian "Democrats in principle" – including Jefferson and Jackson – did *not* favour soft money. They were hard-money fanatics. But for Professor Dawson I should have supposed that the Clear Grits also were. William Lyon Mackenzie was certainly not an advocate of soft money.

[30] Upper Canada, Journal of House of Assembly, Appendix, *Report on the State of the Currency*, 5 March 1830, pp. 21, 24.

[31] Ross II, 398-400.

Society has benefited from the exemption of stockholders from liability for the debts of the corporations they own, as it has benefited from bankruptcy laws that excuse men, in certain circumstances, from the obligation to pay their debts; but it seems to me remarkable that these victories over a simple and primitive moral logic have been achieved. Both were resisted, but the bankrupt had the spirit of humanity to help him against a rigid morality; whereas the exemption of stockholders from personal liability became established in subterranean fashion with almost no formal advocacy and with very little formal recognition – quite as if it were something men liked but were ashamed of. Consequently, that Mr. Mackenzie should have resisted a convention that made it so easy to escape responsibility seems to me natural; an immense number of persons resisted what they considered the immoral innovations of business enterprise for the same reason. And he would not extend that innovation merely to spite a group of men who wished to monopolize it. His idealism was ingenuous and impractical perhaps, but there was no smell of sanctimony about it.[32]

Yet there were plenty of things about which Mr. Mackenzie was confused. The rebellion led by him owed much to the coveting in Upper Canada of the material prosperity that attended business enterprise among the Americans. Though repelled by certain features of business enterprise, he was attracted by its fruits; and he failed certainly, so long as he remained in Canada, to distinguish his own opposition to the Bank of Upper Canada from the Jacksonian opposition to the Bank of the United States – though the Bank of Upper Canada was privileged in fact, its owners being "a junto of government officers, enjoying a monopoly of the paper currency," and the second being a federal institution regulating a private banking system. But when the failure of his violent efforts to overthrow British and Family Compact authority drove him to take refuge in the United States, the spectacle of Jacksonian democracy as it really was chastened his ambitions and impelled him to alter his opinion that the Provinces should emulate the States.[33]

In 1835 the desirability of setting up a provincial bank in Upper Canada was again considered. A select committee held

[32] DuBois, Armand B., *The English Business Company after the Bubble Act, 1720-1800* (New York, 1938), pp. 93-94.
[33] Mackenzie, *Sketches*, pp. 459-60.

hearings and reported favourably on the project. It found that the far larger banking resources of New York State enabled its agriculturists, tradesmen, and mechanics – "although subject to higher taxes, higher prices for land, with a soil and climate by no means superior, with the additional expense of transportation" – to compete successfully with the inhabitants of the province in their own markets. After considering free banking, which the committee called "unrestricted private banking," then being advocated in New York and soon to be adopted there, the committee recommended instead a provincial bank, as had been done in 1819, finding reason to believe that it would "operate as a most salutary check on all chartered as well as private banks, by regulating or restraining any undue issue of paper money; and it will also by lessening the profits of banking prevent so many from entering into the business." This measure also was opposed by William Lyon Mackenzie, presumably again because the stockholders would not be responsible for the corporate debts.[34]

The same year, 1835, the Family Compact was again subdued when it had to acquiesce in chartering the Gore Bank, of Hamilton. The proposed bank's chief sponsor had been associated with the Compact, and when the latter tried to obstruct his charter he began to divulge information about its inner workings, to the delight of its enemies and the public and to its own embarrassment. Besides the Compact's obstruction of new charters, there was a strengthened tendency in general to eschew the experience of the United States, whose banking practices, once thought worthy of emulation, no longer seemed so. As a consequence of this, of the panic conditions that supervened in 1837, and of the inoperable state to which provincial government was falling – with William Lyon Mackenzie leading armed rebellion in 1838 – no new charters were granted till the union of the two Canadas in 1841; and in the upper province till then the incorporated banks, including the offices of the Bank of British North America, were barely a half dozen. In 1837 all the banks suspended but none failed for good, and in the few years succeeding "no permanent changes materially affecting the development of the Canadian banking system took place."[35]

[34] Upper Canada, Journal of House of Assembly, Appendix, *Committee Report on a Provincial Bank*, 13 February 1835.
[35] Ross I, 23, 175; II, 404-05; Shortt, *JCBA*, VIII, 311-12, 317-18, 325.

VII. THE FIRST BANKS IN THE MARITIMES

In the Maritimes a charter had been granted, 25 March 1820, to the Bank of New Brunswick, Saint John; it was the first fully effective charter in British North America – that is, the first enacted, approved, and used. This expedition may explain why there seems to be nothing more to tell of it. The American origin of this charter was obvious, as Professor Shortt observed years ago, but it followed the New England variant of the Hamiltonian pattern. New Brunswick incorporated her second bank, the Charlotte County Bank, at St. Andrews, across the St. Croix River from Maine, 17 March 1825, with a charter like that of the Bank of New Brunswick. In 1834 and 1836 three other banks were chartered, but one was absorbed in 1839 by the Bank of New Brunswick. No other bank seems to have been chartered for nearly twenty years.[36]

In Nova Scotia, as already said, attempts of merchants in 1801 and 1811 to obtain a bank charter had failed. In 1818 the provincial legislature forbade corporate issues altogether and in 1820 forbade issue by individuals of notes of less than twenty-six shilling denomination. These prohibitions, which preceded those in the States, were evidently intended to protect the province's issue of Treasury notes, which were receivable for dues to the provincial government, bore 6 per cent interest, and were not re-issuable. There were further issues in 1813, 1817, 1820, and thereafter occasionally till Confederation in 1867, at which time the outstanding notes were assumed by the Dominion. The issues seem to have been redeemable in practice though not by legal requirement, and in general they served the province well. They were the last of those colonial issues of paper money which began in Massachusetts in the early seventeenth century, reflected a prevailing need in the New World, and displayed the self-reliance, intelligence, and resourcefulness of the colonists. They were imperfect and at times abused in the pressure of the New World's growth, but their merits far exceeded their imperfections. Their use continued for two and a half centuries, and for much of that time they were the occasion of ill-natured disagreement between the new economies that had need of them and the mature, well-capitalized economy overseas

[36] Breckenridge, "Canadian Banking History," *Journal of Canadian Bankers Association* (1894), II, 320-21.

that could not understand such need. And though they were a device of the business world, they have been not only denigrated but ascribed to farmers.[37]

Before the issue of paper money was undertaken in Nova Scotia, a Halifax merchant of substantial wealth, Enos Collins, had built up considerable business in private lending and foreign exchange. This became more important than his merchandising. In 1825 he and his associates, including Samuel Cunard, subsequently the founder of the Cunard line of steamships, asked the legislature for a charter in some respects similar to what had been refused in 1801 and 1811 and in other respects similar to the charters of the Bank of New Brunswick and the Bank of Montreal and contemporary American charters. They asked for a monopoly, however, and the measure, like its two predecessors, failed to pass the Nova Scotian legislature. But the organizers this time went ahead and that same year, 1825, set up a bank, the Halifax Banking Company, under a partnership. Its president and cashier, before it opened, visited Boston and the principal banks there for the purpose of learning how the business should be conducted. The company continued as a partnership for nearly fifty years, with apparently no inconvenience from the lack of a charter. Its business was largely in exchange, Halifax being an important international shipping centre.[38]

The Halifax Banking Company was the financial heart of the merchant and Anglican oligarchy which corresponded in Nova Scotia to the oligarchy of the landed Catholic French in Lower Canada and of the landed Anglicans in Upper Canada, but was the strongest of the three. Five of the banking company's partners were members of the Council of Twelve, which virtually controlled executive and legislative powers in the province. But as elsewhere, the Halifax group did not represent by any means the entire business community, and the dissidents were active. From the business quarter arose a group which wanted to establish a bank of its own, under corporate charter; and from the political quarter arose Joseph Howe, a statesman whose discontent was much like William Lyon Mackenzie's in Upper Canada but whose temper was more moderate and whose

[37] Ross I, 38-39, 411-22; Breckenridge, *Canadian Banking System, 1817-1890*, pp. 205, 215-18.
[38] Ross I, 46-49, 59; II, 426-30.

conduct was more sensible and effective. Against the established but unchartered Halifax Banking Company lay the charge of monopoly; in its favour was the defence that its liabilities were supported by the entire personal fortune of each of its wealthy owners, whereas the owners of the proposed bank would be without any personal liability. And the frequent, notorious failures of chartered banks in the States were cited in evidence of the practical importance of the distinction. The argument was one that might have appealed to William Lyon Mackenzie in his agrarian surroundings, but it was not so persuasive in a business and financial community. The Council of Twelve obstructed the charter but could not prevent its being granted, in 1832, and the new concern, the Bank of Nova Scotia, was organized. Its charter, like those in New Brunswick, was a Boston variant of the American pattern. For some time the two banks followed the usual temptation to mistreat one another all they could by accumulating one another's notes and making peremptory demands for specie.[39]

The controversy over enactment of the Bank of Nova Scotia's charter had "much to do with stirring up the political struggle for responsible government, which did not end until the partners of the Halifax Banking Company had been deprived of their seats on the Council" – as they were in 1840, when the new Lieutenant-Governor, Lord Falkland, pursuant to the new spirit raised up by Lord Durham, obtained their resignations. This action was an achievement which Joseph Howe and his associates had been seeking for years – an achievement which led to responsible government, their further objective, and eventually, with corresponding movements elsewhere, to Confederation.[40]

Yet the tenacity of the Halifax oligarchy and of like groups in other provinces had the conservative and beneficial effect of restraining the infectious ardour for banking, which, had provincial government been more popular and unstable, might have spread from the States. By the time government became popular and responsible, the people of the Provinces had observed to their profit the extravagant course followed in the States and

[39] Egerton, Hugh E., *A Historical Geography of the British Colonies.* Vol. V. Canada, Part II, Historical (Oxford, 1908), pp. 157-58; Ross I, 65, 84; II, 428-30.
[40] Ross I, 70-71, 85-90.

had become satisfied with a modest and patient development adapted to their relatively illiberal environment. The Americans could afford their wastefulness; the Canadians could not.

In 1837 the two banks in Halifax suspended, but for two or three months only – which is better than any other community in the Provinces or States could do. For years they were the only banks in Nova Scotia, except for the office of the Bank of British North America.

VIII. RESERVE AND OTHER REQUIREMENTS

It will be recalled from an earlier chapter that the restriction on the liabilities of the Bank of the United States, 1791, read as follows:

The total amount of the debts which the said Corporation shall at any time owe, whether by bond, bill, note, or other contract, shall not exceed the sum of ten millions of dollars over and above the monies then actually deposited in the bank for safekeeping.

In the charter of the Bank of New York, 1791, the restriction had read:

The total amount of the debts which the said corporation shall at any time owe, whether by bond, bill, note, or other contract, over and above the monies then actually deposited in the bank, shall not exceed three times the sum of the capital stock subscribed and actually paid into the bank.

In the unsuccessful bill of 1808 to incorporate the Bank of Lower Canada the restriction had read:

The total amount of the debts which the said Corporation shall at any time owe, whether by obligation, bond, bill, or note, or other contract whatsoever, shall not exceed treble the amount of gold and silver actually in the bank arising from the capital stock (but exclusive of a sum equal in amount to that of the gold and silver actually in the bank arising from other sources than the said stock . . .).

The charters enacted for the Banks of Upper Canada and for the Bank of Kingston departed from the Lower Canada version and followed the Bank of New York restriction verbatim.

However, the only one of these charters which came into use, it will be recalled, was that of the Bank of Upper Canada at York, opened in 1822. Meanwhile in Lower Canada the articles of association of the Bank of Montreal, 1817, contained a restriction which was repeated verbatim in the consummated charters of that bank, of the Bank of Quebec, and of the Bank of Canada – all three proclaimed in 1822 – except that in the articles the bank was called "the company" and in the charters, where the restriction read as follows, it was called "the said corporation":

The total amount of the debts which the said corporation shall at any time owe, whether by bond, bill or note, or other contract whatsoever, shall not exceed treble the amount of the capital stock actually paid in (over and above a sum equal in amount to such money as may be deposited in the bank for safekeeping).

In the Maritimes, where bank charters followed the Massachusetts pattern rather than New York's, the liabilities of the Bank of New Brunswick, 1820, were restricted as follows:

The total amount of the debts which the said corporation shall at any time owe, whether by bond, bill or note, or other contract whatsoever, shall not exceed twice the amount of the capital stock actually paid in. . . .

This version, used also in the charter of the Charlotte County Bank, St. Andrews, 1825, differs from the versions followed in the Canadas in that the restriction is to twice the paid capital, not treble, and in omitting to exempt or even mention deposits. It is nearly identical with the restriction in the charter of the Philadelphia Bank, 1804:

The total amount of the debts which the said corporation shall at any time owe, whether by bond, loan, bill or note or other contract, shall not exceed double their capital.

Although a restriction to twice the paid capital was typical of Massachusetts, it was not unusual elsewhere, but the omission to say anything about deposits is extremely unusual, either in Pennsylvania or elsewhere. The authors of the earliest Maritime charters must have got a copy of the Philadelphia Bank charter to have reproduced it so closely. In this restriction, they vary from it only to omit the word "loan," which appears in the Philadelphia charter but in no other so far as I know, and to add at another point the word "whatsoever," which was typical of Canadian charters.

All these early provincial charters imposed the same range of conditions as charters in the States and in much the same words. Whether enacted above or below the border, all belonged to one legal family. Reports of condition were customarily required to be submitted, and official inspection was also authorized, but less commonly. The issue of notes below a minimum denomination was usually forbidden, and the failure to redeem notes was usually penalized in one way or another. The one conspicuous difference between state and provincial charters was that the former commonly authorized stock ownership by government and the latter rarely did. Only the charter of the Bank of Upper Canada – the "York Bank" of the Family Compact – had such an authorization; other charters omitted it. And they were doing so before any of the numerous banks in which states had interests had got into trouble from the connection.

Branches, which became ultimately a cardinal characteristic of Canadian banking, were in this early period no more peculiar to provincial charters than to American ones. They were authorized for the two banks at Kingston and York, but apparently no other provincial charters gave specific authorization; the two New Brunswick charters of 1820 and 1825 rather pointedly did not, permitting the directors to "remove" the respective banks to new locations and thereby implying that the bank was to be confined to some one spot. The Bank of Montreal and at least one other bank in Lower Canada were not authorized to have branches but did have them. The proposed Bank of Lower Canada charter of 1808, like its model the Bank of the United States charter, had contained an authorization for branches, but it had been omitted from the 1817 articles of association, and when the latter were taken as a basis of the charter enacted in 1822, the original authorization for branches was not restored, though the bank had branches then in Quebec, Kingston, and New York. Not till 1841 apparently were banks in Canada proper given generally a specific authority to maintain more than one office.[41]

Until the late '30's, bank legislation in both the Provinces

[41] Ross II, 395-405.

and the States, though proliferating in details, remained unaltered and homogeneous in the main. Two patterns were discernible, the New York and the New England, but otherwise from the substance of any given charter, one could not tell where it belonged. All alike were the work of Alexander Hamilton, gradually modified. But in the tense period marked by the destruction of the Bank of the United States, the panic of 1837, the establishment of free banking in Michigan and New York, the political disturbances in the Provinces, Lord Durham's report, and union of the two Canadas in 1841, divergence between bank legislation in the States and that in the Provinces became distinct. The difference arose in the States, where the Jacksonians sought to establish *laisser faire.* In the Provinces the established pattern was not abandoned; nor from that time has any important banking innovation of the Americans been taken over by the Canadians. The result is that though the handiwork of Alexander Hamilton practically disappeared from American banking, it survives still in the Dominion, where it has undergone the changes incident to a long evolution but has retained a continuity otherwise unbroken. To this fact, however, there is the important qualification that the original pattern in the States was itself derived by Hamilton from the British act of 1694 authorizing incorporation of the Bank of England. Banking in British North America, therefore, came from a British source by way of the United States and its first Treasury head.

IX. CANADIAN AND AMERICAN POLICY

The divergence established between American and Canadian banking by 1841 was a matter of both policy and structure. In policy American banking had become committed to free competition and easy money. Federal regulation had been tried, abandoned in 1811, tried again, and in 1836 again abandoned. *Laisser faire* had won. The structure of American banking changed accordingly. The restriction inherent in chartering banks only by legislative act was given up, and free banking laws encouraged the establishment of new banks in unlimited number. In the Provinces and especially in Upper Canada, which was most susceptible to the spirit of American enterprise, the new trends in the States made some appeal but not very

much. The Canadians were aware of the contention that "fictitious capital" in the form of bank credit had "advanced the
prosperity" of the Americans and "that though much capital
has been lost and many individuals ruined, yet the general state
of the people has improved"; but they preferred to stick to the
pattern that in the States was going out of fashion.[42]

This decision was not merely voluntary. In the States, the
ready accessibility, volume, and diversity of natural resources
supported a reckless monetary expansion. In the Provinces,
geography prevented anything so spectacular and even impeded
more modest progress. Moreover, as if geographic impediments
were not enough, just at the time that American enterprise was
turning itself gloriously loose under the expansive leadership of
the Jacksonians, the Provinces were half-strangled in strife with
their respective oligarchies and the British ministry.

It was to correct this situation, which in both Lower and
Upper Canada had sunk to a stage of animosity and bloodshed
such as had hardened the Thirteen Colonies in rebellion sixty
years before, that the Earl of Durham, in one of the happiest
decisions ever made in British statecraft, was sent out to investi-
gate the condition of the two Canadas, taking account also of
Her Majesty's other North American provinces. He acted so
promptly that Whitehall and Westminster turned on him in
anger and closed his career in five months. But in those five
months he set things in train that not merely saved Canada for
the Empire but assured the protracted prosperity of both and
their ability to meet unconceived difficulties generations thence.
The essentials of his recommendation were responsible self-
government and union of the provinces.

These were not achieved fully for about thirty years, the
difficulty of deferring regional interests and sovereignties to the
general interest being almost as stubborn and menacing as in
the States; but the tensions were relieved and improvement
began at once. Lower and Upper Canada were united as the
Province of Canada in 1841, but further union did not take
place till Confederation in 1867.[43] Responsible government,

---

[42] Upper Canada, Journal of House of Assembly, Appendix, *Report on
the State of the Currency*, 5 March 1830, p. 24.

[43] The provinces of Lower Canada and Upper Canada, united in 1841 as
the province of Canada, were again separated under their present
names, as the provinces of Quebec and Ontario, when the Dominion
of Canada was formed in 1867.

however, long exercised by British subjects in Britain itself and vainly claimed in Virginia by George Wythe and Thomas Jefferson before the Revolution, was soon established in the separate provinces generally and successfully. In the Provinces as in the States the virtues of independence were not alone that it was naturally craved but also that the people of North America had a tradition of self-discipline which enabled them to give more fruitful attention to their own affairs than people could who, however excellent, were far across the sea and interested in something else. Lord Durham reported that though dissension had been worst in the two Canadas, it had been almost as bad in the other provinces. "The most serious discontents have only recently been calmed in Prince Edward's Island and New Brunswick; the Government is still, I believe, in a minority in the Lower House in Nova Scotia; and the dissensions of Newfoundland are hardly less violent than those of the Canadas. It may fairly be said that the natural state of government in all these Colonies is that of collision between the Executive and the representative body."[44] Though occasional collisions between the crown and the Commons had occurred in Britain since the revolution of 1688, they had been "rare and transient"; in British North America they were "frequent and lasting." Since, in the New World, the services of government had to be enlisted in providing society with institutions and facilities which the Old already possessed, Lord Durham was inclined to attribute much credit to the American government for that "amazing progress and that great material prosperity which every day's experience" showed the British North Americans was "the lot of the people of the United States." This sounds plausible. Yet the greater governmental efficiency which British North America acquired in consequence of Lord Durham's efforts bore its fruits not in a material prosperity equal to that of the United States but in a greater tranquillity.

Yet there was prosperity too and a gradual laying up of capital. Economic employments became more diverse, exports increased, and capital came in more plentifully. Establishment of the Bank of British North America, in the light of what happened later, was of considerable significance. It was an early and major movement of British capital into the Provinces. It presaged greater future investments, and in a sense it anticipated

[44] Durham, *Report*, Carleton Library edition, p. 52.

federation, taking economic unity for granted and setting up in fact as well as in name a bank of British North America, inter-provincial or national, as other banks so far were not. It was an impressive step by Great Britain as Imperial participant in the internal development of Canada and dominant external influ-ence upon her institutions. It indicated, like Lord Durham's mission and the reforms that followed it, an awakened spirit in the mother country. It occurred at a time, roughly coincident with the Jacksonian revolution, when American example ceased to inspire Canadians as much as it had.

Yet the path to be followed in Canadian development was by no means foregone. There was great doubt in Britain, even in responsible circles, whether it were practicable to hold the Empire together. There was doubt whether the immense area of British North America could ever prove valuable save in spots or ever be drawn into feasible unity. And when as late as 1867, the Americans bought Alaska and actually paid Russia $7,200,000 for it, there were gentlemen in the British Isles who wanted advantage taken of such extravagance in order to get rid of Canada.[45] To have parted with Canada politically would not have stopped British investment there, any more than independence prevented British investment in the States. But it would have meant a different interest. British capital in the Provinces was accompanied by much more managerial respon-sibility. This fostered the conservatism of Canadian business, which found itself backed by British conservatism – particularly in banking. British capital had gone into American banking in great volume at first, but after the United States Bank of Penn-sylvania foundered and altogether too many other American banks besides, much investment was diverted to Canada, and British distrust of the American banking apparatus was added to Canadian distrust of it.[46]

Just before the difficulties of 1837, the Jacksonian prosperity in the States had been highly useful to those British North Americans most determined on political reform. "A people," exclaimed Joseph Howe of Halifax in March 1837, "who num-bered but three millions and a half at the time of the Revolution

---

[45] Whether they could have succeeded is doubtful, for many Americans thought Alaska no bargain, and in the United States Senate its purchase was very nearly prevented.
[46] Breckenridge, *History*, pp. 23ff, 47ff.

– who owed then seventy-five million dollars – and who, though
they purchased Florida with five millions and Louisiana with
fifteen and owed one hundred and twenty-three million dollars
at the close of the last war, are now not only free of debt but
have an overflowing Treasury." America presented "an aspect
of political prosperity and grandeur, of moral sublimity and
high intellectual and social cultivation," which greatly impressed
him. But two months after Mr. Howe wrote this, the banks in
the States stopped specie payments and six months after it the
Jacksonians' Treasury was empty, the "surplus" had disappeared
before they could finish "distributing" it, and the country was
unable to meet its current debts abroad. Mr. Howe's heart could
not have been broken, for his words had been moved less by
admiration for the Americans than by a polemist's need of
things to cast at his adversaries. His position was presumably
the same as William Lyon Mackenzie's, out in Upper Canada,
who had also been citing the splendid example of how things
were done in the States but after a sojourn there and a close
view of his heroes was ready to take back much of what he had
said and quietly become a Canadian once more.[47]

Yet even though political and economic ties with the mother
country improved, there still were enticements to cultivate
American interests and imitate American ways. These arose
only to prove secondary, however, and for the most part
abortive, as it was with free banking.

Free banking had been advocated in Upper Canada before
the debacle of 1837 and almost as soon as in New York. A
measure "to regulate banking" was introduced in the legislature
of Upper Canada in 1831, a measure "to make general the
privilege of banking" in 1833-1834, and a measure "to establish
an uniform system of banking" in 1835. But as in the States,
Michigan's experience dulled the interest in free banking till
1850, when it came again to life, the experience in New York
having meanwhile been encouraging. In that year a bill "to
establish freedom of banking in this province" was enacted by
the legislature of Canada.[48] In a memorandum referring the act
to the British Governor, Lord Elgin, 7 December 1850, the
Inspector General explained: "In the state of New York a

[47] Howe, Joseph, *Speeches and Public Letters*, (ed.) J. A. Chisholm
(Halifax, 1909), I, 135.
[48] Province of Canada, 10 August 1850, 13 and 14 Victoria, c. 21.

system of free banking was established some years ago which has been eminently successful and is likely to be adopted in several other states. It presents the double advantage of effecting ... security to the bill holder and of creating a home market for the public securities." This Canadian free-banking law preceded all the like measures in the States that, beginning in 1851, also followed New York's example. But at this point all similarity to the progress of free banking in the States ceased. Three banks were established under the Canadian law, but in 1855, having obtained special charters, they abandoned their free-banking status. Only two others chose it. The law was practically dead. Its repeal was first proposed in 1857 and in 1866 was effected. Obviously the Canadians did not like free banking.[49]

That they did not care for the farce of free banking in Michigan, Wisconsin, Indiana, and Illinois need arouse no wonder, for contemporary Americans did not like it either. But that they made no good use of free banking at all may seem strange, since American banks did and most were good banks though not required by the law to be. The explanation apparently is that, in the States, free banking usually tolerated no alternative, whereas in Canada, though free banking was authorized, special legislative charters continued to be granted. So long as there was a choice, a good banker was apt to prefer a special charter, for besides the feeling that one conferred according to ancient practice by special legislative act had greater prestige than a new-fangled one handed out at a window by an administrative officer, the free-banking emphasis on note issue was either useless or burdensome. Special charters, in the States and Provinces, invariably authorized note issue, but with no specific requirements. Under free banking, however, notes could not be issued until a quantity of bonds had been purchased and lodged with the state or provincial government, notes obtained from the latter, and agencies arranged for their redemption. To Americans who could get a bank charter on no other terms these requirements were acceptable; but to Canadians with a choice they were a nuisance. For if incorporated by special charter, a bank need buy no bonds − and banks in Canada seem to have found it either difficult or unprofitable to

[49] Breckenridge, *History*, pp. 34, 58, 61-62; Ross II, 412-16; 13 and 14 Victoria c. 21; 29 and 30 Victoria c. 10; Journals of Legislative Assembly, Province of Canada, 1851 (15 Victoria), Appendix ZZ.

mantain a bond portfolio – it need maintain no redemption agencies, and it need have little to do with the provincial regulatory authorities. Intelligent bankers knew that note issue was of minor importance and were less and less interested in charters loaded with obsolescent terms. The Bank of Commerce, New York, the largest and most important bank in the States after 1838, was organized under the free-banking act but never issued any notes and according to Mr. Gallatin would have preferred a special charter had it been possible to obtain one. Most bankers in the States and Provinces still felt it worth while to have at least a small circulation; but in the province of Canada they chose to have it without free banking and there is a strong presumption that in the States the preference of the best bankers would have been the same.[50]

There is still the question why the Canadian legislature did not discontinue the issuance of special charters when it authorized free banking, as was done in the States. I suppose it was because of doubt whether the old arrangement should be wholly abandoned. The Canadian Assembly was under no great pressure to issue many charters though under pressure to issue some. In the States, however, the demand was excessive, and every charter caused a fight. Recourse to bribery was notorious. In New York, indeed, the association of special charters with bribery had been a major reason for making banking free and removing temptations. In Canada there had been no experience to give this consideration force.

The divergence between American and Canadian banks has involved, among other things, the restriction on liabilities to which I have given prominence. The restriction, being one of liabilities to a multiple of capital, assumed that the capital would be held in specie. In the States, when it became recognized that the assumption was vain, then legislative efforts to enforce the retention of specie became common. They took their most important form in 1837 when Virginia enacted the requirement that a bank's specie holdings be not less than 25 per cent of its liabilities, which was the reciprocal of a limitation of liabilities to four times capital. Reserve requirements became in time the chief means of credit control in the States, but not in Canada. The difference is one of many that arose, as American

[50] Breckenridge, *History*, pp. 61-62; Gallatin, Albert, *Writings*, (ed.) Henry Adams (Philadelphia, 1879), III, 434.

banks multiplied in number and the machinery of control was enlarged correspondingly, while the Canadians held to what they had.[51]

The Lords of the Treasury in Whitehall were not struck with admiration for Canada's free banking act of 1850, and the less because it followed American precedent, which Their Lordships thought by no means a safe example for imitation in matters of currency and banking. Instead they criticized directly the two elements of the law that had been called its merits, viz., the security given note-holders and the demand created for bonds. In place of securing note issues by the deposit of bonds they thought it preferable to require cash reserves of one-third, and they doubted the wisdom of creating a market for bonds in the manner intended; "the price thus raised by a fictitious demand would be dependent on the maintenance of circulation based on the deposit of the securities. . . ." Their preference for a reserve requirement to a bond security was, however, academic, for what they really approved, and wisely, was a single bank of issue; and while the Americans made assurance doubly sure by requiring both bond security and cash reserves – but always with care to insure the requirement's not being too effective – both the Provinces and Great Britain herself continued to profit from a sound banking practice under no statutory requirements of the sort at all.[52]

In 1841 there were less than a dozen chartered banks in the Provinces, and over a century later there are still less than a dozen. In the States, with perhaps ten or twelve times the population of the Provinces, there were then more than 700 banks, and now, somewhat more than a century later, there are about 14,000.[53] The average size of Canadian banks was already much greater than that of American banks. By about 1857 or a little later the Bank of Montreal was larger than any American bank and probably the largest and most powerful transactor in the New York money market, where it maintained and employed

[51] In very recent years, however, reserve requirements have been a more important factor in Canadian central banking procedure than previously. There has also been a greater tendency among Canadian banks to lend on documents, as in the States, rather than on overdraft, as in Britain and elsewhere in the world.

[52] Journals of Legislative Assembly, Province of Canada, 1851 (15 Victoria), Appendix ZZ.

[53] In both Canada and the United States the number has in the interval been much greater than it is now midway in the twentieth century.

immense sums. This raised the criticism that the bank, by taking Canada's precious funds abroad to deal with foreigners in Wall Street, was neglecting the domestic borrowers and the Provinces' interest. It was sacrificing Canada to the States. Canadian business and farming struggled as best it could with insufficient credit, America prospered, and Canadian bankers so far from redressing the balance worsened it.[54]

The earth, Thomas Jefferson said, belongs to the living. But it belongs to them a very short time, its condition always determined by the past and its possession indentured to the future. Canadians of the mid-nineteenth century could reasonably complain that the Americans seemed to be having all the fun and making all the money, while their own resources were left in desuetude and their lives were narrowed. But perhaps their mistake was to have lived when they did and not later. In the mid-twentieth century, Canada's resources have a value and her children have a future that are certainly no less for her backwardness a hundred years earlier. They are perhaps greater. I fancy the Canadians of 1850 did better by lending their money in the United States than they would have done in a rash and premature effort to surpass her advantages. It might even be contended that a presiding wisdom restrained Canada in the nineteenth century while America burnt her candles at both ends, and that in the twentieth century Canada is having her turn. This implies that wisdom depends on what century one lives in.

[54] G. Hague, "The Late Mr. E. H. King," *JCBA*, IV (1896-97), pp. 20, 24.

Capital Formation in Canada, 1896-1930

KENNETH BUCKLEY

The production of wheat on the Canadian prairie provided the basic economic opportunity in the economic development of Canada from 1896 to 1930. This opportunity attracted labour and capital to the direct exploitation of virgin land resources and induced investment throughout the economy in major secondary and tertiary industries and, through these, in housing and other community facilities greater by many times than the investment on the agricultural frontier itself. This leverage effect, the most significant aspect of the frontier, was a determining factor in the development of Canada's economic structure and, to a large extent, of its political structure as well. Political and economic behaviour was influenced by the prairie, even in advance of its emergence as a wheat economy, through the anticipations of its impact when it should emerge. Other factors, such as the past experience and failures of the isolated colonies in British North America, the availability of capital funds, the pattern of American experience, and, especially the geography of the country, were important in the development; but the crucial determinant was the opportunity anticipated and finally realized on the prairie frontier.

The British colonies in North America were joined in political union by the British North America Act, 1867, but it was not until after the turn of the century that a significant degree of economic integration was achieved. Meanwhile the powerful anticipations underlying Confederation determined the policies of the new federal government. The nature of these anticipations was frequently expressed: "Coming further east still, let us but have our canal system completed, our connection with the Pacific Railway at the head of Lake Superior, the Northwest

Source: Kenneth Buckley, *Capital Formation in Canada, 1896-1930*, Toronto: University of Toronto Press, 1955, pp. 4-12. Minor deletions in the original text have been made. Reprinted by permission of the publishers.

becoming rapidly settled, the exports of the settlers passing through our canals and the whole system of the Ontario railways complete, and the result will be that the trade of the city of Toronto which has doubled in five years will be quadrupled, and the case will be the same with Hamilton, London, and other cities in the West [Ontario]. Such will be the direct and indirect results of these facilities . . .".[1] The potential frontier, Rupert's Land and the Northwest Territories, was acquired with imperial aid in 1870. The Intercolonial Railway to the Maritimes was completed in 1876 and the Canadian Pacific Railway, from Montreal to the west coast, in 1885. The national policy of protective tariffs was introduced in 1879 to promote indus-trialization and, along with the uneconomic, all-Canadian transportation system, to ensure that the impact of the leverage effects of the new frontier be contained, so far as possible, within the territorial bounds of the new political unit.

In the difficult physical environment of British North Amer-ica, the essential capital formation needed to bring potential resources within the scope of the market passed beyond private means in the early part of the nineteenth century, as durable structures replaced inventories as the major component in the structure of productive capital. Governments were compelled to assume an active role in the investment field and the fulfilment of this role became their major function. A comparison of the period from the mid-seventies to the mid-nineties in Canada with the periods before and after reveals marked contrasts in the efficacy of government intervention in the field of investment. In the three periods governments supported the extension of railways, canals, roads, and other transportation equipment. In the earlier and in the later period, that is from 1840 to about 1870, and 1900 to 1930, large external economies were appar-ently created by these government activities and large-scale booms induced. In both periods basic opportunities were present in the form of an accessible agricultural frontier. Actual re-sources were linked to markets by the new equipment, and these resources attracted a large inflow of settlers whose pioneer ef-forts eventually converted wilderness into prosperous settlement.

[1] From a typical budget speech in the early seventies, in which the minister is justifying federal investment expenditures on canals and railways. (Quoted by W. A. Mackintosh, *The Economic Background of Dominion-Provincial Relations* [Ottawa, 1939], p. 16; reprinted in the Carleton Library [Toronto, 1964], p. 25.)

Secondary opportunities flowed from the basic production: trade and local manufacturing grew to supply the growing production and consumption needs of the pioneer and other marketing facilities were further improved to market his surplus products; demands of the people exploiting these secondary opportunities provided the new opportunities to be exploited by others at third and fourth remove from the initial development, and so on.

From about 1870 to 1895, government efforts were on a larger scale than in the earlier period (1840 to 1870), but the repercussions were brief interruptions in a secular depression extending over twenty-five years. Explosive building and real estate booms were induced, but these were not general, and had a very short life in those localities where they did occur. The absence of basic opportunities in this period accounts for the disappointing results of government action on a large scale. The whole effect, during the period, was virtually limited to the initial impact of each government act.

The prairie frontier finally passed the critical margin separating potential from actual resources when the opportunity it afforded became definitely superior to alternative opportunities open to migrants. This shift in the character of the frontier occurred quite suddenly in the mid-nineties. The determination of the timing of this major turning point in Canadian economic development has been attributed to many factors. . . . Two factors were fundamental. The interior of the continent is a single, continuous plain and the movement into western Canada was a natural extension of the American frontier after the occupation of more accessible free land in the United States. This natural movement of population was accelerated by a sharp upturn in the price of wheat in the mid-nineties. At the outset investment was largely the expenditure of personal effort and savings upon opportunities recognized by those close at hand. Most of the first arrivals on the frontier were North Americans. Their expenditures embodied knowledge gained from experience in a similar environment. Outside capital was not attracted on a significant scale until the boom was well under way. At the turn of the century, from 1896 to 1901-2, the United Kingdom was experiencing an investment boom on a scale that provided ample domestic opportunities for labour and capital and at the same time affected favourably, from Canada's point

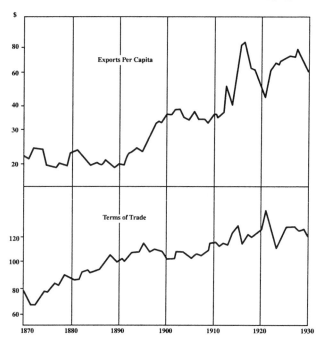

FIG. 1. Real exports per capita and the terms of trade, 1870-1930. (Source: Taylor and Mitchell, Statistical Contributions, and Dominion Bureau of Statistics.)

of view, the price of wheat.[2] When the domestic cycle in the United Kingdom had run its course, and after the nature of new frontier opportunities in Canada had been thoroughly demonstrated and the rising trend in the economic activity of the dominion was well advanced, the flow of British labour and capital to Canada began.

The sudden shift in real opportunity in Canada is reflected in the real exports per capita which are shown in Figure 1. The rate of Canada's economic growth has varied with the availability of virgin resources and the relative ease of convert-

[2] In 1900 and 1901, gross home investment in the United Kingdom reached the highest levels achieved from 1870 to 1913. This boom even attracted foreign, particularly American, capital to the United Kingdom in the finance of the London underground railway system. (See A. Cairncross, *Home and Foreign Investment in Great Britain, 1870-1913*, (Doctoral thesis, Cambridge University), pp. 246-47 and Table 21).

ing these into cash sales in the world markets. Expanding exports of primary commodities were the means of acquiring manufactures essential to the further expansion of domestic production and consumption, and they generated the profits necessary to attract and service foreign investment. Only when conditions conducive to the expansion of the rate of exports prevailed, could the expansion of the productive capacity of the country, in terms of its capital, human, and natural resources, proceed over an extended period beyond the rate fixed by domestic savings and domestic population growth. In their relation to exports, natural resources were the lever inducing rapid growth in the other (human and capital) dimensions of productive capacity.

Real exports per capita, as shown in Figure 1, followed a flat trend from 1875 to 1896 and then began to rise.[3] This shift in trend after 1896 indicates an expansion in opportunities that accelerated for some time at a faster rate than the spectacular growth of population which it induced. The change took place before the flow of foreign capital began and was, in fact, a cause of that flow. The terms of trade over the years when the shift in opportunity occurred are also shown in the figure; they reflect favourable price trends which served to reinforce the change in real opportunity. But the terms of trade, like the cheapening of transportation and the decline in interest rates, had been more or less steadily improving Canada's position since the eighteen-seventies and, like them, was a contributing rather than a causal factor in the turning point.[4]

[3] The pattern of Canadian economic experience appears to conform with Schumpeter's scheme, wherein the second long "Kondratieff" cycle from 1843 to 1897 reaches a peak about 1870. (J. A. Schumpeter, *Business Cycles* [New York, 1939].) Because of the importance of international prices and price trends to a simple staple-producing and exporting economy and the fact that Kondratieff derived the shape of his cycles from data heavily weighted by prices, this conformity is not surprising. However, the relative secular stagnation in Canada from the seventies to the nineties was not the product of any rhythm in general international business activity, but of a closed frontier in the east and the absence of resources in the West. The relative flatness in the trend in Canadian activity from the seventies to the nineties, evident in the chart, reflects the status of the prairies in those years when, like other parts of the continental plain before they became resources, they were vacant.

[4] See W. A. Mackintosh, *Economic Problems of the Prairie Provinces* (Toronto, 1935), chapter 1, for trends in transportation costs and the cost of borrowing through this period.

Variations in the rate of growth of population in a new country like Canada were largely the net product of movements into and out of the country.[5] Whatever may be the explanation of the worldwide migrations that occurred, the experience of each new country was determined to a large extent by the nature of the economic opportunities available for individual migrants relative to opportunities available among its competitors in the field of immigration. In Canada, from 1870 to the mid-nineties, these opportunities were directly related to government actions of various kinds, and their short-lived character was reflected in the flows of immigrants and emigrants during the period. In spite of large numbers of arrivals in the decades from 1870 to 1900, net migration was negative in each. After the change in the opportunities in 1896, net migration became positive and contributed almost 40 per cent of the 100 per cent increase in the population that occurred in the following thirty-five years.[6]

SUMMARY OF THE INVESTMENT BOOM

The rate of expansion of the capital equipment of the country which occurred from 1901 to 1930 is shown in Table 1. Global estimates of domestic capital formation per capita expressed as annual averages for each quinquennium are shown in the first column. Reducing the expenditures to a per capita basis brings out the high rates of investment activity achieved before 1915 during the period of the first heavy movement of population into the West. The true intensity of the process in this period is masked by the upward drift in prices. An indication of the bias introduced by price changes may be seen in columns 2 and 3 of the table, where the annual average gross investment in structures – the largest of the three major components of domestic capital formation – is shown in current and constant prices. The highest rate was achieved from 1911 to 1915. During this period the all-time peak, that of 1912-13, sustained the average despite the sharp recession and depression

---

[5] Birth and mortality rates have played an important role, and in recent years the principal role, in determining the rate of growth of Canada's population, but in the period from 1870 to 1930 migration was chiefly responsible for the wide *variations* in the decade rates.

[6] The population increased from 5.4 million in 1901 to 10.4 million in 1931. Net migration in this period was 1,928,000. (Cf. *Monthly Review*, Bank of Nova Scotia, July 1954.)

TABLE I

GROSS DOMESTIC CAPITAL FORMATION AND
GROSS CONSTRUCTION, 1901-30
EXPRESSED AS ANNUAL AVERAGES PER CAPITA

	1 Gross domestic capital formation (current dollars)	2 Gross construction (current dollars)	3 (constant dollars)
1901-5	45	24	33
1906-10	70	44	51
1911-15	86	53	55
1916-20	98	52	35
1921-25	81	50	30
1926-30	119	63	39

of 1914-15. The average for the preceding quinquennium was almost as high because annual expenditures, although lower than those later achieved, were better maintained. A mild depression in 1908 had little effect on construction. The rate during the war and post-war boom compared favourably with that of the following period of agricultural depression and was not a great deal lower than the rate from 1926 to 1930 when the final large scale movement into the West occurred.

Direct investment on prairie farms absorbed large absolute expenditures. The size of these and their relation to gross domestic capital formation from 1900 to 1930 are shown in the first three columns of Table II. . . .

It is apparent from the last four columns of Table II, which show the absolute and relative size of investment in transportation, that railway investment did not reach the same level of intensity as prairie farm investment until after 1905. The lag is suggestive. Following the initial burst of activity in the West, investment in the railway field rose to a remarkable level and high rates of investment were maintained until 1915. After 1915 a downward trend set in. Investment in other transport – canals, harbour work, etc., highways and bridges, trucks and automobiles for business use – continued to grow as a result of the innovation of the automobile. However this growth was not great enough to offset the decline in railway expansion. The relative importance of the whole transport group declined after 1915. Prairie farm investment was at its relative peak from 1901 to 1905 (column 3), continued at a slightly lower level until 1915, and then declined. Relatively speaking, transport rose after 1905 (column 7), remained at remarkable levels until 1915, then declined.

TABLE II

PRAIRIE FARM AND TRANSPORT INVESTMENT COMPARED
WITH GROSS DOMESTIC CAPITAL FORMATION
(millions of dollars)

	1	2	3	4	5	6	7
	Gross domestic capital formation	Prairie farm invest-ment*	Per-centage 2 is of 1	Transport investment			Per-centage 6 is of 1
				Railway	Other	Total	
1901-5	1,283	221	17.2	165	36	201	15.7
1906-10	2,287	319	13.9	473	66	539	23.6
1911-15	3,279	463	14.1	682	166	848	25.9
1916-20	4,033	370	9.2	423	238	661	16.4
1921-25	3,641	245	6.7	386	367	753	20.7
1926-30	5,831	454	7.8	583	642	1,225	21.0

*Including buildings, equipment, trucks, inventories, but excluding passenger cars.

The expansion of steam railways was directly related to wheat. The prairie offered little resistance to the construction of the network of lines which were built within the region. Mileage grew from 3,300 in 1897 to 4,000 miles in 1901, 6,000 in 1906, 8,000 in 1911, and 14,000 in 1916. In post-war years when extensive railway construction was quiescent elsewhere in the dominion, the construction of branch lines continued on the prairies, raising the total mileage to nearly 18,000 by 1929. This construction would have been induced in the normal course of events. But unfortunately prairie expansion also induced the construction of two complete transcontinental systems and these, built like the Canadian Pacific within the framework of national policy, traversed the barren wilderness of the Canadian Shield at very great cost.

Early prairie roads were mere trails following the square pattern laid down by the survey system, sufficient for the moving of grain to loading platforms and elevators along the railroad and of supplies from the villages back to the farms; but the automobile revolutionized local demands, not only on the prairie but throughout the country, and as a result road construction became a major field of investment. . . .

Had the expanding export region exchanged the proceeds of its sales directly for imports as it would largely have done in the absence of a nationally planned transport system and tariff, the economic prosperity of the eastern provinces would have been dependent on local developments. But the expenditures of the new region were channelled to the east, and protected manufacturing industries expanded greatly to meet the demands. British Columbia, on the west, redirected the lumber products of its forests from exports to the prairie market which absorbed up to 70 per cent of the total. The Maritime provinces in the far east shared in the boom so long as the extensive phase of railway construction which accompanied prairie expansion persisted on a national scale. Its iron and steel industry was unable to compete effectively with firms located in the central provinces when the peak demands for railway equipment subsided. The central provinces were the chief beneficiaries of national policy. Capital invested in their manufacturing industries increased from $357 million in 1900 to $4,091 million at the peak in 1929. The greatest relative expansion occurred in iron and steel and textiles under a tariff designed to give maximum protection to finished goods, with the materials, equipment, and other items affecting the costs of production of the finished commodities entering free or at a nominal duty.[7] The concentration of production of manufactured goods in the central provinces and its distribution between Ontario and Quebec are indicated in Table III. The selected items shown cover about one-third of the national production, and the geographical pattern reflected is representative of the total.

Opportunities for capital and labour in manufacturing were considerable, but the most spectacular increase in opportunities came in the tertiary industries. Transportation has already been mentioned. The high degree of capital intensity in the transportation industry and the geographical extent of the country implied very large investment outlays. Apart from certain other utilities the degree of capital intensity among the remaining service industries was relatively low; but in absolute and relative terms the largest job opportunities were opened up in these

[7] W. A. Mackintosh, *Economic Background of Dominion-Provincial Relations* (Ottawa, 1939), p. 35; Carleton Library edition, pp. 49-51.

TABLE III

NATIONAL MANUFACTURING OUTPUT IN THE CENTRAL PROVINCES IN 1929[a]

	1	2	3
Industrial group	Percentages of net national production		
	In Ontario	In Quebec	1+2
Automobiles	96	—	96
Rubber tires	95	4	99
Machinery	72	25	97
Castings and forgings	69	21	90
Railway rolling stock	23	53	76
Hardware and tools	68	29	97
Agricultural implements	95	3	98
Cotton yarn and cloth	18	75	93
Boots and shoes	36	60	96
Rubber footwear	38	62	100
Clothing, men's	36	61	97
Clothing, women's	56	40	96
Hosiery and knit goods	72	22	94
Electrical apparatus and supplies	77	22	99

(a) Source: Amended from Mackintosh, *Economic Background of Dominion-Provincial Relations*, p. 50; Carleton Library edition, p. 97.

service fields. The total labour force increased by 120.2 per cent from 1901 to 1931. The farm labour force increased by only 57.9 per cent. (The process of mechanization in agriculture was relevant here.) Other primary occupations increased by 113 per cent. The labour force in manufacturing rose by 65 per cent, and in construction by 128.1 per cent. Thus primary plus secondary occupations increased by less than the national average. A 218 per cent increase (on the average) occurred among workers reporting the following occupations: transportation (252 per cent), trade (253 per cent), clerical (339 per cent), other service (161.4 per cent).[8] It is apparent that the expansion of job opportunities in the service industries contributed more than other industrial fields to the expansion of non-farm population and, through the accompanying process of urbanization, to the demand for housing – the largest single component of the volume of construction – and to roads,

[8] If unskilled workers not allocated were all treated as manufacturing, the increase in manufacturing would still be lower than the national average. Actually these unallocated workers were working in construction and transportation as well as in manufacturing. (Cf. D.B.S. *Census Bulletin, No. 0-6, Occupations and Industries* [Ottawa, 1944].)

streets, sidewalks, schools, hospitals, public utilities, and other community facilities. The importance of this relation of the service industries to the expansion and pattern of investment expenditures is sometimes overlooked.

Table IV compares the investment in railway structures in value and percentage terms with the investment in housing. The value of direct government construction (excluding railway construction) is also shown in the table. In the whole field of construction during the period under review housing was the

TABLE IV

MAJOR COMPONENTS OF GROSS CONSTRUCTION, 1901-30
(millions of dollars)

	1	2	3	4	5	6
	Gross constr.	Railway constr.	Per-centage 2 is of 1	Housing constr.	Per-centage 4 is of 1	Govern-ment constr.
1901-5	681	124	18.2	222	32.6	79
1906-10	1,439	381	26.5	468	32.5	149
1911-15	2,007	537	26.8	568	28.3	342
1916-20	2,122	253	11.9	641	30.2	256
1921-25	2,271	253	11.1	742	32.7	436
1926-30	3,109	389	12.5	1,060	34.1	578

Direct railway construction by the federal government is included in column 2 and excluded from column 6. The total federal railway investments for the six quinquennia in millions of dollars were: 15, 99, 98, 36, 3, 24.

only component to rival transportation in fundamental importance and to surpass it in size. In absolute value terms, investment in residential housing over the whole period was almost as large as the total investment in all transport structures and equipment (see Table II). In addition, the relative stability of the housing component, reflected in column 5 of the table, contrasts markedly with the railway component. The latter rose from 18.2 per cent of gross construction in 1901-5 to over 26 per cent in 1906-10 and 1911-15, and then fell off to average about 12 per cent of gross construction in the following three quinquennia. Meanwhile housing was fairly close to 30 per cent of gross construction in each quinquennium.

The relation between tertiary occupations and basic production in western Canada was obvious and direct. The bulky character of wheat held the producing units within a short road haul of the railways.[9] Stations were erected at intervals of approximately eight miles along the track,[10] and around these clustered the local distributive agencies adapted to the needs of the prairie wheat economy. Three to six grain elevators, a loading platform, and, at some points, a small stockyard lined the track.[11] Terminal elevators were built at Fort William and Port Arthur at the head of Lake Superior at an early date. The bulk of the grain was moved by water to lower lake terminals and then to New York by the Erie Barge Canal or to Montreal. A small capacity was provided on the Canadian Atlantic seaboard to handle winter shipments. Interior terminals were built on the prairie after 1912. Pacific terminals were built following the completion of the Panama Canal.[12]

The high degree of specialization of prairie agriculture and the character of local resources implied dependence on primary and secondary producers in other regions and an extensive marketing structure to facilitate supply. In addition to the assemblers each small market centre supported a variety of merchandising and service establishments, professional men, and financial institutions.[13] The cities that emerged in the three provinces displayed the same general pattern as the towns and villages with the addition of many wholesale institutions and, substituting for the country general store, a somewhat more specialized structure of retail outlets. In short, the cities, towns, and villages were centres of tertiary producers. Among secondary producers, building and construction workers were the more numerous, with manufacturing virtually limited to pro-

[9] V. C. Fowke, "The Distributive Pattern in the Prairie Provinces," *The Commerce Journal*, 1945, p. 70.

[10] *Ibid.*, p. 71.

[11] The capacity of country elevators increased from 12.8 million bushels in 1900 to 192.9 million bushels in 1930. The cost of constructing these at 1930 prices would exceed $70 million, with no allowance for those destroyed or demolished during the period. Capacities are from *Canada Year Book* and unit costs from D. A. MacGibbon, *The Canadian Grain Trade* (Toronto, 1932), p. 93.

[12] Terminal capacity increased from 5.6 million bushels in 1900 to 201.7 million bushels in 1930.

[13] Cf. Fowke, "The Distributive Pattern in the Prairie Provinces," for a description of the institutional pattern of the typical market centre in the western provinces.

cessing of farm products, particularly the production of flour. Winnipeg became the wholesale centre for the prairie provinces and was the only large city in the West until the opening of the Panama Canal enlarged Vancouver's opportunities. But Winnipeg was subsidiary to Montreal and Toronto. The two eastern cities became national metropolitan centres with the whole economy shared as a hinterland between them. The concentration of the wholesale trade of Canada was reflected in the first full census of merchandising which was taken in 1931: 69.7 per cent of all wholesale sales in Canada in 1930 were made in the four largest cities, with 23.1 per cent in Montreal, 20.1 per cent in Toronto, 19.1 per cent in Winnipeg, and 6.4 per cent in Vancouver. Head offices of national wholesalers, of large department and chain store retailers, and of the various financial services were concentrated in Montreal and Toronto. The two cities also attracted manufacturing industries with the result that a large part of the secondary industries was located within or near their boundaries. The rapid growth of these and other urban centres in Canada from 1896 to 1915 was largely the result of prairie expansion. The accident of war, which added a stimulus of its own, the gradual emergence of important new staple exports, and the substitution of capital for labour in agriculture were among the major factors contributing to urban growth after 1915. . . .

TABLE V

DOMESTIC INVESTMENT, FOREIGN INVESTMENT,
AND GROSS NATIONAL PRODUCT, 1901-30
(millions of dollars)

	1	2	3	4	5	6
					Per-	Per-
	Gross	Gross	Foreign	Gross	centage	centage
	national	domestic	invest-	invest-	2 is	4 is
	product	capital	ment	ment	of 1	of 1
		formation		(2 + 3)		
1901-5	5,650	1,283	-301	982	22.7	17.4
1906-10	8,482	2,287	-784	1,503	27.0	17.7
1911-15	12,178	3,279	-1,515	1,764	26.9	14.5
1916-20	20,923	4,033	-262	3,771	19.3	18.0
1921-25	22,589	3,641	72	3,713	16.1	16.4
1926-30	28,758	5,831	-563	5,268	20.3	18.3

Table V emphasizes in a different way the investment opportunities that accompanied the opening of the Canadian West. Here gross capital formation and gross investment are compared with the gross national product. The aggregates are shown in millions of dollars for each quinquennium from 1900 to 1930. In the final two columns of the table gross domestic capital formation and gross investment are expressed as percentages of gross national product. Gross domestic capital formation exceeded 25 per cent of the gross national product from 1901 to 1915. An average of almost 27 per cent was maintained from 1906 to 1915. The 26.9 per cent average for the years from 1911 to 1915, which include two years of recession, suggests the unusual levels attained in the peak years, 1911-13. The average dropped off to 19.3 per cent from 1916 to 1920, reached a low for the thirty-year period of 16.1 per cent from 1921 to 1925, and recovered to 20.3 per cent after 1926. The remarkably high levels of domestic capital formation before 1915 were made possible by large inflows of British and foreign capital funds. The inflows of British and foreign funds are shown in column 3. Adding these algebraically to gross domestic capital formation yields the gross investment shown in column 4. The importance of foreign savings varied considerably over the period. They were relatively more important before 1915 than after and also absolutely more important from 1905 to 1915 than from 1926 to 1930. Only in the depressed period from 1921 to 1925 were they not a factor at all. An approximation of the relative importance of gross domestic savings appears in column 6, where gross investment is expressed as a percentage of gross national product. Direct government investment would have to be deducted from gross investment and the residual adjusted for the net surplus or deficit of governments to obtain a conceptually accurate measure of domestic savings offsets. . . .

Defensive Expansion: The State and Economic Growth in Canada

H. G. J. AITKEN

> I know of no difference in the machinery of government in the old and
> new world that strikes a European more forcibly than the apparently
> undue importance which the business of constructing public works
> appears to occupy in American legislation. . . . The provision which in
> Europe, the State makes for the protection of its citizens against
> foreign enemies, is in America required for . . . the "war with the
> wilderness." The defence of an important fortress, or the maintenance
> of a sufficient army or navy in exposed spots, is not more a matter of
> common concern to the European, than is the construction of the
> great communications to the American settler; and the State, very
> naturally, takes on itself the making of the works, which are a matter
> of concern to all alike. – Lord Durham, *Report on the Affairs of
> British North America* (1839).

In the statement quoted, Lord Durham contrasted the role
of the state in the development of North America with its role
in Europe. A modern historian would probably not accept
Durham's generalization without question, though he might
admit that in 1839 the contrast had some validity. The British
provinces in North America – particularly Upper Canada, or
what is now Ontario – at the time Durham became Governor
General had brought themselves to the verge of bankruptcy by
undertaking capital investments for development on a greater
scale than their slim fiscal resources could support. Their situ-

Source: Hugh G. J. Aitken (ed.), *The State and Economic Growth*,
New York: Social Science Research Council, 1959, pp. 79-114. Reprinted by permission of the author and publishers.

ation, as Durham saw it, was analogous to that of a European nation whose government had bankrupted itself by undertaking a military effort beyond its means. The responsibility for this failure to maintain a satisfactory rate of growth lay, in Durham's view, with the state, just as in the case of a European country that had failed to provide for its own external security.

Durham's opinion that in Europe the primary function of the state was defence while in North America it was development reflected his reaction to the wave of internal improvements that had swept over most of the states and provinces of North America in the 1820's and 1830's. Historians have long recognized that governments played an important role in promoting and financing these early internal improvements. After 1840, however, according to the conventional interpretation, the federal and state governments in the United States tended increasingly to follow a *laissez-faire* policy. This tendency is alleged to have continued until the 1890's, when the growth of industrialism and public resentment against the trust movement led again to a policy of government intervention.

No analogous interpretation of Canadian development has ever found acceptance among economic historians. On the contrary, the standard interpretation of the entire history of the Canadian economy assigns to the state a major role in guiding and stimulating development: on any reading of the historical record, government policies and decisions stand out as the key factors. The creation of a national economy in Canada and, even more clearly, of a transcontinental economy was as much a political as an economic achievement.

The system of concepts suggested by Hoselitz[1] has one major advantage for the student of Canadian economic history: it enables him to put the Canadian experience in perspective, by comparison with the experience of other national economies. This is, of course, the characteristic virtue of the "ideal type" method. Therefore, if in the following discussion I appear to be emphasizing the discrepancies between the actual course of events in Canada and the pattern suggested by Hoselitz, this should be taken not as an implicit criticism of the schema but as the implementation of the remaining steps in the method.

As a preliminary step, several points should be noted in the

[1] "Patterns of Economic Growth," *Canadian Journal of Economics and Political Science*, 21:416-431.

case of Canada. First, the relevant area changed significantly over time, as a result of the expansion of settlement and also of constitutional changes. The nation state that today we call Canada dates only from 1867. Before that date we are dealing with a number of distinct and very different regional economies which, in respect to the role played by the state in economic development, cannot be classed together without serious distortion. To find a single pattern in the experiences of these different regions, which faced different problems and opportunities, is difficult. The role of the state in the Maritime provinces, seeking their development in maritime trade and the fisheries, was poles apart from its role in central Canada, where development was considered to depend on the perfection of a transportation artery between the midwest and the Atlantic.

All the colonies were of course within the general sphere of control of the British government in London. This to some extent offsets the heterogeneity of separate legislatures and varying situations, but only at the cost of introducing further complexity. We must bear in mind that the locus of the "state" was neither single at any one time nor constant over time. For example, financial assistance to railroad construction in Canada was provided by governments at all levels – municipal, provincial, federal, and imperial. There was no single locus of decision making, nor even a single hierarchy. Each level of government operated within its particular limitations to achieve its own objectives, and these did not always coincide in all respects. Much the same could be said of banking legislation and fiscal policy.

Thus a plurality of government bodies influenced the direction and rate of economic devlopment in Canada. All these bodies might well be included in our concept of the state, and discussion of its role in Canadian development would then involve the activities of all levels of government in the "direct line of sovereignty" from the British crown and parliament down to the municipality. The difficulty with this procedure is that at several points in Canadian history a government outside this line of sovereignty – that of the United States – has exercised an influence on Canadian development certainly no less than that of any British government. Throughout its history Canada has been an economic satellite of both Great Britain and the United States.

These difficulties do not make it impossible to apply the Hoselitz schema to the case of Canada, but they do remind us that any theoretical framework involves some degree of over-simplification. The classification of Canada as expansionist, satellitic, and autonomous, however, raises other problems which are more serious and call for careful scrutiny.

I. THE PERIOD BEFORE CONFEDERATION

The Canadian provinces in the period before Confederation fall into two general groups: the Maritime provinces of New Brunswick, Nova Scotia, and Prince Edward Island; and Canada proper, which included under a single legislature after the Act of Union of 1840 the two earlier provinces of Upper and Lower Canada (roughly present-day Ontario and Quebec). In addition there was the territory under the control of the Hudson's Bay Company. This included not only the drainage basin of Hudson Bay but also the entire prairie region, the Rocky Mountains, and the Pacific coast, including until 1846 part of what is now the state of Oregon, and the territory that became the province of British Columbia in 1858.

The Maritime Provinces

Development in this region in the period from 1783 to 1840 depended on fishing, shipbuilding, maritime trade, and lumbering.[2] In terms of the general economic organization of the British colonial empire, these provinces performed the functions that the New England colonies had performed before the American Revolution. The Maritimes were a source of agricultural produce, dried fish, and lumber for Newfoundland and the British West Indies; they served as a base for the coastal

---

[2] See W. Thomas Easterbrook and Hugh G. J. Aitken, *Canadian Economic History* (Toronto: Macmillan Company, 1956), Chapters 7, 9, 11; Harold A. Innis, *The Cod Fisheries* (New Haven: Yale University Press, 1940); Arthur R. M. Lower, *The North American Assault on the Canadian Forest* (Toronto: Ryerson Press, 1938); Donald G. Creighton, *British North America at Confederation: A Study Prepared for the Royal Commission on Dominion-Provincial Relations* (Ottawa, 1939); F. Lee Benns, *The American Struggle for the British West India Carrying-Trade*, Indiana University Studies, No. 56 (Bloomington, 1923); and Stanley A. Saunders, *Economic History of the Maritime Provinces: A Study Prepared for the Royal Commission on Dominion-Provincial Relations* (Ottawa, 1939).

and Banks fisheries, exporting their catch – as New England had done – partly to the West Indies and partly to southern Europe; their magnificent stands of white pine provided timber for civil and naval construction in Great Britain; and their shipbuilding industry not only served as a valuable supplement to the output of English shipyards but also furnished ships for a multilateral maritime trading system based on Halifax and Saint John.

As far as Nova Scotia was concerned, the important frontiers of development were those of maritime trade and the fisheries. In agriculture progress was disappointing. Prince Edward Island alone achieved self-sufficiency in foodstuffs. In neither Nova Scotia nor New Brunswick was there a continuous frontier of agricultural settlement in the classic American sense. Immigration into these two provinces from the United Kingdom was insignificant before 1815, reached a peak in the 1840's, and declined in the 1850's; at all times the volume was smaller than the influx into the St. Lawrence colonies and considerably smaller than that into New England. Immigrants into Nova Scotia – mostly Highland Scots and southern Irish – tended to cluster in the small fishing villages scattered along the Atlantic coast. When immigrants ventured into agriculture, they were inclined to concentrate on livestock and dairy farming, where the competition of imports from the United States was less severe than in breadstuffs. Partly because of the intrinsic poverty of the area's arable land, partly because of the competing employment opportunities in the fisheries, agricultural development in Nova Scotia was slow and haphazard. Nothing that can be described as a continuous expansion of the frontier of settlement can be discerned.

New Brunswick differed from Nova Scotia in the important role played by the lumber industry in the provincial economy. Nova Scotia after 1815 retained sufficient forest resources to support a prosperous shipbuilding industry, but exports of native timber to Great Britain and the West Indies were insignificant. In New Brunswick, on the other hand, lumbering was the major industry from the American Revolution to the 1850's, surpassing the fisheries and agriculture in numbers employed and in export earnings.

In encouraging the development of the New Brunswick timber industry – and later that of Upper and Lower Canada also – the state, in this case the British government, played a major role. Without preferential tariff protection, the only variety of New Brunswick timber that could be marketed profitably in England was high-quality white pine, used for the masts and spars of naval and commercial vessels. Freight costs from New Brunswick to England in the early nineteenth century were on the average three times as high as from the Baltic ports. Labour costs in the North American colony were very much higher than in northern Europe. And the timber trade of the Baltic ports had been brought to a high degree of organization and efficiency. In these circumstances New Brunswick timber other than large masts could not be sold at a profit in England.

Dependence on Baltic timber supplies was the Achilles' heel of British naval power throughout the seventeenth and eighteenth centuries, but little was done to remedy matters. The outbreak of the Napoleonic wars, however, compelled a sudden change in policy and led the British government to encourage by tariff protection a general export trade in timber from the North American colonies. Duties on foreign timber were sharply increased from 10 shillings a load in 1795 to 25s. in 1805, 34s.8d. in 1810, and 65s. in 1814. Reduced to 55s. in 1821, they remained at that figure until 1842. Colonial timber entered Great Britan duty free, except for a nominal registration duty between 1821 and 1842.

On the foundation provided by these preferential duties there developed the North American trade in square timber – the economic mainstay of New Brunswick, and to a large extent of Upper and Lower Canada also, from 1810 to the early 1850's. Rapid industrialization in Great Britain provided a growing demand for timber, the universal construction material for factories and residential buildings; the rich forest resources of the St. Lawrence, Ottawa, and St. John rivers furnished an ample supply; and the British consumer paid in the form of higher prices the difference between freight costs from the Baltic and from North America.

The frontier of the lumber industry in New Brunswick was also a frontier of settlement. In this colony there was no sharp division between natural forest land and natural farm land, as there is in some areas. The rivers, particularly the St. John, by which the lumberman floated his rafts down to the sea also gave the settler easy access to the fertile valleys of the interior. The lumber camps provided both markets for agricultural produce and opportunities for the farmer to obtain part-time employment during the winter and early fall. This close connection between the lumber industry and agricultural settlement produced an approximation to an advancing frontier of settlement, and in this sense the tariff preferences granted by the British government to colonial lumber contributed to the formation of an "expansionist" pattern of development in New Brunswick.

Let us turn to maritime trade and the fisheries. In both these fields development depended on active support from the state, primarily the British government. The central issue in maritime trade after 1783 was whether the United States should be permitted to trade directly with the British West Indies. The merchant capitalists of Nova Scotia and New Brunswick wished the ports of the British West Indies closed to all but British and colonial shipping, hoping that in this way they could monopolize the lucrative carrying trade in breadstuffs, livestock, staves, dried cod, molasses, and rum. The owners of the sugar plantations in the British islands − still a powerful group in British politics, although their influence was not as great as before 1776 − wished to obtain their necessary imports as cheaply as possible, and consequently to have the British West Indies thrown open to the shipping of all nations. New England merchants, in their turn, regarded access to the British islands as a prize worth fighting for, and exerted effective pressure on Congress and the President to retaliate in kind against any attempt on the part of the British government to discriminate against American shipping.

No one, I think, can analyse the tangled history of the retaliatory legislation that this conflict of interests produced (the American Tonnage Act of 1816 and Navigation Acts of 1817, 1818, and 1820, the British Free Port Act of 1818 and Trade Acts of 1822 and 1826) without wondering whether the prize was worth all the complicated manoeuvring that it occasioned. Certainly the policies that the British government pursued − if such a series of expedients can be called a policy − were influenced by considerations of more general import than the political pressures that the Maritime provinces and the West Indies planters could exert. Chief among these I would place the still influential mercantilist doctrine that the carrying trade of the Empire should be restricted to British and colonial shipping, combined with an overall strategy of restraining American expansionism in the Caribbean. On the American side, of course, the struggle to secure access to the British West Indies was the last major issue on which the New England mercantile oligarchy was able to use the federal government as its instrument. The election of Andrew Jackson as President ended this phase and made possible the compromise solution in the so-called "reciprocity agreement of 1830." By this time New England merchants had found other fields for their enterprise: South America, the Pacific coast, and the Orient.

Throughout this period of bitter economic warfare, the mercantile interests of the Maritime provinces looked to the British government to represent and safeguard what they regarded as their rights as citizens of the Empire. They realized clearly that they laboured under serious handicaps in open competition with American shippers – greater distance from markets, smaller capital resources, and inadequate sources of agricultural produce – and therefore sought to induce the British government to preserve intact the code of navigation that had been the heart of the old empire. In this they were finally unsuccessful; the American government was a much more formidable adversary to the consolidation of the new imperial system than Holland or France had been to the old. In both Nova Scotia and New Brunswick the concessions that the United States forced from the British government in 1830 were felt as serious economic reversals. The Maritime provinces had relied on the state to aid them, and the state – necessarily concerned with wider interests than those of the North American colonies – had failed them.

An analogous pattern of state action may be seen in regard to the fisheries. Here expansionism certainly entailed establishing control over the country's resources, but in rather a particular sense. The point in dispute was what in fact and in law were the country's resources, and to decide this question the intervention of the state was required. The Treaty of Paris which ended the American Revolution stated that citizens of the United States were to continue to enjoy unmolested the right to fish in the inshore waters of British possessions in North America as well as on the Banks and in the Gulf of St. Lawrence; and that they should be permitted to dry and cure fish on any unsettled parts of the coasts of Nova Scotia, the Magdalen Islands, and

Labrador. On the conclusion of the War of 1812, the British government took the position that by declaring war the United States had forfeited these treaty rights and that the inshore fishing privileges had been automatically cancelled. The United States government, on the other hand, argued that the Treaty of Paris had not granted a privilege but merely recognized a right that could not be cancelled unilaterally. Internal dissension prevented the American delegation from taking a firm stand on the issue, however, and the Treaty of Ghent did not mention the fisheries.

This controversy over the inshore fisheries bedevilled Anglo-American relations for the next half-century. As far as Nova Scotia and New Brunswick were concerned, the issue was one of establishing control over resources that were rightfully theirs. To make good this claim they relied on the power of the state, in the form of the British government. A brief review of later developments will illustrate how this power was exercised.

Immediately after 1815, the British government reinforced its naval squadron in Nova Scotian waters and issued instructions that American vessels were to be warned from fishing within the three-mile limit or using Nova Scotian ports for any purpose connected with the fisheries. Seizure of several American ships produced an attempt to settled the issue by diplomacy. This culminated in the signing of a Convention in 1818 by which, in return for concessions in other areas, the United States renounced any liberty which had previously been enjoyed to take, dry, or cure fish "within three marine miles of any of the coasts, bays, creeks, or harbors" of the British provinces in North America.

Unfortunately for the prospects of a permanent settlement, the Convention of 1818 suffered from the characteristic diplomatic vice of ambiguity. Was the Bay of Fundy a bay within the meaning of the Convention, or was it part of the open sea? Were American fishing ships entitled to pass through the convenient alleyway of the Gut of Canso, even though this brought them within three miles of the shore, or were they not? American fishing captains, as might be expected, adopted a loose construction of the Convention; the Nova Scotia goverment insisted on a strict interpretation. The dispute was a minor matter in the whole range of Anglo-American relationships but, as is sometimes the case with minor diplomatic frictions which are not alleviated, became a focus of strong feelings on the part of the interests immediately concerned.

For more than three decades the issue was allowed to smolder, principally because neither Great Britain nor the United States felt that much was to be gained by forcing a decision. This situation changed abruptly in the early 1850's when Great Britain opened negotiations in Washington for reciprocal free trade in natural products between the United States and the British North American colonies. Particularly in central Canada the attainment of reciprocity was regarded at this time as of prime importance. In the Maritimes opinion was divided. In the United States there was little strong feeling on the subject either way. The principal obstacle that the British and Canadian negotiators in Washington had to surmount was simply the indifference of the American Congress. Attempts to secure the abolition of duties on natural produce by parallel legislation were abandoned as hopeless in 1852; thereafter efforts were directed toward securing action by treaty. To this end the British government looked around for some issue that could be used to force decisive action, and found the still unresolved controversy over the inshore fisheries. Late in 1852 the British government announced that it intended to enforce its interpretation of the Convention of 1818; the British naval squadron in Nova Scotian waters would be reinforced, and American ships would thenceforth be strictly excluded from the Bay of Fundy.

Whether Great Britain was actually prepared to go to war over the fisheries issue may well be doubted. The threat of armed force, however, provided the diplomatic gambit necessary for securing prompt and favourable action on reciprocity. The President was now assured of congressional support for a settlement that would include both reciprocity and the inshore fisheries, and in June 1854 the Reciprocity Treaty became law. Import duties were abolished on a wide range of natural products passing between the United States and the British North American colonies, and American shipping was admitted to the use of the St. Lawrence canals on the same terms as British and colonial vessels. American ships were permitted free access to all the coastal fisheries of the British colonies and were allowed to land on the shores of the colonies to dry their nets and cure their fish. Fishing ships from the British colonies received corresponding privileges in the American coastal fisheries north of the thirty-sixth parallel.

Throughout this protracted and often acrimonious dispute, the hopes of Nova Scotians of establishing control over what they regarded as their resources depended on the actions of the British government. The power of the state, exercised through diplomacy and on occasion the threat of armed force, was the primary instrument of development. It cannot be argued that this power was always exercised in the best interests of the colonies concerned. In the Convention of 1818, the Reciprocity Treaty of 1854, and the Washington Treaty of 1871, the Maritime provinces believed – with some justification – that their interests were being sacrificed as "a burnt offering on the altar of Anglo-American friendship."[3] Throughout this period the British government was the state, as far as the relations of the North American colonies with foreign nations were concerned. But the interests of the British government transcended those of the colonies, and British policy could not be directed exclusively or even principally to advancing colonial economic interests. Business and political opinion in the colonies inclined increasingly toward a greater measure of local control over the secular decisions that determined the course of development.

Central Canada

Meanwhile in central Canada events were following a very different course. By the Constitutional Act of 1791 the old province of Quebec had been divided into two provinces, Upper and Lower Canada, each with its own legislature. The hope was that this would enable Upper Canada, in which English-speaking people were in the majority, to work out its development independently of French-speaking Lower Canada. Montreal, the seaport of both provinces, was included in Lower Canada – an act that contained the seeds of much later conflict, as the policies that the English-speaking merchant capitalists of the port wished to pursue, such as improvement of the navigation of the St. Lawrence, came to be opposed by the highly unsympathetic French-Canadian Assembly. The division of the provinces also led to a series of disputes over the division of the customs

[3] Donald G. Creighton, *Dominion of the North* (Toronto, 1957), p. 319.

revenue. Import duties levied at Montreal provided both provincial governments with their principal source of revenue. The rates could not be altered without the consent of both legislatures, and the total had to be divided in some ratio set by arbitration. The ability of the government of Upper Canada to expend moneys for internal improvement was therefore limited by the willingness of that of Lower Canada to raise import duties and agree on the way in which revenues should be divided.

The administrative inconveniences that resulted from the separation of the provinces, it can be argued, were the price that had to be paid for enabling Upper Canada to attract British immigrants and British capital, for neither of these necessary resources would have been attracted to the province had it not been free from the encumbrances of French land law and a French-dominated legislature. Whether the price was not too high may well be asked, for Upper Canada was not insulated from the conflicts of Lower Canada. Politically the provinces might be divided, but economically they were a unit. No constitutional act would obscure the fact that the St. Lawrence River bound the provinces together in a single commercial system. The whole development of Upper Canada hinged on free access to the ocean via the St. Lawrence and the port of Montreal. The division of the provinces divorced the merchants of Montreal from the political support they would otherwise have received from their commercial hinterland and hamstrung their efforts to improve the navigation of the river by government financing. Upper Canada alone could not remove or bypass the obstacles to navigation and her access to the ocean, for the most serious of these – the rapids in the St. Lawrence below Cornwall – were in Lower Canada. The merchants of Montreal could not overcome the inertia and hostility of the Lower Canada Assembly once the lines of political conflict between the French- and English-speaking elements in the province had been irrevocably drawn.

In any evaluation of the role of the state in the development of central Canada, the adverse repercussions of the division of the provinces by the Act of 1791 must be weighed against any positive aid that was provided later. The delay in undertaking improvement of the navigation of the St. Lawrence was not the only unfortunate result; there is also evidence that political separation impeded the flow of capital from Montreal to its commercial hinterland in Upper Canada.[4] Certainly in the construction of the Welland and Cornwall Canals, the two major improvements in navigation undertaken in Upper Canada before the provinces were reunited in 1840, Montreal capital played only a minor role. Montreal's relationship to its hinterland was subtly different from that of Boston or New York or Philadelphia.

Until 1821 the commercial life of Montreal was dominated by the fur trade. The trade in agricultural exports and manufactured imports that developed along with the expansion of settlement in Upper Canada and the American Old Northwest was at first merely a modest adjunct to the trade in furs. In 1821, however, the North West Company of Montreal was absorbed by the Hudson's Bay Company and within a few years the fur trade had deserted Montreal entirely, to be carried on thenceforth from bases on Hudson Bay and the Pacific coast. This reversal drove several of the leading commercial houses of Montreal into bankruptcy; those that survived did so by switching their capital into the entrepôt trade between England and the settlements of the interior. In future Montreal's commercial prosperity was to depend entirely on how effectively it could compete with the other metropolitan centres on the Atlantic seaboard and the Gulf of Mexico – Boston, New York, Philadelphia, Baltimore, and New Orleans – for the trade of hinterland. Success in this endeavour depended on the construction and maintenance of a low-cost transport route from the interior settlements to tidewater.[5]

Montreal's commercial aspirations extended far beyond the political boundaries of the British North American colonies. There were only three natural water gateways to the interior of the continent: the Mississippi, the St. Lawrence, and Hudson Bay. The St. Lawrence provided the shortest route from England to the interior, and Montreal commanded the St. Lawrence. During the French regime and until 1821 the natural advantages of the St. Lawrence route had enabled Montreal to monopolize

[4] Hugh G. J. Aitken, "A Note on the Capital Resources of Upper Canada," *Canadian Journal of Economics and Political Science*, 18:525-533 (November, 1952).

[5] See Donald G. Creighton, *The Commercial Empire of the St. Lawrence, 1760-1850* (Toronto: Ryerson Press, 1937); Easterbrook and Aitken, *op. cit.*, Chapters 12, 14, 16.

the whole fur trade of the trans-Appalachian region, save only what the Hudson's Bay Company could garner from its northern bases, and a trickle of low-quality pelts to New Orleans. The fur trade had now disappeared, thanks to the superior capital resources of the Hudson's Bay Company; but for Montreal the grand strategy of commercial expansion remained essentially unchanged. The objective of this strategy was the control of trade of the North American hinterland, including not only those areas north of the international boundary but also the rapidly growing settlements between the Alleghenies and the Mississippi – an ambitious design but, in an age as yet ignorant of the railroad, not unrealistic.

The expansion of settlement in Upper Canada was an important component in this overall strategy. The export and import trade of Upper Canada at least would pass down the St. Lawrence corridor and through the warehouses of Montreal, no matter what happened to the trade of the American Old Northwest. In encouraging immigration into Upper Canada, however, neither Montreal capital nor any government played a major role. Before 1812 most of the immigrants came from the United States – some of them "late loyalists," others frontier settlers and land speculators of the familiar type. After 1815 restrictions were placed on American immigration. For a few years immigration declined seriously, but in the early 1820's arrivals from Great Britain began to climb, stimulated by the low passage rates which the timber ships, returning empty, offered for the transatlantic voyage. Large numbers of immigrants arrived in each year from 1826 to 1832. Epidemics of cholera and disturbed political conditions in Canada caused a slump in arrivals in the middle and late 1830's but in the 1840's the influx again increased, stimulated by famine in Ireland. The population of Upper Canada, estimated at 157,923 in 1825, reached 791,000 in 1850, by which date most of the good agricultural land in the province had been occupied.[6]

Until 1825 not only Upper Canada but the whole basin of the

[6] Gilbert Patterson, *Land Settlement in Upper Canada, 1783-1840* (Toronto: Ontario Bureau of Archives, 1921); Robert L. Jones, *History of Agriculture in Ontario, 1613-1880* (Toronto: University of Toronto Press, 1946); Helen I. Cowan, *British Emigration to British North America, 1783-1837* (Toronto: University of Toronto Library, 1928).

lower Lakes, including the American Old Northwest, was tributary to Montreal. The natural advantages of the St. Lawrence River as an export-import route were sufficient to neutralize the international boundary, in an economic sense, despite the fact that the route was almost wholly unimproved (it was interrupted by geographical obstacles at Niagara and between Kingston and Montreal). When De Witt Clinton reminded the New York Legislature in 1819 that it cost a Buffalo merchant four times as much to send a ton of produce to Albany as it did to Montreal, he stated only what was common knowledge: the Old Northwest, the political development of which had been so carefully mapped by Congress in the Ordinance of 1787, was economically tributary to a British colony. Commercial control of the interior went to the cities that commanded the water gateways: Montreal and New Orleans.

Within a few years of its completion in 1825, the Erie Canal had completely undermined Montreal's position. New York now controlled a route to the interior which was far cheaper than the unimproved St. Lawrence. Montreal's commercial hinterland was now confined strictly to the area that could be protected by British and colonial tariffs, that is, to Upper Canada, an area in which expansion of settlement to the north and west would always be shut off by the vast wall of pre-Cambrian granite so that nothing like a continuous westward-moving frontier was possible. And even this limited hinterland could not be monopolized by Montreal, for Upper Canada farmers had always the option of shipping their produce across the Lakes to Buffalo or Oswego and thence to New York, whenever the price differential was larger than the American tariff. Montreal's commercial future depended on recapturing Upper Canada and invading the American midwest; and this in turn depended on the improvement of the St. Lawrence route. This was the challenge that faced the economy of central Canada. It was to call for a continuous series of capital expenditure for canals, harbours, and railroads which for the next half-century set the pace for Canadian development.

In these transport improvements the state played a major role. To be sure, the first Welland Canal, between Lakes Erie and Ontario, was constructed by a private company, but extensive financial aid was received from the provincial and imperial

198 - APPROACHES TO CANADIAN ECONOMIC HISTORY

governments.[7] In 1841 the private stockholders were bought out, and the canal was rebuilt and enlarged at government expense. The other canals on the St. Lawrence – the Cornwall, Williamsburg, Beauharnois, and Lachine – were constructed by the government of the province of Canada between 1841 and 1848, while the Rideau Canal between the Ottawa River and Lake Ontario was built by the British government.

Early railroad building followed a different pattern, in which the initial promotion and construction were generally the work of private entrepreneurs. But here, too, the government provided essential financial assistance.[8] The Guarantee Act, passed by the Canadian legislature in 1849, provided a government guarantee for half the bonds of any railroad over 75 miles in length, if half the line had already been built. In 1851 the provisions of this Act were restricted to the three major railroads then under construction – the Northern, Great Western, and St. Lawrence and Atlantic – and to roads forming part of the projected trunk line system from southwestern Ontario to the Maritime provinces. Financial aid extended by the provincial government under this Act and later acts to assist the Grand Trunk Railway totalled approximately $33,000,000. Considerable sums were also disbursed by municipal governments under the Municipal Loan Fund Act of 1852, a measure designed to make it easier for municipalities to float bond issues in London by pooling their credit in a single fund. The debt incurred under this Act, amounting to some $12,000,000, was assumed by the provincial government in 1859.

The extensive financial obligations undertaken by the Canadian provincial government in this period reflected partly the scarcity of large pools of private capital in Canada at this time and the difficulty experienced by Canadian canal and railroad companies in raising capital in London, and partly a conviction that the improvement of internal transportation was the key to the future development of the Canadian economy and therefore a suitable sphere of government action. In this connection it should be pointed out that the pattern of development in central Canada in this period can be called "expansionist" in

[7] Hugh G. J. Aitken, *The Welland Canal Company: A Study in Canadian Enterprise* (Cambridge: Harvard University Press, 1954).

[8] George P. deT. Glazebrook, *A History of Transportation in Canada* (Toronto: Ryerson Press, 1938; reprinted in the Carleton Library, 1964), Chapter 5; Easterbrook and Aitken, *op. cit.*, Chapter 14.

two quite different senses. In the first place, there was the expansion of settlement in Upper Canada, a process characterized by a moving frontier, large immigration, and a gradual extension of control over the province's resources. Terminal dates are of course rather arbitrary, but in general the process may be said to have begun around 1800 and to have spent its force by 1850. This is expansionist development in the sense most clearly indicated by Hoselitz's definition. Government action was relatively unimportant except in the initial separation of the province from its seaport (as already suggested, probably a net retarding influence), the provision of legal and administrative procedures for the orderly distribution of crown lands, and certain changes in tariff policy which may have assisted the growth of agricultural exports.

Whereas an expansionist pattern in this first sense may properly be contrasted with an "intrinsic" pattern of development, expansionism in the second sense, namely, the strenuous and continued efforts to improve the St. Lawrence route as a corridor for freight originating outside Canada, calls for some other contrast. This was the expansionism of a commercial economy, whose potentialities for development were conceived as lying not so much in production as in trade. For close parallels one must look to the Dutch economy in the seventeenth century or the economy of New England in the eighteenth. Certainly in central Canada in this period few conceived of the future of the economy as lying in either manufacturing or a continued expansion of agricultural settlement. The key to the development of central Canada was thought to lie in trade or, in other words, in attracting down the St. Lawrence corridor the exports and imports of the American midwest. This was the final goal of Montreal's commercial ambitions.

This conception of the role of central Canada as an artery of commerce persisted throughout the first half of the nineteenth century. Its influence was slow in dying, although by the late 1860's it was being challenged by the newer conception of expansion into the western prairies. The goal was never achieved – Montreal never captured more than a small fraction of the American midwestern trade – but its attainment was never so far distant as to kill all hope that, with a little more effort or ingenuity, it might be. A few cents cut from the costs of the through route, a canal here, a branch railroad there, a train ferry at Detroit, a railroad bridge at Montreal, and the prize might yet go to Montreal. Such at least was the vision; the Welland Canal, opened in 1829, the St. Lawrence canals, completed in 1848, the Grand Trunk Railway, with a line from Sarnia to Portland in 1859, and its competitor, the Great Western, linking Windsor, Toronto, and Hamilton in 1856, were attempts to translate the vision into reality.

The Western Prairies and the Pacific Coast

Developments on the western prairies and the Pacific coast in the period before Confederation can be summarized briefly. Until the discovery of gold in British Columbia in 1856, the dominant economic activity throughout this area was the fur trade.[9] The expansionist phase of the fur trade had ended in 1821, when the long struggle between Montreal and Hudson Bay was concluded by the absorption of the North West Company by the Hudson's Bay Company. By this date the area of exploitation had been extended from its original limits around the Great Lakes across the prairies, into the Mackenzie River basin, across the Cordilleras, and onto the Pacific slope. Throughout this area the trade was controlled by a single organization – the Hudson's Bay Company, operating under an exclusive charter received from the Crown in 1670.

The policy followed by the Company after 1821 was one of planned conservation. The destructive struggle with the North West Company had resulted in ruthless exploitation of fur resources, unsound trading practices, and uneconomic duplication of trading posts. Under the energetic direction of George Simpson, governor of the Company in North America, these wastes were largely eliminated by 1826. The organization of the trade was brought under tight centralized control and a policy of conserving fur resources in areas that had been over-trapped during the period of competition was instituted. Such a policy was possible only under conditions of monopoly.

In certain areas, however, the Company was still exposed to competition, and conservation policies could not be applied.

---

[9] Easterbrook and Aitken, *op. cit.*, Chapters 10, 15; Harold A. Innis, *The Fur Trade in Canada* (New Haven: Yale University Press, 1930), Chapter 4, and his Introduction in R. H. Fleming, ed. *Minutes of Council, Northern Department of Rupert Land, 1821-31* (Toronto: Champlain Society, 1940).

The first of these was on the Red River, near the present-day city of Winnipeg, where a small agricultural colony had been established by Lord Selkirk in 1812, partly in an attempt to relieve distress in the highlands of Scotland, partly as a tactical move designed to interfere with the North West Company's pemmican supplies. In general the attitude of the Hudson's Bay Company toward agricultural settlement was hostile, because the trade in fur could not survive in any area where settlers managed to gain a foothold. The colony on the Red River, which had been established under the auspices of the Company, was a partial exception; it served as a labour pool for the supply brigades and as a convenient location for retired or superfluous personnel. But even there the Company did all it could to hold agricultural expansion within bounds, to keep the colony economically and politically dependent on the Company, and above all to prevent the development of economic ties with the United States. This last objective led to continual friction, for American traders from Minneapolis, St. Paul, and Pembina regarded the colony as an important source of furs and a market for manufactures, and the possibility of American annexation of the colony, with the consent of a majority of its inhabitants, was never far distant. By 1865 it was clear that the Hudson's Bay Company could not restrain American expansionism much longer in this area and that the colony could not indefinitely be denied a measure of self-government.

On the Pacific coast, as on the Red River, the Company met the spearheads of American expansionism, adopted a policy of containment, and finally was compelled to make a strategic withdrawal. The movement of American settlers into the Oregon Territory was the dynamic factor in this instance. Immediately after 1821 the Company had begun intensive exploitation of the fur resources of the Columbia and Snake River area. The commercial prospects of this region were not at first considered encouraging. But the Columbia area was one of the last remaining untapped fur preserves, and furthermore the Company's operations there would make possible a "defence in depth" against American expansion. By the Convention of 1818, it will be remembered, Great Britain and the United States had agreed to joint occupancy of the Oregon Territory, but there was never very much doubt that the latter would in the end annex most if not all of the territory so occupied (although the exact boundary remained in dispute). The Company's policy therefore was to exhaust the fur resources of the area as quickly as possible and at the same time to restrain, by all peaceful means, the spread of American settlement. In Governor Simpson's words, the Columbia–Snake River area was "a rich preserve of beaver . . . which for political reasons we should endeavour to destroy as fast as possible."[10]

Throughout the period of joint occupancy, up to 1846, the Hudson's Bay Company functioned explicitly as the agent of the British government on the Pacific coast, maintaining close contact with the Foreign Office in London and executing (and to some degree forming) official British policy. The final withdrawal to the forty-ninth parallel was far from unexpected, and full preparations had been made. The entire policy of containment and planned withdrawal must be considered a success, for certainly a fur-trading organization never could have been expected to hold the line against the stream of American immigrants pouring in over the Oregon Trail. Almost completely unexpected, however, and a far greater shock to the Company's position, was the discovery of gold on the Fraser River in 1856-57. Against agricultural settlement the Company had fought a successful delaying action; a gold rush was something against which a fur-trading organization could not hope to stand. Nevertheless, the Company was then the sole representative of the British crown in the area and had to accept responsibility for the maintenance of law and order. To be sure, a colony had been formed on Vancouver Island in 1849, but its governor and the local governor of the Company were the same man, and its employees formed the majority of the population.

The influx of gold miners, many of them from California, completely transformed the situation and ended the rule of the Company. Sir James Douglas formally severed all connection with the Company upon accepting the governorship of the new colony of British Columbia in 1858, and in the same year the Company's exclusive trading rights on the mainland were revoked. By 1859 the population of British Columbia had risen to 17,000, excluding Indians. The problems that remained included finding some relatively secure economic base for the colony (especially after the decline of gold production in 1865), pre-

[10] Frederick Merk, ed. *Fur Trade and Empire: George Simpson's Journal, 1824-1829* (Cambridge: Harvard University Press, 1931), p. 40.

venting its annexation by the United States, and connecting the colony economically and politically with the other British colonies in North America – the province of Canada on the St. Lawrence, the isolated colony on the Red River, and the Maritime provinces. Confederation in 1870, with its promise of a transcontinental railroad within ten years, was expected to solve these problems.

It requires little imagination to regard the Hudson's Bay Company as playing the role of "the state" throughout western Canada from 1821 to 1870. The pattern of development encouraged by the Company in this period was the very antithesis of expansionist. In most of the Company's territory in western Canada the keynote of policy was conservation, and the overall goal was to preserve the area as a source of furs for the markets of Europe. Such a policy could not be followed in the Red River colony, the Oregon Territory, or British Columbia after the discovery of gold, and the Company was compelled to cede part of its control to other agencies. Forces of expansion, emanating principally from the United States, could not be contained by any defensive measures available to a fur-trading organization. Only by union with the other British colonies could the necessary resources be mobilized to hold the lines of defence against American expansionism and create a national transcontinental economy.

II. CONFEDERATION AND THE "NATIONAL POLICY"

During the 1840's Canadians had seen the economic structure of the British Empire dismembered piece by piece, as the Corn Laws and the Navigation Acts were repealed and the differential timber duties reduced to a nominal level. Cast off, as they felt, by the mother country, they had flirted briefly in the late 1840's with the idea of annexation to the United States. Later the idea of reciprocal free trade in natural products seemed to offer an acceptable substitute for annexation; and in 1854, with the signing of the Reciprocity Treaty, central Canada and the Maritimes seemed content to accept the status of an economic satellite of the United States. With the victory of the protectionist North in the Civil War and the abrogation of reciprocity in 1866, this prospect also disappeared. Unable to secure preferential tariffs from either Great Britain or the United States, Canadians finally and hesitatingly turned to the possibility of transcontinental federation. Political deadlock between the French and English factions in the legislature of central Canada provided one urgent stimulus to action. The possibility of agricultural expansion into the western prairies, already threatened by American encroachment, served as another.

The passing of the British North America Act in 1867, uniting under a federal legislature the provinces of Canada, Nova Scotia, and New Brunswick, paved the way for a federation of all the scattered colonies. This was accomplished by the purchase of Rupert's Land from the Hudson's Bay Company in 1868 and the admission of Manitoba, British Columbia, and Prince Edward Island as provinces in 1869-70. The political details of the confederation arrangements are familiar and need not be repeated here. The economic policies which were to strengthen the political skeleton are of prime importance for our purpose, however, for in these measures the role assigned to the state in the development of a transcontinental economic system becomes clearly evident. These measures are known to Canadian historians as the "National Policy," a term applied in a narrow sense to the system of protective tariffs adopted in 1878, and in a broad sense to the general strategy of defensive expansionism adopted by the new federal government after 1867.[11] In these measures we see for the first time a fading of the older conception of the St. Lawrence as an artery of trade for the midwest, and a dawning of the newer conception of transcontinental expansion.

At the heart of the National Policy was the determination to strengthen Canada's east-west axis by the construction of a transcontinental railroad. This would offset the increasing north-south pull of American markets and at the same time make possible agricultural expansion into the western prairies beyond the intervening barrier of the pre-Cambrian Shield. Central Canada – now the provinces of Ontario and Quebec – would become the manufacturing and financial centre of the new dominion, and by the transcontinental railroad manufactured goods could be sent west to the prairie market and agricultural

---

[11] Vernon C. Fowke, "The National Policy – Old and New," *Canadian Journal of Economics and Political Science*, 18:271-86 (August, 1952, and reprinted in this volume, pp. 237-58); and "National Policy and Western Development in North America," *Journal of Economic History*, 16:461-481 (December, 1956).

produce east to the St. Lawrence provinces and Europe. To this grand design all other aspects of the National Policy were to contribute. The protective tariff would check the importation of American manufactures and funnel freight of Canadian origin along the east-west artery. The retention by the federal government of the natural resources of the western provinces, to be administered "for the purposes of the dominion," made possible centralized direction of immigration and settlement policy and the use of land grants to facilitate railroad construction.[12]

Agricultural expansion in the west was basic to the whole design. Wheat was the new staple to which the transcontinental economy was geared. The first essential was construction of the transcontinental railroad. British Columbia had been assured in 1870 that such a road would be begun within two years of admission of that province to the dominion and completed within ten, but it soon became evident that this promise could not be carried out. The principal railroad then operating in Canada – the Grand Trunk – was willing to extend its system to the west only on condition that it could build south of the Great Lakes, through the traffic-producing territory of Michigan, Illinois, Wisconsin, and Minnesota, rather than across the barren lands north of Lake Superior. This was unacceptable to the federal government: Canada's transcontinental axis had to pass entirely through Canadian territory – it was unthinkable that the United States should be permitted to control any part of it. This stipulation excluded the Grand Trunk from participation in the transcontinental project for the time being. The federal government also received an offer to build the railroad from a group of capitalists ostensibly headed by Sir Hugh Allen, a prominent Canadian steamship operator, but actually representing the Northern Pacific group in the United States under the leadership of Jay Cooke. This offer also was refused on the ground that the railroad had to be under Canadian control. For a time no further offer was received. The federal government undertook preliminary surveys of the prairie and Rocky Mountain areas and began building a line south from Winnipeg to the United States boundary to connect with the St. Paul and Pacific. It began to

[12] Arthur S. Morton and Chester Martin, *History of Prairie Settlement and "Dominion Lands" Policy* (Toronto: Macmillan Company, 1938); Herbert Heaton, "Other Wests than Ours," *Journal of Economic History*, Vol. 6, Suppl. (1946), pp. 50-62.

appear as if the nationalistic insistence of the federal government on Canadian control and an all-Canadian route had indefinitely postponed construction of the transcontinental line.

The assistance offered by the federal government to any company contracting to construct the Pacific railroad had originally been generous and became increasingly so. During the first period of Canadian railroad construction, in the 1850's and 1860's, government aid had typically taken the form of guarantees of bonded debt, and the provincial governments had been in financial difficulties as a result. Remembering this experience, the federal House of Commons, in approving the resolution for a transcontinental railroad, stipulated that government assistance should consist of land grants and cash subsidies. In line with this policy the government in 1872 offered a grant of not more than 50 million acres and $30,000,000 in cash. This was later amended to $10,000 in cash and 20,000 acres per mile of track, and again amended in 1878 to a total grant of 100 million acres – according to estimates made at that time, about two-thirds of the total area suitable for agriculture and pasture in the prairie region.

It was not regarded as feasible or desirable that the government construct the railroad itself. This had already been tried on the Intercolonial Railway between Montreal and the Maritimes with dubious results, and this experience, combined with the slender and inexperienced administrative resources available to the federal government, may have made contracting with a private syndicate appear more attractive. Opinion differed, however, between the Liberal and the Conservative parties: the latter insisted on construction by private enterprise, while the former toyed with the idea of step-by-step government construction across the prairies westward from Lake Superior, with the line never advancing far beyond the area of settlement. Some measures were actually taken to put this latter conception into effect. It never caught the public imagination in the way the more ambitious project did; on the other hand, the possibility of relying on shipping on the Great Lakes for the connection between the prairies and central Canada was attractive from the cost viewpoint. It would have avoided the necessity of laying rails through the barren area of the pre-Cambrian Shield north of Lake Superior – the reason for the reluctance of private enterprise to accept the government's offer.

Not until 1880 did a group of private entrepreneurs come forward who both met the government's requirements as to national affiliation and possessed the resources and talent required for the task. Paradoxically, these men had made their reputation in railroading by their successful reorganization of a twice-bankrupt American road, the St. Paul and Pacific. Two of them, however, Norman W. Kittson and James J. Hill, were of Canadian origin, and their principal associate, Donald A. Smith, was a chief commissioner of the Hudson's Bay Company. The other members of the original Canadian Pacific Railway syndicate, George Stephen and Richard B. Angus, were president and general manager respectively of the Bank of Montreal. None of them was associated at this time with any major American Pacific railroad (although Hill later withdrew and devoted himself to expansion of the Great Northern system). These affiliations and the increasing evidence that it would be long before another offer would be made, if this were rejected, satisfied the government's insistence on Canadian control. The contract satisfied the government's insistence on Canadian control. The contract with the government was signed in October 1880 The C.P.R. was to receive $25,000,000 in cash and 25 million acres of land; all sections of the railroad already completed by the government were to be handed over to the Company without charge, and sections already under contract were to be completed at government expense; the construction of competing railroads between the C.P.R. line and the American boundary was to be prohibited for 20 years; and other concessions of minor importance were added.[13]

With this assistance and later emergency financial help from the government, highly competent management and construction techniques already perfected in the United States, the through line of the C.P.R. from the Pacific coast to central Canada was completed in 1885. Before World War I its facilities were supplemented by two additional transcontinental lines, the Canadian Northern and the Grand Trunk Pacific, both constructed with federal and provincial government assistance; the whole formed a transport network considerably in excess of the

[13] Easterbrook and Aitken, *op. cit.*, Chapter 18; Glazebrook, *op. cit.*, Chapters 6-11; Harold A. Innis, *A History of the Canadian Pacific Railway* (Toronto: McClelland and Stewart, 1923), Chapters 1-3; James B. Hedges, *The Federal Railway Land Subsidy Policy of Canada* (Cambridge: Harvard University Press, 1934).

country's needs at the time. Thus did the problem of excess capacity, which had plagued central Canada after the completion of the canals in 1848, reappear in the first half-century of the new dominion.[14] Defence against American economic expansion necessitated transcontinental expansion in Canada; but its costs, borne originally by the government but finally by consumers of high freight rates and a high tariff, made the maintenance of national economic unity extremely difficult.

Meanwhile in 1878 the second foundation stone of the National Policy, the protective tariff, had been firmly laid. Here the power of the state was applied directly to forging national economic unity and erecting bastions against American expansion. The question is not why Canada turned to protection, but why protectionism came so late. Lingering hopes for a renewal of reciprocity are part of the explanation; the strenuous opposition of the Maritime provinces, another part; and the weaknesses of domestic industries, a third. Yet as early as 1858 A. T. Galt, Minister of Finance, had stated the function that the protective tariff was to perform as a means of stimulating traffic along east-west transport routes and encouraging the development of manufacturing in central Canada. Not until two decades later, however, was Galt's policy of "incidental protection" converted into an admittedly protective tariff, and then only under the pressure of the major depression of 1876-79. By this date hopes for reciprocity had dwindled; railroad construction, by lowering transport costs, had increased the vulnerability of Canadian manufacturers to foreign competition; and a more rapid rate of industrialization was coming to be recognized as essential if the overall conception of a transcontinental national economy was to be realized. In addition, the emergent spirit of Canadian nationalism, already noticed in its effect on the planning of the Pacific railroad, fostered a conviction that the nation must reduce its dependence on outside conditions by developing its own sources of manufactured goods.

Between the protective tariff and railroad construction in the west there was a close connection. When the tariff kept out foreign goods and encouraged manufacturing within Canada,

[14] Harold A. Innis, "Unused Capacity as a Factor in Canadian Economic History" and "The Political Implications of Unused Capacity," in *Political Economy in the Modern State* (Toronto: Ryerson Press, 1946), pp. 201-228.

prospects of freight on the east-west transport artery and an adequate level of earnings by the railroads were improved. When goods entered over the tariff barrier, customs revenue could be applied to meet railroad deficits and support the debt incurred by the state for western expansion. This was the philosophy first stated by Galt in 1858. It underlay the whole National Policy program from 1878 onward and was not seriously modified until the onset of depression in the 1930's.

Both in tariff legislation and railroad construction the state after Confederation assumed an active role in promoting Canadian development. The responsibility for creating a national economy and the conditions in which it could survive lay with the state. Extending far beyond the basic constitutional framework of government, internal security, and justice, this responsibility embraced also the construction, in partnership with private enterprise, of the east-west transport system; the erection of tariff barriers behind which an industrial complex could develop; and the promotion of immigration and a flow of investment capital from Europe. The overall objective of the policy was to make possible the maintenance of Canadian political sovereignty over the territory north of the American boundary: that is to say, to prevent absorption by the United States and to build a nation state that could guide its own economic destiny, and assert its independence from both the mother country and the United States, within limits no more restrictive than those necessarily applicable to an economy dependent on staple exports for its overseas earnings. Sustaining the policy was an emerging sense of national identity and purpose, analogous to the sense of manifest destiny which had coloured the expansion of the United States.

Whether the initiative in stating and implementing this policy is to be ascribed to private enterprise or to the state is a question on which opinions will differ. The assertion that the state in the form of the federal government was merely acting as the agent or instrument of private economic interests – the same interests that had worked to achieve Confederation, the sale of the Hudson's Bay Company's lands, and the chartering of a Pacific railroad – could probably be supported. But if the distinction between "the state" and "private enterprise" is to be retained (as applied to Canada, the distinction often seems artificial), the weight of the evidence seems to indicate a contrary view.

The secular decisions at this stage of Canadian development were made by governmental bodies; the basic developmental policies to be pursued were stated by government officials; and the implementation of these policies involved the exercise of initiative by governments.

III. THE TWENTIETH CENTURY

I propose to use three aspects of Canadian development in the twentieth century to exemplify the ways in which the state has continued to influence the rate and direction of economic change: the fostering of the pulp and paper industry in central Canada; the construction of the St. Lawrence Seaway; and the control of the oil and natural gas industries.

Pulp and Paper Industry

The primary instrument of state assistance to the pulp and paper industry has been the tariff. Exploitation of Canada's forest resources for the manufacture of paper and allied products dates from the introduction of the first methods of manufacturing paper from wood pulp in the 1860's. Today the manufacture of pulp and paper is Canada's leading industry, whether the criterion be value of output, capital invested, or wages paid. The spectacular growth of the industry has been due partly to Canada's rich resources of timber and hydro-electric power; partly to a mass demand for cheap newsprint in the United States; and partly to a consistent government policy of discouraging the export of raw pulpwood and encouraging its manufacture into newsprint and pulp within Canada.

Government policy concerning the industry has centred in a systematic attempt to induce pulp and paper mills to migrate toward the source of the raw material.[15] Basic to the success of this policy has been the secularly buoyant demand for newsprint in the United States and the progressive exhaustion of its pulp-wood supplies. By 1900 it was clear that American newsprint consumers could no longer rely exclusively on domestic supplies unless they were prepared to pay considerably higher prices.

---

[15] John A. Guthrie, *The Newsprint Paper Industry: An Economic Analysis* (Cambridge: Harvard University Press, 1941). See also "The Pulp and Paper Industry in Canada," *Canada Year Book, 1952-53* (Ottawa, 1953), pp. 467-475.

The cheapest and most convenient source of imports was Canada, where costs of production were generally somewhat lower and the danger of exhaustion of supplies was more remote. Canadian provincial governments controlled by far the largest proportion of the country's forest resources and recognized at an early date that they were in an unusually strong position to reinforce the pull of cheap raw materials by imposing duties on the export of the unmanufactured product. The implementation of this policy clearly involved the risk of retaliatory action by the United States, not to mention the hostility of politically influential newspaper chains, but was nevertheless pushed through with surprising consistency. British Columbia led the way in 1891 by prohibiting the export of timber cut on crown lands; Ontario followed with a similar prohibition in 1902; and Quebec in 1900 imposed in effect an export duty on pulpwood by reducing the fees on timber cut on crown lands by about one third on condition that the wood was manufactured within the province. Within the next thirteen years the remaining provinces adopted similar legislation.

The ability of the United States to retaliate by imposing higher import duties on Canadian pulpwood was limited by the reluctance of newspaper publishers to pay the cost in higher newsprint prices. A compromise passed by the American Congress in 1909 reduced the tariff on the lowest grade of paper to three sixteenths of one cent, on condition that the exporting country removed all restrictions on pulpwood exports. When the Canadian provincial governments refused to reverse their policy, a retaliatory duty of $2 per ton was imposed on Canadian paper. The burden of this tariff, however, was borne principally by American newspapers, whose demand for Canadian newsprint was highly inelastic. Pressure for the removal of the retaliatory duty resulted in a provision for free admission of Canadian newsprint in the proposed reciprocity agreements of 1911, which, however, were rejected by Canada after having been accepted by the Congress. In 1913 American newsprint consumers finally won a conclusive victory in the Underwood Act which provided for the free admission of newsprint paper valued at not more than 2.5 cents a pound, together with mechanical and chemical pulp. Subsequent increases in the price of Canadian newsprint have been met by raising the

2.5-cent limit, so that since 1913 Canadian pulp and newsprint have entered the American market free of duty.

The history of the Canadian newsprint industry is important principally as the only instance wherein Canadian producers and governments have been able to exploit a quasi-monopoly in the marketing of a staple product. The embargoes and restrictions on the export of the raw material admittedly would not have been effective without the underlying locational pull of cheap pulpwood and hydro-electric power. Nevertheless, the determination of the provincial governments to exploit fully the strong bargaining position given them by control of pulpwood supplies undoubtedly hastened the migration of newsprint production to Canada.

St. Lawrence Seaway

We have noted the construction of a system of canals between Lake Erie and tidewater at Montreal as the dominant theme of economic development in central Canada from 1815 to 1849; the inspiration of this series of transportation improvements by a vision of central Canada as an artery of commerce between the American midwest and Europe; and the slow transition from this phase of development to that of transcontinental economic expansion.

The recent construction of the St. Lawrence Seaway constitutes an emphatic restatement of the older theme. The conception of a transport system that would permit ocean-going vessels to go to the heart of the continent by way of the St. Lawrence was never abandoned; rather, it was cast into the shadow by the newer and more practicable proposals for a transcontinental railroad. Now, with the opening of new resources of iron ore in Quebec and Labrador and the pressure of new conceptions of continental defence strategy, the original idea has been translated into action. The agreement to build the Seaway signed by the Canadian and United States governments in 1954 was, in essence, the realization of an idea that has influenced Canadian development for more than 150 years.[16]

---

[16] Easterbrook and Aitken, *op. cit.*, Chapter 21; "The St. Lawrence Seaway," *Canada Year Book, 1955*; pp. 885-88; U. S. Senate, 83rd Congress, 2nd Session, Document No. 165, *The St. Lawrence Seaway Manual* (1955); Royal Institute of International Affairs, *Springs of Canadian Power* (London, 1953).

Since 1841, when the private interests that had constructed the first Welland Canal were bought out by the Canadian government, the completion, maintenance, and enlargement of the St. Lawrence–Great Lakes canal system has been regarded as a responsibility of the state. By the early years of the twentieth century, successive governments had brought into existence a chain of canals between Montreal and Lake Ontario giving a minimum depth of 14 feet throughout, and deepened the ship channel below Montreal to 35 feet. Between Lake Ontario and Lake Erie the Welland Canal, which had been deepened between 1873 and 1887 to 14 feet, was already proving inadequate for the traffic; and construction of the Welland Ship Canal, to provide a channel 25 feet deep, was begun in 1913. Between Lake Huron and Lake Superior, at Sault Ste. Marie, an American canal had been built in 1853-55; and a similar canal on the Canadian side was begun in 1887 and completed in 1895.

Despite these successive enlargements and extensions, it was still impossible for the large steamships that operated on the Great Lakes to pass down the St. Lawrence to Montreal, and for the ocean-going vessels that touched at Montreal to proceed to the Lakes. The bottleneck of the 14-foot St. Lawrence canals meant that water-borne traffic had to be transshipped twice between the Atlantic and Lake Erie – at Montreal and at Kingston. By enlarging and deepening these canals, Canada could have overcome this bottleneck without help from the United States. Its participation was highly desirable, however: better use could be made of the natural channel of the St. Lawrence (the international boundary over much of the distance above Montreal), and the heavy financial burden involved could be borne more easily by two federal governments than by one.

Early attempts to find some formula for joint construction proved abortive. Commissions of inquiry appointed by both federal governments in 1895 produced no positive results. In 1921 the International Joint Commission, which was established in 1909 to arbitrate questions involving the boundary waters of Canada and the United States, recommended joint construction, but no decision to implement the recommendation followed. Later inquiries and recommendations produced the St. Lawrence Deep Waterway Treaty of 1932, which was rejected by the U.S. Senate in 1934, when opposition came principally from the eastern seaboard states and American railroad interests. The Great Lakes–St. Lawrence Agreement of 1941 also failed to secure congressional approval. Faced with the prospect of indefinite further delay, the Canadian parliament in 1951 created the St. Lawrence Seaway Authority, a crown corporation authorized to construct a deep waterway between Montreal and Lake Erie either wholly within Canada or in conjunction with the United States if Congress finally agreed to participate.

Meanwhile the economic significance of the project had been completely transformed. Originally regarded almost exclusively as a transport improvement, it was increasingly considered as a power resource. Industry in central Canada has developed on an energy base made up partly of bituminous coal imported from the United States and partly of hydro-electricity generated within Canada. In 1945 Canada had a total installed hydro-electric turbine capacity of just over 10.25 million horsepower, of which 5.9 million was in Quebec, and 2.7 million in Ontario. Of the total energy consumed in Ontario and Quebec in 1943, water power contributed 37.8 per cent, and coal 52.6 per cent.[17] The rate of industrial development in these two provinces since 1900 has hinged on the rate of hydro-electric power development. The principal power sites have been at Niagara Falls and on the St. Lawrence and the rivers of its drainage system.

Recognition of the importance of the St. Lawrence Seaway project as a potential source of cheap hydro-electric power dates from the late 1920's, when it was partly responsible for a marked growth of interest in the project in the United States. Several large American corporations were keenly interested in the hydro-electric aspects and threw their influence on the side of American participation, in alliance with the Lake cities, such as Cleveland, Detroit, and Chicago, which had always been attracted by the transportation aspects. Not until after World War II, however, did hydro-electric power become the critical factor. In Ontario, where primary load requirements had increased by 88 per cent from 1945 to 1954, an acute shortage of electric power was imminent. In New York State and Quebec it seemed certain that existing generating facilities would be

[17] *Report of the Royal Commission on Coal*, W. F. Carr, chairman (Ottawa, 1947); John H. Dales, "Fuel, Power, and Industrial Development in Central Canada," *American Economic Review*, 43:181-198 (May, 1953).

inadequate within a few years. In these circumstances the development of the last remaining water power resource of any significance in the area – the St. Lawrence River – became imperative. The total power available from the St. Lawrence between Lake Ontario and Montreal is estimated at 5.4 million horsepower; of this, only some 1.4 million had been developed at that time.

Joint participation in the development of hydro-electric power proved easier to secure than in the navigation improvements. In 1951 the Canadian government announced its intention of proceeding independently with the Seaway development. Negotiations on the electric power aspects continued, however, and in 1952 parallel petitions for approval of joint development of the hydro-electric facilities were submitted to the International Joint Commission by the two federal governments. Permission was readily obtained and plans were approved, with Canada still accepting exclusive responsibility for the construction and operation of the deep waterway.

In the meantime another major development had taken place: the opening of the iron ore deposits in the Quebec-Labrador region.[18] The existence of large iron ore deposits in this region was known to Canadian geologists as early as 1893, but the impossibility of extracting the ore and delivering it to Canadian and American smelters, with the existing transportation facilities, at prices competitive with Mesabi and Newfoundland shipments prevented commercial devlopment. Commercial surveying did not begin until 1938. Between 1942 and 1944 extensive surveys revealed very large deposits of low-phosphorus iron ore, and by 1944 reserves of more than 300 million tons of high-grade ore had been proved. The first shipments of ore from this development were made in July 1954. Production was geared initially to a rate of 10 million tons a year. Meanwhile plans were pushed for a similar development of iron ore deposits in Ungava, north of the original discoveries.

The capital for the initial exploration of the Quebec-Labrador deposits came from Canadian mining interests. The

[18] Royal Institute of International Affairs, *op. cit.*; Dominion Bureau of Statistics, *Chronological Record of Canadian Mining Events from 1604 to 1947 and Historical Tables of Mineral Production in Canada* (Ottawa, 1948); "Canada's Mineral Resources," *Canada Year Book, 1954*, pp. 482-506; "The Iron-Ore Resources of the Quebec-Labrador Region," *Canada Year Book, 1950*, pp. 505-12.

Iron Ore Company of Canada, however, the concern now working the deposits, represents a union of Canadian and American capital; five leading American steel corporations are large shareholders. Development of the Steep Rock deposits in Ontario has been similarly financed and organized. In both cases American interest stems largely from the approaching exhaustion of the higher-grade deposits in the Mesabi range. It has been estimated that by 1960 Canada will be one of the world's largest exporters of iron ore. Despite the rapid growth of the Canadian steel industry, it seems clear that most of Canada's iron ore exports will go to the United States.

The relevance of these developments for the St. Lawrence Seaway project is obvious. If iron ore from the Quebec-Labrador deposits was to be transported to the iron and steel producing centres south of Lake Erie, radical improvements in the existing canal facilities were indispensable. The increased cost of reliance on either the existing 14-foot canals or rail transportation would have destroyed the economic feasibility of the scheme.

Opinions can reasonably differ as to whether the United States would have agreed to participate in construction of the Seaway in the absence of these developments in Quebec-Labrador. It seems, however, that the prospect of obtaining competitively priced high-grade iron ore from Canada was a major influence producing American participation after almost three-quarters of a century. Estimates by the U.S. Department of Commerce, made shortly before construction of the Seaway began, put the total annual traffic between the Gulf of St. Lawrence and Lake Erie at not less than 57 million tons. Of this total, it was estimated that iron ore from Ungava and Quebec-Labrador would contribute 30 million tons. Economic and strategic considerations combined to emphasize the importance of a transportation improvement that would open this massive new resource to the industrial centres of the American heartland. In the absence of these considerations the bills for American participation in the Seaway that were finally approved by Congress in May 1954 might well have had a much rougher passage.

The construction of the Seaway represents, as has been said, the realization of one of the most persistent aspirations of Canadian development. The role of the state has included not only the obvious responsibility for construction and finance but also that of exerting diplomatic and political pressure on the government of an interested, friendly, but disappointingly uncooperative power – the United States. This is of course a developmental function that no other organization could have performed. It may be emphasized, however, that the Seaway illustrates Canada's changing satellitic role vis-à-vis the United States and Great Britain. The Seaway was originally thought of as a means of enabling Canada to capture and control part of the transit trade between Great Britain and the American midwest: the idea reflected Canada's role as an economic satellite of the former. In its final form, however, the Seaway is largely facilitating the export of Canadian raw materials to the United States. The St. Lawrence River, throughout most of Canada's history a symbol of a dominant orientation toward Europe, now serves to strengthen Canada's economic ties to the United States.

Oil and Natural Gas Industries

Until the years immediately after World War II, Canada's production of crude oil and natural gas was insignificant. Oil fields in the southwestern peninsula of Ontario, between Lake Huron and Lake Erie, were first exploited in 1858 and reached a peak production of 795,030 barrels in 1890. Thereafter they were important only for local supplies of natural gas. The Turner Valley oil field in Alberta was discovered in 1914 and by 1930 was producing one million barrels a year. Canada remained, however, a large net importer of crude oil.

During World War II the speed of exploitation for new Canadian resources of crude oil increased markedly, partly as a result of tax concessions by the federal government, and new discoveries were made in areas distant from the Turner Valley field. In 1946 the Conrad and Taber oil fields near Lethbridge, Alberta, came into production, and were followed within a few months by the Lloydminster field lying across the Alberta and Saskatchewan boundary. These finds, important in themselves, dwindled into relative insignificance with the opening of the Leduc field near Edmonton in 1947, which was of first-class importance. A period of intensive surveying followed, with American oil companies playing a leading role, and within a few years several major oil deposits were discovered. Most of the early discoveries lay within Alberta, but by the end of 1953 the area of active exploration included Saskatchewan and Manitoba, the northeast corner of British Columbia, and the Northwest Territories south and west of Great Slave Lake. By 1954 proven recoverable reserves had reached a total of 2.5 billion barrels. Total crude oil production rose from about 8.5 million barrels in 1945 to 29 million in 1950 and almost 61 million in 1952.

These discoveries represent completely new development potentials for the Canadian economy, and their full significance will not be apparent for some time.[19] They have posed certain problems of national policy, which have centred around the construction of pipelines for the export of natural gas to the United States. There is a certain understandable suspicion in Canada concerning the extent to which its resources have come to be owned and controlled by American corporations. It is recognized, on the one hand, that American capital is important in stimulating and supporting Canadian development, particularly since this capital tends to flow into the more venturesome and speculative projects.[20] On the other hand, Canadians, who have only recently attained full independence and self-determination in the political sense, are reluctant to see their natural resources – the full richness of which is just coming to be appreciated – exploited in the interests of industries of another country. This sentiment is particularly marked in the case of the spectacular new developments of resources such as prairie oil and gas.

In comparison with the Texas and California fields, for example, the original oil and natural gas discoveries in the western prairies suffered from one major handicap: their distance from water transportation. The markets that Alberta oil and gas could reasonably expect to serve were in central Canada and on the Pacific coast. To reach these markets the construction of pipelines was indispensable. In the case of oil pipelines no

[19] Easterbrook and Aitken, *op. cit.*, Chapter 21; "Canadian Crude Petroleum Situation," *Canada Year Book, 1954*, pp. 540-44; The Royal Bank of Canada, "Oil and Gas Bulletins"; Royal Institute of International Affairs, *op. cit.*

[20] Easterbrook and Aitken, *op. cit.*, Chapter 23; A. E. Safarian and E. B. Carty, "Foreign Financing of Canadian Investment in the Post-war Period," in American Statistical Association, *Proceedings of the Business and Economic Statistics Section . . . , September 10-13, 1954*, pp. 72-79.

government restriction of any importance was encountered. In 1949 the Interprovincial Pipeline Company, a subsidiary of Imperial Oil, began construction of a line from Edmonton to Superior, Wisconsin. This was completed late in 1950, and construction was begun on an extension south of Lake Superior, across the Mackinac Straits to Sarnia, Ontario. During 1952 an additional line was constructed to carry refined products from Sarnia to Toronto. In 1952 construction also began on the Transmountain Pipeline from Edmonton to British Columbia, and plans were made for its continuation to new refineries to be constructed in the state of Washington. No Canadian government interposed any obstacle to the construction of these pipelines, despite the fact that part of the eastern line ran through the United States and the western was planned to terminate at refineries in that country.

A very different policy was adopted concerning natural gas pipelines. At an early date the government of Alberta announced that exports of natural gas from the province would not be permitted until reserves had been proved adequate to provide a 30-year supply for the province and to meet the prior needs of the dominion. The first of these two conditions was satisfied in 1951, and in 1951-52 government approval was given for two pipelines to carry natural gas to the United States: one to serve the Anaconda Copper Company's plant at Butte, Montana, the other to serve industrial consumers in Portland and Seattle. With these two exceptions, the export of natural gas to the United States was prohibited. A statement by the Canadian federal government in March 1953 made clear the policy: no permits would be granted for the export of natural gas until the government was convinced that there could be no economic use, present or future, for that gas in Canada.

Literally interpreted, this statement implied an indefinite embargo on natural gas exports. By what rational process could a government ever convince itself that there could be no present or future use for a major energy resource within Canada? In practice, however, the government's policy has been interpreted to mean that sanction will not be given for the export of natural gas to the United States until a pipeline has been constructed entirely through Canadian territory to convey natural gas from the prairie provinces to Ontario and Quebec.

The apparent discrepancy between the Canadian federal government's policy concerning oil and uranium, completely free export of which has been permitted, and that concerning natural gas and hydro-electric power, export of which has been permitted only under very unusual conditions, has occasioned considerable critical comment. The rationale of the policy is that hydro-electric power and natural gas are considered sources of industrial energy, whereas oil and uranium are not. Access to cheap Canadian industrial power will be restricted to plants within the political boundaries of Canada; it is hoped that this inducement, combined with the protective tariff, will encourage manufacturing within Canada and counteract the tendency for Canadian resources to be exported in their natural condition to industries in the United States.

The analogy with the policies successfully pursued in the case of the newsprint industry is obvious, as is the analogy with the federal government's insistence in the 1860's and 1870's on the construction of a transcontinental railroad entirely within Canadian territory. In all three cases the state has acted to offset the pull of markets in the United States. The state has interpreted its function as the preservation of national economic unity along an east-west axis as a defence against the divisive north-south pull of the United States.

IV. CONCLUSION

In broad outline the story of Canadian economic development until the early years of the twentieth century is a simple one. The rate and direction of developments have been determined by the economic characteristics of a number of staple products: fish, fur, timber, wheat, and minerals. Each of these staples has posed its own particular problems of organization and marketing, and each has cast Canada in the role of an economic satellite and marginal supplier of other more advanced areas, chiefly Great Britain and the United States. Fish, fur, wheat, and square timber kept Canada within the economic orbit of the former; lumber, metallic minerals, and more recently crude oil drew Canada closer to the latter. Great Britain and the United States have also been the principal sources of capital imports and of the immigrant labour supply.

The role of the state in Canadian development has been that of facilitating the production and export of these staple products.

This has involved two major functions: planning and to some extent financing the improvement of the internal transport system; and maintaining pressure on other governments to secure more favourable terms for the marketing of Canadian exports. In relation to economic development, the escape from colonial status and the achievement of political independence in Canada have meant primarily the creation of a political apparatus competent to perform these functions effectively.

The course of economic development in Canada can be called expansionist, but with two qualifications. First, expansionist tendencies have not infrequently been frustrated, partly by changes in demand conditions in foreign markets, partly by the temporary inability or unwillingness of the state to underwrite the capital investments required for further growth. Second, expansionism in Canada has been largely induced rather than autonomous. It has been contingent on state action both in the political integration of widely separated regional economies and in the provision of indispensable transport facilities. Throughout Canadian development expansionism has been defensive in character. It has been part of a general strategy of containing the expansionism of the stronger and more aggressive economy of the United States and preserving a distinct political sovereignty over the territory north of the present international boundary. Each phase of expansion in Canada has been a tactical move designed to forestall, counteract, or restrain the northward extension of American economic and political influence. Primary responsibility for maintaining and strengthening this policy of defensive expansionism has fallen on the state.

The Economic Background
of the Rebellions of 1837

D. G. CREIGHTON

I

In 1837, the Canadian economy was subjected both to the stresses inherent in its own unstable organization and to the strains of a temporary financial and commercial panic. The last crucial stages of economic change and social conflict within the Canadas coincided unhappily with a general financial collapse in the English-speaking world; and the coincidence of these two crises produced a violent exaggeration of all the weaknesses to which the Canadas had been subject. From the very beginning the trades of the St. Lawrence had suffered from persistent fluctuations and shared a common instability; but to these chronic infirmities were now added all the special difficulties of the shift from the trades in fur and timber to the production of wheat and flour. The discord between trade and agriculture, the disagreement between the organization of the commercial system and the demands of the rural communities, had reached the last stages of their development. While the old trading system of the St. Lawrence was expressed politically in the commercial state, the agricultural interest had become vociferously articulate in the reform parties of both provinces. And these economic contradictions and social conflicts were evidently nearing their climax at the very moment when the financial panic broke in England and the United States.

The special maladjustments and conflicts which distracted the Canadas in the 1830's were, in the main, the product of that

Source: D. G. Creighton, "The Economic Background of the Rebellions of Eighteen Thirty-Seven," *Canadian Journal of Economics and Political Science*, Vol. 3, No. 3, August 1937, pp. 322-34. Reprinted by permission of the author and publishers. This paper was read at a joint session of the Canadian Historical Association and the Canadian Political Science Association.

great series of changes which began with the advent of the
loyalists in 1783 and closed approximately at the middle of the
nineteenth century. In the past the Canadas had formed a
commercial state. The St. Lawrence, in the minds of those who
controlled and directed its activities, was a great imperial trade
route rather than a centre of populous North American communities. The northern trading system, which was the obsession
of successive generations of Canadians, was vast in its extent. It
bound Canada to the metropolis of the Empire; and in North
America it had inspired a continental strategy which extended
far beyond the international boundary between Canada and the
United States. The first tiny settlements on the St. Lawrence and
the lower lakes were dwarfed by a commercial system which
was largely independent of their existence and which, in fact as
well as in design, transcended their limited activities. The fur
trade, which had been hostile to the last against settlement, had
ended only in 1821. The trade in square timber which succeeded
it was, in a large measure, carried on independently of the new
settlers. And it was not until the early 1830's, which witnessed
an enormous increase in the exports of wheat, that the value of
the wood shipped to Great Britain was exceeded by the total
value of all other commodities exported from Quebec to British
ports.[1]

Yet within this commercial system, which had been organized to serve interests largely different and far more ambitious
than their own, the little agricultural settlements developed, at
first slowly and then with rapidly increasing speed. The French
Canadians, on the St. Lawrence and the Richelieu, and the
loyalists on the edges of the lower lakes, had been steadily
recruited by the advent of American frontiersmen and assisted
British immigrants; but in the late 1820's there began the first
great spontaneous migration of British peoples to Canada. It
arose out of the chronic, only occasionally relieved, depression
which in Great Britain followed the conclusion of the Napoleonic wars; and its volume, the calamities which were associated
with it, and the amazing consequences to which it led, aston-
ished, dismayed, and delighted the people of the Canadas. The
population of the two puny provinces shot upward. In 1827, the
number of inhabitants in Upper Canada had been estimated at
177,174; in 1837 the total population of the province was

[1] *Montreal Gazette*, March 5, 1836.

reckoned at 397,489.[2] The immigrants, who were packed away
in the holds of the empty timber ships returning to Canada,
helped to solve some of the problems of the heavy one-way
traffic in the timber trade.[3] But this temporary balance was
purchased at the price of a more important disequilibrium. The
shift from the older trades to agriculture was accelerated; the
demand for new markets and a better transportation system
grew more imperative; and the intensification of the agricultural
interest created new requirements, new commitments, and new
problems which unsettled the bases of the old commercial state.

These weaknesses and maladjustments in the Canadian
economy were reflected in the social disputes and political
rivalries which in 1837 approached their climax. Though it
drew inspiration from various different sources and assumed a
variety of forms, the conflict in the Canadas was in large
measure a social conflict which grew naturally out of the
disturbed economy of the St. Lawrence. The governing class –
the "Chateau Clique" in Quebec, the "Family Compact" in
Upper Canada – was less a company of blood-relations than it
was a fraternal union of merchants, professional men, and
bureaucrats; and the Reformers of both provinces, though they
are usually described in terms of their racial characteristics,
their religious affiliations, or their political principles, drew their
main support from the countryside and took on all the characteristics of a rural protest movement. The controversy between
agriculture and commerce, farm-lands and trade-routes, North
American parochialism and the old colonial system, had already
found expression, a quarter-century before, in the quarrels between the merchants of Quebec and Montreal and the peasants
and lawyers of Lower Canada; and now, as the migration
peopled the western part of Upper Canada, the conflict was
extended territorially and deepened in import. In Lower Canada,
which was still devoted to subsistence agriculture and to a
debased feudal land-holding system, the peasants' opposition to
commercialism was deepened by a touch of archaic misunder-
standing and hatred. But in both provinces there was the same
struggle against the institutions and programs of the commercial

[2] *Census of Canada*, 1870-71, vol. IV, pp. 83-171.
[3] H. A. Innis, "Unused Capacity as a Factor in Canadian Economic
History" (*Canadian Journal of Economics and Political Science*, vol.
II, Feb., 1936, pp. 1-15).

class and the same dislike of commercial wealth and privilege. As it developed, the conflict aroused political loyalties and expressed itself in rival political philosophies; but action continued, nevertheless, to hover around definitely economic issues. In the new age, with the emergence of the agricultural west, the merchants were determined to solve the few problems which seemed alone to delay the realization of their enormous opportunities; and it was their design to build a new international commercial empire upon the bases of the staples, wheat and timber, to reconstruct a second unity of the St. Lawrence upon the ruins of the fur-trading unity of the past. They intended, by free trade, to encourage the import of American products into Canada: they hoped, through the old mercantile system, to obtain protected imperial markets for the exports from Quebec; and the St. Lawrence trading system which connected these far markets and these distant depots of supply was to be improved by canals, harbours, and ship channels, developed by banks, commercial companies, and government enterprises, and peopled by a horde of immigrants from the British Isles. The governing class was the party of commercialism, the party which hungered to develop the country by private capital and public expenditure; and in support of a commercial system which was at once transatlantic and transcontinental, the merchants were prepared to break by force through feudal law, antiquated custom, and rural inertia.

The Radicals in both provinces viewed all this with indifference, suspicion, or positive hostility. It was true that among the frontiersmen of Upper Canada these feelings of apathy and distrust were not so instinctive nor so obstinate as they were among the peasants, priests, and lawyers of the lower province; but in time, as the political engagement became general, the attitude of the Upper Canadian Radicals came to differ comparatively little from that of the Patriotes of Montreal. It was the belief of the leaders of both parties that the institutions, projects, and expenditures desired by the commercial class would either divert attention from rural needs, or would impose intolerable burdens and inflict definite injuries upon the countryside. While in Lower Canada the Assembly absolutely refused to begin its part of the St. Lawrence Canals, the Radicals in Toronto criticized Upper Canada's share of the undertaking and repeatedly attacked the Welland Canal.[4] "My opinion is," declared Perry, in opposing a new provincial loan in aid of the Welland Canal, "you would injure the agricultural interest of Upper Canada . . . and I never will give up the interest of Upper Canada for the Welland canal. Is all to be subservient to this great Moloch, and everything bow to it?"[5]

It was the same with all the other institutions and projects characteristic of the commercial state. The Canada Company was attacked by the Radicals in Toronto with only less ferocity than the British American Land Company was denounced at Quebec; and Papineau's hostility to the Montreal Bank was paralleled by Mackenzie's relentless pursuit of the Bank of Upper Canada. "Let them run to the Banks," declared Papineau, anticipating Mackenzie's language of a few years later, "and, in the terms of the law, demand gold and silver for their notes. . . . The most efficacious and the most immediate means which the Canadians have to protect themselves against the fury of their enemies, is to attack them in their dearest parts – their pockets – in their strongest entrenchments, the Banks."[6] The Radicals engineered a run on the Lower Canadian banks in 1834 and on the Bank of Upper Canada in 1837. While Papineau and his followers criticized the timber trade and questioned the timber preference, the Radicals in Upper Canada campaigned against the free-trade policy by which American products were admitted into Canada for export by the St. Lawrence.[7] Fundamentally, Mackenzie was hostile to the whole Canadian commercial system; and he was even anxious that the United States should be requested to permit Upper Canada to import and export via the New York route.[8] These economic disputes were not unimportant, subsidiary, and ephemeral. They were continually agitated; they helped to bring on the deadlock in the Canadas and to prepare both parties for politics of force; and when in 1834 the Montreal Tories formed their Constitutional Association, they solemnly declared that they would no longer "submit to the domination of a party averse to Emigration, to commerce,

[4] *Montreal Gazette*, March 6, 1834; *The Patriot*, Feb. 14, 1834; *Colonial Advocate*, Feb. 17, 1831.
[5] *The Patriot*, Feb. 4, 1834.
[6] *Montreal Gazette*, Dec. 11, 1834.
[7] *Colonial Advocate*, Oct. 2, 1834; *Belleville Intelligencer*, quoted in *The Patriot*, Nov. 28, 1834.
[8] *The Patriot*, Jan. 19, 1836.

to internal improvements, and to all those interests which may
be regarded as British . . .".[9]

The economic changes which disturbed the old commercial
system, the economic issues which embittered the conflict between the farmers and the governing class, were not, however,
the only material factors in the political situation of 1837. The
weaknesses and inconsistencies in the Canadian economy, the
growing animosities among the Canadian people, were paralleled by the increasing financial instability of the commercial
state. Its obligations and resources, which ought to have been
consolidated, were, in fact, divided between the two provinces;
and these two quarrelling provinces could not combine in joint
policies or share a common burden. The disputes over the
division of the customs revenue collected at Quebec were settled
periodically, though with difficulty; but though it was possible
to divide income, it was impossible to equalize expenditure.
The problem of the canals was as indivisible as the river they
were designed to improve; but while Lower Canada obstinately
refused to begin its part of the construction, the upper province
optimistically took up its own heavier share of the task. The
province, which was financially stronger, made no attempt to
use its borrowing power, while the financially weaker province
proceeded to acquire a large debt. Before 1837, Upper Canada
had exhausted the market for provincial bonds within the
Canadas and had placed debentures to the value of £600,000
(stg.) with Baring Brothers and Thomas Wilson & Co. in
England.[10] Upper Canada was beggaring itself in an effort to
finish a great undertaking which, in fact, could never be completed without the co-operation of the unwilling sister province.
So long as the two colonies remained divided, their finances
would continue unstable and the canalization project would
remain incomplete. The Constitutional Act, which had divided
the old province of Quebec into Upper and Lower Canada, had
proved an impossible political vehicle for the commercial state.
The energy and extravagance of Upper Canada and the inertia
and parsimony of the lower province had been left in isolation,

[9] Public Archives of Canada, *Secretary of State's Papers*, Lower Canada, Molson *et al.* to Craig, Nov. 22, 1834.
[10] *Journal of the House of Assembly of Upper Canada*, 1835, appendix,
vol. I, no. 17.

to contradict rather than to modify each other; and both provinces, in their different but equally potent ways, contributed to the gradual unsettlement of the whole political machine.

By 1837, the weaknesses of the Canadian economy, the instability of Canadian public finance, and the clashes among the Canadian people had reached a state of ominous exaggeration and strain. Under the grinding stresses imposed upon it, the whole northern system was visibly disintegrating; and the forces which divided and distracted it were now expressed in militant political parties. The quarrel between feudal and frontier agriculture on the one hand and commerce and bureaucracy on the other, approached the final limits of exasperation; and the inexorably approaching crisis was welcomed as much as it was feared. Both parties in both provinces began to declare their anticipation of a civil war; and as the meetings, parades, and disturbances grew in number, as the speeches and riotings increased steadily in violence, each party found in the other's menaces the justification for its own appeal to force.

II

At this point, when the crisis in the Canadas approached its climax, the financial and commercial panic broke in the British-American world. The Canadian provinces could no more hope to escape the economic influences of Great Britain and the United States than they could expect to avoid the distempers inherent in their own economic and social condition. Canada, a dependent, staple-producing country, tied by innumerable and binding connections to the markets of Great Britain and the United States, had always followed the ups and down of their trade cycle with submissive fidelity; and in 1836 the British-American business world was travelling through the last erratic stages of a speculative prosperity towards an imminent financial collapse. In Great Britain the first great railway boom approached its climax. In the United States, the proliferation of banks and the vast expansion of credit had encouraged a quickening activity which invaded every sphere of business life;[11] and the unappeasable demand for canals, banks, railways, and other public improvements goaded the American legisla-

[11] W. B. Smith and A. H. Cole, *Fluctuations in American Business, 1790-1860* (Cambridge, 1935), sec. 2.

tures into more ambitious projects and more lavish expenditures.[12]

In the Canadas, though the prosperity of the early 1830's followed its usual course, it was checked by the embarrassments peculiar to a staple-producing country. The exports of timber and sawn lumber, encouraged by gradually rising prices in the United Kingdom, had reached a new peak in 1835 and 1836.[13] During the early thirties, the exports of wheat and flour had enormously increased. But in 1834-5 the glut forced down prices; the British corn laws for a while prevented the import of Canadian wheat into the United Kingdom; and the Canadas were forced to turn to their second and inferior market in the other British North American provinces and the West Indies.[14] It was in 1836 that this over-supply was succeeded by a disastrous scarcity which affected the entire continent. The crop failed in Lower Canada, as well as in the northwestern American states; Upper Canada disposed of its supply in the United States, despite the tariff; and before the end of the year North America had already begun to import breadstuffs from Europe.[15] Flour, which had opened at 28s. 6d. a barrel in Montreal at the beginning of 1836, reached 42s. 6d. in December and 60s. in February, 1837;[16] and the savage bread riots which occurred in New York City were paralleled by the distress and real destitution which visited the French-Canadian parishes on the lower St. Lawrence.[17] The boom still continued, but it had grown excessive, erratic, and onerous. And in these exciting circumstances the Upper Canadian Legislature met during the winter and held one of the last prosperity sessions of that period in North America.

It was at this moment that the financial crisis was precipitated in the United States. For years the Democratic administration under President Jackson had fought the Bank of the United States and had unsettled the money market by the transference of federal banking deposits and the distribution of federal

[12] R. C. McGrane, *The Panic of 1837* (Chicago, 1924), pp. 1-42.
[13] *Quebec Gazette*, Feb. 13, 1836; Jan. 25, 1837.
[14] F. W. Burton, "Wheat in Canadian History" (*Canadian Journal of Economics and Political Science*, vol. III, May, 1937, pp. 210-7).
[15] *The Constitution*, Jan. 18, 1837.
[16] *Ibid.*, Dec. 19, 1836; Feb. 13, 1837.
[17] Public Archives of Canada, *Series Q*, vol. 237-1, pp. 28-31, Gosford to Glenelg, May 6, 1837.

surplus revenues. In the summer of 1836, the administration concluded its long warfare with the bankers and the speculators by issuing the notorious specie circular, which abruptly demanded specie in payment of public lands. In the meantime, decline and retrenchment had already begun in England. The London and Liverpool houses, burdened with vast credits in America, were vulnerable before the demands of the English bankers; and their embarrassments, promptly transferred to their clients in America, helped to upset the toppling speculative prosperity in the United States.[18] In March and April the commercial houses began to fail in New York and Philadephia; and on May 10, 1837, the New York banks suspended specie payments.

In these spring months of 1837, the crisis in Canadian affairs was set in motion irresistibly. In March, when the financial crash was imminent in the United States, the British parliament endorsed Lord John Russell's provocative resolutions; and this blunt imperial manifesto broke the political deadlock in the Canadas, and blasted the hopes of the Canadian Radicals. By a sinister coincidence, the impact of the American financial panic was timed to accompany the impact of British political interference; and under this combined blow the northern commercial state fell apart into its conflicting interests, its rival groups, its antipathies and fears and hatreds. While in Lower Canada the Radicals organized a new series of protest meetings and denounced the policies of Great Britain in shriller tones, the whole populace of both provinces awaited breathlessly for the effects of the financial panic. The bankers feared for the safety of their institutions; the bureaucrats in Upper Canada were worried for the security of their London loans; the merchants in both provinces grew suddenly apprehensive for the continuance of their loans and discounts; and the farmers and mechanics, agitated by the tirades of Mackenzie and the other Radicals, were frantic to exchange their bank notes for coin.

The next few weeks were filled with confused activity and angry agitation. In Lower Canada, the banks could suspend specie payments without forfeiting their charters; and the Montreal bankers, with the entire support of the commercial community, abruptly stopped the payment of gold and silver on

18 McGrane, *Panic of 1837*, pp. 40-42.

May 17.[19] So far as was possible the lower province had avoided a severe contraction of credit; but Upper Canada was faced not only with the problem of financial stringency but also with a probable crisis in provincial finance. Of the loan of £600,000 negotiated in London, £147,000 still remained to the credit of the province.[20] Upper Canada had drawn its bills of exchange for part of the balance; and if the houses of Baring Brothers and Thomas Wilson failed, as so many feared they would, then the protestation of the bills would inevitably entail the bankruptcy of the province. W. H. Draper, a member of the executive, was hurriedly dispatched to England;[21] the receiver-general, J. H. Dunn, followed him at once, gloomily warning the executive to curtail the expenditure for public works as much as possible.[22] The stoppage of the canals on the St. Lawrence was generally expected: it was feared by some that the idle labourers might riot.[23] And in those first anxious days of May, the crisis in public finance created even more consternation than the approaching contraction of credit. No doubt the merchants complacently expected the suspension of specie payments, while the Radicals denounced it in advance. But they made, both of them, a lamentable miscalculation. They had forgotten their unforgettable governor, Sir Francis Bond Head.

Sir Francis, who had dramatically entered Upper Canadian politics in January, 1836, was an operatic character whose chief political attributes were a talent for rhetoric and a relish for grandiloquent gestures and heroic attitudes. In his romantic imagination the quarrel of local interests in Upper Canada had been transformed into a grand conflict of political loyalties and moral principles. He attacked Canadian radicalism like a paladin on a crusade: he won the election of 1836 with the impetuosity of a cavalry leader. And until that fatal May of 1837, the gratitude and admiration of the Tories could scarcely be contained within the straining limits of the English language. It was the banking crisis which disillusioned the merchants. It was then that the governor revealed his purpose to act in character as an officer and a gentleman with most undiscrim-

[19] *Montreal Transcript*, May 18, 1837.
[20] *Q*, vol. 396-4, pp. 567-71, Head to Glenelg, April 23, 1837.
[21] *Ibid.*, pp. 620-3, Head to Glenelg, April 29, 1837.
[22] Public Archives of Canada, *Upper Canada Sundries*, Dunn to civil secretary, May 5, 1837.
[23] *Ibid.*, Macaulay to Hagerman, n.d.

inating consistency. He decided the question of specie payments on a point of honour and dismissed the problem of credit on a moral principle. In his opinion, the banks were morally bound to pay out specie on demand, as they had promised to do. "Upper Canada," he declared, "would prefer to lose its specie rather than its character. The principle of Monarchy is honour and from that principle the Lieutenant Governor will never consent to depart."[24]

The Bank of Upper Canada, influenced by these inspiring sentiments as well as by the more mundane consideration of its connection with government, decided, on May 17, to continue specie payments.[25] For a few days the Tory papers talked admiringly of these decisions; and the *Patriot* asserted that the Bank of Upper Canada's "bold and gallant bearing . . . appeals with irresistible force to all the better feelings of man." But in a few days it began to be appreciated that the continuance of specie payments would in all probability entail a discontinuance of discounts, loans, and "banking accommodation" in general. Sir Francis Bond Head might talk with gentlemanly distaste about "accommodation" as if the term were a kind of deplorable coinage of the American vernacular; but the business of Upper Canada was largely based on credit; and before the end of May the merchants were urging the immediate suspension of specie payments and a special session of the Legislature to deal with the financial crisis.[26]

The governor, whose popularity in commercial circles had descended almost as rapidly as it had arisen, yielded uneasily; and towards the end of June the provincial parliament met. The Assembly, which was dominated by the commercial element, was determined to break the contraction of credit; and its plan, as finally drafted in legislation, was to suspend specie payments and make bank notes and provincial debentures legal tender.[27] To the governor it was unthinkable that borrowers should be encouraged at the expense of the honour of monarchy and the character of Upper Canada; and, with the help of the Council, he defeated the Assembly's bill and forced through another which permitted the banks to suspend only at the discretion of

[24] *Q*, vol. 397-1, pp. 154-79, Head to Glenelg, May 23, 1837.
[25] *The Patriot*, May 19, 1837.
[26] *Ibid.*, May 30, 1837.
[27] *Ibid.*, June 20, 27, 1837.

the Governor-in-Council.[28] The protests of the dismissed Assembly were followed by a general indignant clamour when Sir Francis published the terms upon which he would permit the banks to suspend; but the governor remained firm, with that steadfastness which invariably afforded him such lively gratification. The Bank of Upper Canada practically gave up its ordinary commercial discounting, abandoned the local shopkeepers to their misfortunes, and waxed fat upon the profitable business of foreign exchange.[29] When the anxious merchants and traders of Upper Canada turned from their own banks to the institutions of the lower province, they were met with adamant, if regretful, refusals. "We all here feel the importance of affording facilities to the purchase of wheat in Up: Can:", wrote Peter McGill of the Montreal Bank to W. H. Merritt, " – but the Banks of L: Can: cannot give them, and but few Individual Houses will be able to supply their Correspondents with the needful from hence, because their Capital is already in Up: Canada Credits, and nothing coming down. – In my day such times have never been experienced."[30]

During that summer and autumn, the financial stringency continued to embarrass the ordinary commercial activities of the province and to hold up the ambitious program of public works. Though Messrs. Glyn, Halifax & Co. took up the bills of exchange drawn by Upper Canada upon the bankrupt house of Wilson & Co., there was no more money forthcoming from London at the moment;[31] and during the summer the commissioners for the St. Lawrence canals struggled on under great difficulties and by September were £10,000 in debt to the contractors.[32] The commercial slump, which throughout the United States had followed swiftly on the heels of the financial panic, was accentuated in Upper Canada by the unrelieved and exceptional contraction of credit; and during the spring and summer the whole carrying trade of the St. Lawrence dried up

[28] Q, vol. 397-2, pp. 475-9, Head to Glenelg, July 12, 1837.
[29] Adam Shortt, *The History of Canadian Currency, Banking and Exchange*, part 8: *Crisis and Resumption* (Toronto, 1902), pp. 5-8.
[30] Public Archives of Canada, *Merritt Papers*, vol. IV, McGill, to Merritt, Aug. 16, 1837.
[31] Public Archives of Canada, *Series G*, vol. 291, Glenelg to Head, July 22, 1837.
[32] *Journal of the House of Assembly of Upper Canada*, 1837-8, appendix, pp. 154-56.

to a mere lethargic trickle of business. Late in May it was reported in Montreal that business in Upper Canada was almost at a standstill;[33] and for weeks there was little or no produce coming down the river to the ports. "An excessive languor," wrote one reporter in Montreal, "pervades nearly every branch of commerce, and our streets have, so far as relates to business, the appearance they are wont to exhibit on a close holiday or a Sunday."[34] In a long, dull, weary season, which showed only a slight flurry of activity towards the end of September, the volume of the timber trade was alone comparable to that of the previous year. There were no exports of wheat, for Montreal was steadily importing from Europe until late in the autumn; the export of flour had declined by over a half; and the value of free goods and goods paying the general 2½ per cent duty, imported from Great Britain, had fallen off over £500,000 from the high of £1,800,000 established in the previous year.[35]

A winter of high prices and real scarcity, a winter which distressed the villages of Upper Canada and brought some parishes in the lower province to the verge of starvation, was followed by an abrupt financial panic and a commercial slump. The credit with the local shopkeeper, the summer employment on the public works, were more than ever necessary to a frontier population distressed by want and suffering; but the public works were half suspended, the commercial operations of the country were distracted, and, while the two provinces waited anxiously for the harvest, Montreal continued to import expensive European wheat. "During my residence in this province," wrote one observer to Sir Francis Bond Head, "I have not witnessed so much absolute distress at any period as now exists."[36] Mackenzie told the farmers that "the days of brass money and wooden shoes" were returning; and the agricultural and commercial depression was put forward as one of the main reasons for the summoning of the Reform Convention at Toronto.[37] It was in this atmosphere that the crises in the Canadas reached its paroxysm. It was through these oppressive scenes that the two provinces travelled on the last stages of their journey towards armed revolt.

[33] *Montreal Courier*, quoted in *Quebec Gazette*, May 26, 1837.
[34] *Montreal Transcript*, Aug. 12, 1837.
[35] *Quebec Gazette*, Jan. 25, 1837; March 20, 1838.
[36] *Upper Canada Sundries*, May 8, 1837.
[37] *The Constitution*, Aug. 9, Sept. 26, Oct. 4, 1837.

III

In this explosive coincidence the two crises came together. The quarrel between commerce and agriculture had reached the limits of aggravation at the time of a financial panic and a commercial depression; and at the moment when Great Britain had exhausted its remedies and its patience, the Canadian Radicals and loyalists were ready to resort to force. In these last few weeks before the rebellions, when men were actively preparing for a struggle or dubiously regretting its approach, their final decisions, of necessity, were determined by a multitude of factors. The old loyalty to empire, the acceptance of custom, the fear of disorder, and the respect due to the solemn warnings of the Roman Catholic and Methodist Churches – all these served to arrest angry men and to curb disaffected communities. But those who did enter eagerly or drift irresolutely into revolt were moved by the old, simple animosities; and to them it was probably of more importance to right economic wrongs and attain vague social objectives than it was to win political independence from Great Britain. In one important sense the rebellious were simply the final expression of the conflict between agrarianism and commercialism, between feudal and frontier agriculture and the commercial state; and when Mackenzie in the Draft Constitution for the state of Upper Canada outlawed incorporated trading companies and declared that labour was the only means of creating wealth, he expressed, in final theoretical form, the old attack upon the institutions, powers, and privileges of the commercial state.[38]

As the inevitable end approached, the constitutionalists in both provinces were recruited by increasing numbers of neutrals and repentant Reformers; but to the end it was the magistrates, bureaucrats, and merchants who were the most determined defenders of the existing order. The towns were the strongholds of the governing class; the most powerful and unified of its various divisions was the commercial group; and it was appropriately enough in Montreal, the focus of the whole trading system of the St. Lawrence, that Toryism found its most

[38] R. A. MacKay, "The Political Ideas of William Lyon Mackenzie" (*Canadian Journal of Economics and Political Science*, vol. III, Feb., 1937, pp. 1-22).

provocative and violent expression.[39] Even in the countryside, as Mackenzie found in his famous crusade "north of the ridges," the local shopkeepers were active and their influence apparent. "It is most provoking," wrote Mackenzie, "to see the Storekeepers continually against Reform. . . . At Equesing who were more indefatigable in raising recruits to put down the voice of the town and its 5,000 inhabitants than Squires O'Reilly, Brown, Chalmers, and Chisholm, and Mr. Salisbury, all Merchants? So it was in Caledon, Albion, and Chinquacosy."[40]

In the end the rebellions were precipitated by the riot in Montreal, which occurred on November 6.[41] In the fighting which raged up and down the city streets, the Patriotes were defeated. Their hold upon the town was broken; their leaders were forced from it in retreat. And when the executive, misinterpreting their equivocal movements, sought to effect the arrest of the principal Radical leaders, the countryside was driven to resistance and the resistance swelled into armed revolt. It was a rebellion without a plan of operations and without a chance of success. Disorganized, sporadic, hopeless, the *jacqueries* drew towards their inevitable conclusion; and the defeat of the Lower Canadian peasantry was the prelude to the defeat of the frontiersmen in the west. Though there were Reformers in Toronto, they were not prepared to test their strength in the city as the Patriotes of Montreal had done. The rebellion was directed, as it had to be, from the countryside against the town. It was Mackenzie, Lount, Matthews, Anderson, and the farmers from "north of the ridges" who made the last effort of that protest movement which had always been so largely agrarian in character. And in the mistakes and absurdities of the revolt can be seen the tragic inexpertness of a farming population which had little but its angry sense of injustice to sustain it.

---

[39] *Quebec Gazette*, Oct. 25, 1837; *Montreal Herald*, quoted in *The Patriot*, Nov. 7, 1837.
[40] *The Constitution*, Aug. 16, 1837.
[41] *Q*, vol. 239-2, p. 372, Wetherall to Gosford, n.d.; *The Patriot*, Nov. 14, 1837.

The National Policy—Old and New

V. C. FOWKE

I

The Canadian system of protective tariffs has long been known as the National Policy. Professor Underhill describes this designation as a stroke of genius.[1] We gladly bow to the judgment of Professor Underhill, with one proviso, namely, that we may regard this description of the protective system as a stroke of *political* genius, and not necessarily as genius in the abstract and absolute. No one can doubt the political sagacity of the appeal made to the Canadian electorate in 1878 which claimed for the Conservatives an exclusive proprietary right to the formula for nation building. In retrospect we can readily recognize the contribution of the protective system to the creation of the Canadian nation. We are, nevertheless, by no means able to identify the protective system as the only nation-building instrument of the past century of Canadian history.

Professor Underhill does not, of course, attribute to Sir John A. Macdonald the genius which he finds implicit in the designation of the protective system as the National Policy. This indicates the exercise of proper caution, for it is clear that Macdonald displayed little originality in thus describing the tariff system. Many years ago Professor O. D. Skelton stressed the evolutionary nature of the concept of the National Policy and referred to the term as "a phrase which Rose devised,

Source: V. C. Fowke, "The National Policy — Old and New," *Canadian Journal of Economics and Political Science*, Vol. 18, No. 3, August 1952, pp. 271-86. Reprinted by permission of the author and publishers.

This paper was presented at the annual meeting of the Canadian Political Science Association in Quebec, June 5, 1952.

[1] F. H. Underhill "Political Parties and Ideas" in George W. Brown, ed., *Canada* (Berkeley and Toronto, 1950), p. 336.

Hincks stamped with his approval, and Macdonald made current."[2]

The Canadian protective system itself was more evolutionary in its origins than is commonly suggested, and Macdonald merits rather less credit, or blame, depending on the point of view, than is traditionally accorded him for the formulation of the system. The name of Sir Alexander T. Galt is inseparably linked with the introduction and defence of the policy of "incidental protection" in the pre-Confederation years. The first tariff of the dominion government contained a 10 per cent tax on bread-stuffs and Sir Francis Hincks instituted a considerable range of protective duties in 1870. All these were removed within a short time under pressure from the Maritimes. The Liberal ministers of the 1870's were able to argue convincingly that their tariff schedules were designed exclusively for revenue, and half way through their term of office they specifically rejected the protective principle. In 1878, while still in the Opposition, Macdonald proposed[3] the adoption of a National Policy involving a "judicious readjustment of the Tariff." The proposal became an election pledge and this pledge at least was honoured. The "judicious readjustment" of the tariff was begun by the Conservatives in 1879 and was furthered throughout their term of office. The Liberals who fell heir to the protective system in 1896 preserved it faithfully in fact, while denouncing it vigorously in the true oral tradition of the Manchester School.

It matters little, however, who gets the credit or blame for Canada's protective system. The term "National Policy," with its origins in historical accident, has become firmly rooted in Canadian thought and expression. The capitalized phrase will undoubtedly long continue to designate the historic milestone at which Canadians abandoned the idea of tariffs for revenue only, discarded even the euphemism, "incidental protection," and deliberately set foot on the pathway marked "Protection."

[2] Cf. Skelton "General Economic History, 1867-1912" in Adam Shortt and A. G. Doughty, eds., *Canada and Its Provinces* (Toronto, 1914), IX, 146.

[3] On March 7, 1878, as the House moved to go into committee on the Budget, Macdonald introduced the resolution: "That this House is of the opinion that the welfare of Canada requires the adoption of a National Policy, which, by a judicious readjustment of the Tariff, will benefit and foster the agricultural, the mining, the manufacturing and other interests of the Dominion. . . ." See *Canada, House of Commons Debates*, 1878, p. 854.

Firmly rooted though it be, the usage is unfortunate. National policy ordinarily means simply the policy of a national government. As such, it is as comprehensive as the field of constitutional competence of the government in question. No nation would tolerate a national government which for generations had but a single policy, the imposition and maintenance of protective tariffs. Canadians know well that tariff protection has been but one of a countless number of the policies of their national government.

However, governmental policies, although innumerable, are not of equal importance, and when the policies are grouped according to their collective purposes gradations of importance can readily be distinguished. Some groups clearly relate to minor or temporary, others to fundamental and persistent governmental aims. The decision of the Canadian government to foster the industrialization of the country by means of tariff protection was a policy of the latter type. It was of considerable importance in itself, and was one of a group of policies directed toward the accomplishment of the most basic and persistent of the purposes of the Canadian government. In this regard it must be emphasized that the national policy predated the creation of a national government in Canada and envisaged the establishment of such a government as one of its indispensable instruments.

In its broadest aspects the national policy was the design of creating a national political and economic unit in the British North America of a century ago. The areas of which the national unit was to be formed comprised some or all of the geographically dispersed British provinces, colonies, and territories in North America. These areas were to be united politically and economically in order that they might cope more effectively with alterations in imperial and continental relationships which rendered existing arrangements obsolete, if not wholly inadequate.

Political and economic alterations, both internal and external, indicated an urgent necessity for changes in the relationships among British North American territories after 1850. Politically there was the domestic stalemate over representation as well as the increasing reluctance of the imperial government to maintain the burden of colonial defence. A national government would, so it was reasoned, end the statemate of representation and assume responsibility for defence on a national scale. As for the economic forces which contributed to the national policy, the decision to create and develop an integrated national economy arose from the disappearance of not one but two more highly regarded alternatives – imperial economic integration and continental economic integration. The removal of imperial preferences at mid-century not only ended hope of extending imperial integration immediately, but also seriously reduced existing integration. The Reciprocity Treaty with the United States in the 1850's restored temporarily to full vigour the persistent belief among British North American economic groups that continental integration offered a practicable and preferable alternative to close imperial economic relationships. This belief waned in proportion as the conviction grew that the Americans would not renew the treaty upon the expiration of its first term. The collapse in quick succession of hopes for closer imperial co-operation and for a satisfactory measure of continental interdependence made increasingly urgent the need for a national economy as the one adequate instrument of economic survival.

In turning from continental to national economic objectives the Anglo-Canadians on the St. Lawrence abandoned, or appeared to abandon, a quest of long duration. From the days of its first European occupation the St. Lawrence had been regarded as a continental trade route, a means of access to the trade and commerce of the continental interior. The French fur traders had fully utilized its potentialities, and after the fall of Quebec the Anglo-Americans, with headquarters in Montreal, had extended the fur-trading empire to its continental limits on the Arctic and the Pacific. This empire ended after a struggle with the absorption of the North West Company by the Hudson's Bay Company in 1821. Significantly enough, American national expansion contributed to the decline of the North West Company by an increasing curtailment of that company's southern and southwestern fields of operation.

Agricultural expansion westward from the Atlantic coastal regions was the most important element in North American economic life in the decades after the Revolutionary War. The expansion was continental, and the settlers, whether from the older settlements to the eastward or from across the Atlantic, paid scant attention to the invisible political boundary which was projected across the continent by American national aspirations. Agricultural expansion meant the expansion of trade and commerce in agricultural products and in agricultural supply. Potash and wheat were among the first agricultural products to move commercially from the continental agricultural frontier. Between 1790 and 1850 new agricultural settlement enveloped the lower Great Lakes in its westward advance and provided North America with its first wheat economy and with its first staple-producing agricultural community.

Two points must be emphasized in regard to this agricultural expansion. First, the agricultural commerce which succeeded the fur trade in northeastern North America at the turn of the nineteenth century was potentially continental rather than national in scope. Second, the merchants in Canada regarded the St. Lawrence as the "natural" trade route for the agricultural commerce of the continental interior as they had for the continental fur trade. At the very least, so they reasoned, they should be able to share in the agricultural trade of the American frontier regardless of political boundaries. Such reasoning was challenged, and effectively challenged, by American merchants. Public and private developmental expenditures improved the American trade route – the Hudson-Mohawk river system – first by the construction of the Erie Barge Canal and later by the construction of a system of railways joining the American Middle West with New York. Efforts to make good the Canadian claims in this matter fostered the construction of St. Lawrence canals and the Grand Trunk Railway, burdened provincial governments with heavy debts, and created serious constitutional difficulties. Persistent failure to establish competitive competence in relation to American interests left only the difficult choice between accepting defeat and instituting some boldly imaginative new method of attack upon the problem.

The British colonies which created the American national state in the late eighteenth century did so after they had willingly withdrawn from the imperial economic framework. The national government was assigned the duties of defence and economic development which the colonies would no longer entrust to Britain and which, as individual states, they could not perform themselves. In contrast to the American colonies of the late eighteenth century, Britain's American colonies of the mid-nineteenth century did not willingly repudiate imperial economic integration or imperial defence. Rather they found themselves, contrary to their wishes, substantially rejected by Britain on both counts. At the same time their problems of economic development and defence were greatly intensified by the outstanding success which had attended the efforts of the American nation. In Confederation they created the framework of a second national state in northern North America on the familiar principle of fighting fire with fire.

A number of important steps were necessary to the creation of a national economic and political unit in British American territory. The first of these was the creation of a national constitution; the main outlines as well as much of the detail of such a constitution were provided in the British North America Act of 1867. Development and integration were the indispensable and inseparable economic requirements, both resting heavily upon the possibility of facilitating trade among the existing colonies or provinces. Confederation removed the tariff barriers which had existed between the separate units, and the British North America Act provided for the completion of an intercolonial railway by the national government. Further development, however, would require the exploitation of some vast new area of resources, and attention was thus directed even before Confederation to the uncertain prospects in Rupert's Land and in the Pacific colonies. These prospects, doubtful though they were, might be developed by the national government if ownership and transportation facilities could be assured. Thus the liquidation of the Hudson's Bay Company's proprietorship in Rupert's Land and the construction of a Pacific railway were seriously considered, but no decision was reached in the years before 1867.

In this paper the term "national policy" includes collectively the group of policies sketched in outline above which were designed to transform the British North American territories of the mid-nineteenth century into a political and economic unit. As thus defined the national policy was fully formulated in its main outlines prior to Confederation, which was its major constitutional instrument. Other instruments of the national policy, such as western lands and settlement, the Pacific railway design, and the system of protective tariffs, took shape in the decades after 1867. No one of these policies, but all of them together, merit the title "national policy."

II

Economic and political historians may come to regard the century from 1825 to 1925 or 1930 as the era of the first Canadian national policy. It may appear unrealistic to hint at the beginnings of the national policy more than half a century before the phrase became current with the introduction of the protective system, and over forty years before the British North America Act provided the constitutional framework for a Canadian nation. Nevertheless the historical perspective is necessary. The economic objective of the first national policy was the creation of a new frontier of investment opportunities for the commercial and financial interests of the St. Lawrence area. By the middle of the nineteenth century these interests thought of investment opportunities in terms of large-scale agricultural immigration and settlement, which in the experience of both Canada, and the United States during the second quarter of the nineteenth century had been associated with great increases in economic opportunities.

Altogether there have been less than half a dozen periods of sustained and relatively substantial immigration into territory which now forms the Dominion of Canada. The twenty-five or thirty years following the middle 1820's was one of these. During this period some hundreds of thousands of immigrants came to eastern Canada and transformed the forest wilderness into the flourishing agricultural and commercial community of pre-Confederation Upper Canada. The immigrants of that generation came unsolicited and on many occasions unwanted. Their emigration was sponsored by the old land rather than the new. Yet the economic benefits which resulted from their coming and which spread with unequal but generally expansive force throughout the total economy were unmistakable. Eventually there was established the firm conviction that agricultural occupation of new territory provided a wide range of opportunity for the profitable employment of capital, labour, and entrepreneurship. The near-cessation of immigration and the exhaustion of the Canadian agricultural frontier in the late 1850's coincided with economic recession. The obvious inference was that the failure of agricultural expansion was largely responsible for the general economic distress.

The concept investment or real-capital formation as used by

the present-day monetary theorist provides a helpful instrument for the demonstration of the economic implications of large-scale immigration and agricultural settlement. The self-sufficient agricultural pioneer who serves as the stereotype in Canadian history of the folk-lore variety would, by definition, possess no economic significance for other segments of the community. But the Canadian agricultural pioneer was by no means self-sufficient. He bought the services of ocean and land transportation companies, of innkeepers, of the legal and medical profession, of the processors of timber, grains, and livestock, and of credit-granting agencies. He bought equipment, clothing, and even provisions sold if not manufactured in the market centres which grew up as the indispensable counterpart of the agricultural frontier. The establishment of an agricultural community with its urban, commercial complement requires real-capital formation on a scale dependent on a number of variables, among the more important of which is the extent of the agricultural economy which is being created. The second quarter of the nineteenth century was important for the first national policy because the experiences of that period convincingly demonstrated in Canada the investment opportunities of an agricultural frontier.

It was suggested above that the first national policy occupied a century of Canadian history, the span of years from 1825 to 1925 or 1930. Whether the earlier years should be included, some may doubt; but all agree on the remainder of the period. The economic and political life of the last half of the nineteenth century in Canada was focused upon the formulation of the national policy and the establishment of constitutional, economic, and physical facilities to render that policy effective. The policy was not fully implemented until after 1900, but its economic effects at least had been achieved by 1930. There is no intention of elaborating in detail in this paper the historical incidents of any part of the century under review. Reference has already been made to the significant economic developments of the decades before 1850 and to the various steps taken after 1850 toward the establishment of a new agricultural frontier and a Canadian nation. Apart from a brief consideration of the fulfilment phase, and particularly its end, little more can be said about the first national policy in this paper.

A few points, however, require further elaboration. It has

already been pointed out that the national policy pre-dated Confederation and the creation of a national government in Canada. The federal government which was established by the British North America Act was the creature of the national policy and its most prominent instrument. After 1867 the further elaboration and pursuit of the national policy became the leading, if not the sole, objective of the national government. If one looks back only as far as Confederation, therefore, it is an understandable error to regard the federal government as principal rather than as agent in its relationship to the national policy. Although understandable, the error is none the less real. The federal government was created an agent within the framework of the first national policy and continued to act as agent until, with the attainment of the objectives of the national policy, it had exhausted its usefulness to its original principals, the commercial, financial, and manufacturing interests of the central provinces.

It is important to recall the main elements in the original division of powers between the federal government and the provinces. The division arrived at was well designed for the accomplishment of the first national policy, but quite unsuited to the national requirements once that policy had been fulfilled. In general terms, and at considerable risk of over-simplification it can be stated that the dominion government was given the responsibility for defence and development. Particular care was taken to enumerate the commercial and financial features of the developmental responsibility. The provinces and the dominion were given concurrent jurisdiction over agriculture and immigration with an overriding dominion power in case of conflict. The provinces were left with matters of local control, with education, with what today would be classed as public welfare functions, and with the disposition of unalienated public lands.

The provision giving control of crown lands to the provinces led to what was perhaps the first major modification of the national constitution. With the liquidation of the Hudson's Bay Company's title to Rupert's Land the dominion government came into possession of the Canadian counterpart of the American public domain, many millions of acres of arable land which would serve as an attraction for immigrants and a source of revenue for railway-building. The early necessity of creating the province of Manitoba posed a serious threat to the concept of a national public domain. To accord to Manitoba equal constitutional status with the existing provinces would deprive the dominion of ownership and disposition of a substantial proportion of the most fertile lands in the western territories. A simple expedient was adopted. Manitoba was implicitly classified as a province of inferior constitutional status, and the Manitoba Act specified that the crown lands in the new province should be retained by the dominion "for the purposes of the Dominion." The Manitoba principle was applied to Saskatchewan and Alberta when they were established as provinces in 1905.

Obviously it introduces arbitrary discreteness to say that the Canadian wheat economy was established and the first national policy fulfilled within the period beginning in 1900 and ending in 1930. There were many settlers in the West before 1900; a good deal of land was occupied and substantial crops of wheat were grown annually by the turn of the century; the establishment of the wheat economy did not commence all at once. Nor, of course, did the processes of its establishment terminate within a single calendar year. Relatively speaking, however, the rate of economic expansion in the Prairie Provinces and the corresponding stimulus to the integration of the entire Canadian economy set the first three decades of the present century apart from any preceding or succeeding time.

Within the generation after 1900, 4½ million immigrants came to Canada, three times as many as had come within the preceding half-century. During the thirty-year period the Canadian population all but doubled, to total 10,377,000 in 1931. Meanwhile the population of the Prairie Provinces increased more than fivefold to a total of 2,354,000. In 1901 only 8 per cent of the population of Canada lived on the central plains; by 1931 almost one-quarter were there. The area in farms increased sevenfold and the improved acreage elevenfold from 1901 to 1931. By 1931 there were upwards of 300,000 farms in the three provinces with 60 million acres of improved land. Approximately 25 million acres were in wheat. As early as 1920 wheat had become the most valuable Canadian export. In 1901, wheat exports yielded less than 10 million dollars; in 1929, 495 million dollars. During 1929 Canada exported an average of one million bushels of wheat per day.

The transfer of natural resources from the dominion to the

individual prairie provinces in 1930 symbolized the end of the establishment phase of the wheat economy and the completion of the first national policy. The terrific impact on the prairie economy in the 1930's of the world depression and of the drought cycle which coincided with it temporarily concealed the implications of the transfer of resources. Undoubtedly the disinvestment and real-capital consumption in the Prairie Provinces during the 1930's were due to drought and depression. But these were merely superimposed upon a situation in which, by the late 1920's, the possibilities of settlement in the Prairie Provinces were rapidly approaching their limit, and in which a further significant extension of the wheat economy was out of the question. The remaining natural resources which were transferred to the Prairie Provinces in 1930 would not have tempted any railway company, or any hard-bitten farmer from Ontario, or scarcely even the unsuspecting immigrant.

III

It will occasion no surprise that the outlines of the new, or second, national policy are as yet by no means firmly fixed or clearly visible. In previous parts of this paper it was pointed out that the first national policy took shape throughout the course of more than half a century. In contrast, the earliest tentative efforts on the part of the federal government toward the discovery of a new policy or group of policies are now not more than twenty-five or thirty years old. Some will no doubt argue that it is much too soon to seek for any facet of federal activities or viewpoint sufficiently concrete to be called a policy, or for anything, in fact, more tangible than a persistant pursuit of the expedient. Nevertheless, even at the risk of being proven wrong by future developments, it seems worth-while to attempt to review the major incidents of the past two decades in the perspective of the national policy concept.

The hypothesis which will be advanced here is that after 1930 the federal government worked gropingly and against substantial constitutional difficulties toward the formulation of a new set of national policies to replace the old which had been accomplished. It is argued that the main outlines of this new collective policy can be observed with reasonable clarity in two or three areas of activity: the broad field of public welfare; agricultural policy; and possibly monetary management. Within the limited space of this paper, attention will be centred on the first, that of public welfare.

The first decade and a half between the wars show as little trace of policy at the national level as one could find in a century of Canadian history. Briefly speaking, the old policy was at an end and nothing had as yet been devised to take its place. One cannot escape the impression that political and administrative leaders in the national government during this period either failed to realize that the national purposes originally assigned to the federal government had been achieved, or else thought it a matter of little importance.

One of the national purposes appeared quite obviously to have been completed by 1920. That was the contingent obligation to provide defence. The contingency had arisen after nearly half a century of Canadian national existence and had been effectively met. Canada had been defended. That job was done. A generation that has talked freely and stoically of a third world war almost ever since the end of the second may find it difficult to recall that it was upwards of twenty years after the end of the Great War before the possibility of a second came to appear worthy of serious consideration. As far as defence was concerned the federal government rested after 1918, and through two decades of inactivity sought convalescence from the political and economic injuries incurred in the unprecedented national effort of world conflict.

Gradually, after 1920, the federal government turned back to pick up the tasks of national development where they had been dropped in 1914. What they found, however, was not a great project waiting to be set in motion again but a number of comparatively minor chores which required completion in order that the Canadian economy might operate satisfactorily within its existing limits. There were already too many transcontinental railways, for example, but there remained the uninspiring task of salvaging two of them by co-ordination into a single system. The resultant administrative unit, the Canadian National Railways, was poorly equipped with feeder lines, and hundreds of miles of branches were added to it in the Prairie Provinces. The dominion government added a terminal elevator at Prince Rupert by 1925, and completed the Hudson Bay Railway and a terminal transfer elevator at Churchill by 1931. At the same time the Welland Ship Canal, which was begun before World War I, was brought to completion and a five million bushel terminal elevator was built at Prescott to make the new canal an effective channel for the movement of western wheat.[4] The dominion government facilitated the restoration of the immigration movement to substantial proportions in the late nineteen-twenties but was not concerned that so few of the settlers homesteaded in the Prairie Provinces. The restoration of the natural resources to the provincial governments was imminent and merely awaited the conclusion of a dominion-provincial agreement.

There can be no suggestion that the decade of the twenties was one of economic stagnation in Canada. From 1920 to 1929 the population of the country increased by one-sixth, the real national income by one-half and the volume of exports by three-quarters.[5] Investment in all forms of capital equipment throughout the country during the decade is estimated at more than six billion dollars.[6] The wheat economy grew throughout the decade as a whole. From 1921 to 1931 the population of the Prairie Provinces increased by one-fifth, the area of occupied farms increased by one-quarter, the area of improved land by one-third and the acreage of wheat by one-half. The tractor, truck, and combine first appeared in significant numbers in the wheat-growing area during the latter part of the decade.

Of fundamental significance for the relative status of the dominion and provincial governments, however, was the expansion of non-agricultural activities and the real-capital formation associated therewith. The twenties saw a tremendous expansion in the installation of hydro-electric facilities and in the equipment for pulp and paper production and base-metal mining. From 1920 to 1929 the developed water-power in Canada increased from 2.5 million to 5.7 million horsepower, the gross value of pulp and paper production increased from $151 million

[4] From 1920 to 1924 the dominion government spent $236 million on waterways and harbours. Over the same period the two railways spent $700 million on road and equipment and $150 million on hotels, telegraphs, and steamships. Of a total increase of $200 million in current expenditures by all governments in Canada from 1921 to 1930, the dominion proportion was only $33 million. Of a total increase in outstanding debt of one and one-quarter billion dollars over the same period the dominion proportion was only one-quarter of a billion including the Canadian National Railways. See *Report of the Royal Commission on Dominion-Provincial Relations* (Ottawa, 1940), Book I, 116, 128; reprinted in the Carleton Library (Toronto, 1963), p. 142.
[5] *Ibid.*, Table 30, 117.
[6] *Ibid.*, 116.

to $244 million and that of non-ferrous metals from $76 million to $154 million.[7] During the 1930's, when all other types of productive activity were seriously depressed, the Canadian gold-mining industry expanded apace. All these lines of production were concentrated in the central provinces and in British Columbia. They involved the utilization of provincial natural resources, and the active promotion of these developments was a welcome and rewarding responsibility of the respective provincial governments. The stature of the provincial governments in comparison with that of the dominion rose steadily throughout the first decade between the wars.

Federal leadership was remarkably slow in recognizing the fact that only a government with significant functions and responsibilities would continue to be regarded as significant by the electorate or by other governments within or without the country. It may be too soon to outline fully the new and continuing functions which the federal government has found for itself within the past twenty or thirty years. It is not too soon to note the change in the attitude of federal leaders when they eventually realized that a government without functions would be a government without respect. The federal government of 1867 found a national policy awaiting it; the dominion government between the wars had to formulate its own.

The oldest and most clearly defined elements of the new national policy are to be found in the field of public welfare activities. The federal Old Age Pensions Act of 1927 represents perhaps the first substantial commitment of the national government to a new kind of responsibility. The care of the aged had been a matter of repeated discussion by the dominion legislature and by special committees of the House since 1906. Special committee reports in 1924 and 1925 led to legislation which was rejected by the Senate in 1926 but was passed and assented to in 1927. The Act offered federal grants-in-aid to provinces which would pass enabling legislation, the grants to pay one-half[8] the

[7] *Ibid.*, 116 n.
[8] The federal proportion was increased to 75 per cent of the total as of July, 1931. The special committee of the House investigating the possibility of a pension plan in 1924 estimated that their proposals would involve a total eligible list of under one hundred thousand and that the annual cost to the dominion would approximate ten or eleven million dollars. By 1950, 282.6 thousand persons were drawing the pension at a cost of $90 million to the dominion and $30 million to the provinces.

cost of non-contributory means test pensions with a maximum of twenty dollars per month to persons seventy years of age or over who met certain qualifications regarding citizenship and residence. By the time the Old Age Pensions Bill came before the House in 1926 and 1927, Canada was so far retarded in social security provisions, compared with areas such as Britain and Scandinavia, that the only serious criticism of the proposed legislation concerned its constitutionality.

The argument that care of the aged lay within provincial jurisdiction surprised no one. Nor, indeed, did anyone deny it. By the 1920's it was generally recognized that practically anything that might be thought of by way of social reform would be excluded from dominion jurisdiction by the current judicial interpretation of the Property and Civil Rights clause of the British North America Act. A suggestion concerning a federal unemployment insurance scheme had been dismissed in 1922 as obviously unconstitutional. The grant-in-aid fiction would, however, serve to circumvent the constitution in certain limited circumstances. It had made possible federal intervention in the fields of education, highway construction, and relief. It would do the same for pensions. The government's faith in the middle twenties that by the miracle of the grant-in-aid a national old age pension scheme could be made to fit the Procrustean bed of provincial jurisdiction was fully justified. The old age pension scheme in Canada has rested on that comfortable fiction throughout a quarter of a century. Meanwhile the entire philosophy of the scheme has been transformed. Pension cheques which were of necessity accepted by the recipients as governmental charity in 1927 may, since the practical abolition of the means test as of January 1, 1952, be accepted without ignominy as social security payments.

Apart from instituting and partially financing the old age pension plan the federal government showed little if any anxiety to embark on new areas of responsibility before the middle 1930's. There was, in any case, little pressure upon them to do so in the general prosperity of the later 1920's. The onset of the depression in 1930 changed the circumstances suddenly and with impelling necessity. Constitution or no constitution, the municipal and provincial resources immediately proved inadequate to meet the emergency and the dominion government extended grants-in-aid to bridge the gap. The grants were made on a temporary basis in view of "extraordinary conditions," and because the distress "had become so general . . . as to constitute a matter of national concern."[9] Administration was left with the provinces and their constitutional responsibility to bear the burden of relief was not brought in question. Year after year of temporary emergency went by and each year the dominion renewed its emergency relief legislation. Over the eight years from 1930 to 1937 inclusive, the dominion assumed 40 per cent of the total relief cost for the country as a whole, a proportion which amounted to three-quarters of a billion dollars.[10] It may be that the anomalous experience with the relief problem during the thirties was largely instrumental in setting the federal government to work in a serious attempt to secure a measure of constitutional competence in the field of public welfare. To this day, however, and despite the enlarged measure of constitutional ambition which the federal authorities have displayed over the past eighteen or twenty years, they have made no move to acquire responsibility for relief.

Mr. Bennett's "New Deal" legislation of 1935 and the treatment accorded it by the Supreme Court of Canada and the Privy Council mark a turning point in the attitude of the federal government toward the enlargement of constitutional responsibility. In August, 1934, the Prime Minister proposed to the provinces a conference to discuss a number of matters, including the question: "Are the provinces prepared to surrender their exclusive jurisdiction over legislation dealing with such social problems as old-age pensions, unemployment and social insurance, hours and conditions for work, minimum wages, etc., to the dominion parliament? If so, on what terms and conditions?"[11] The provincial reception of this proposal was entirely lacking in enthusiasm. Mr. Bennett thereupon announced a program of "reform" legislation despite the constitution. In a series of radio talks in January, 1935, he outlined his proposals, and before the end of the month took the first step toward their implementation by introducing an unemployment and social

[9] Cf. *Report of the Royal Commission on Dominion-Provincial Relations,* Book I, 163; Carleton Library edition, p. 176.
[10] *Ibid.* In addition the dominion advanced $106 million to the four western provinces to assist them in carrying their share of the burden.
[11] Quoted by Brooke Claxton, "Social Reform and the Constitution," *Canadian Journal of Economics and Political Science,* I, no. 3, Aug., 1935, 410.

insurance bill. During February he introduced three conditions-
of-work bills; before the end of the session he introduced two
measures for the control of industry stemming from the recommendations of the Royal Commission on Price Spreads. All
these bills were enacted along with amendments to the Natural
Products Marketing Act and the Farmers' Creditors Arrangement Act which had been passed in the previous year. These
eight diverse measures[12] – four concerned with labour control,
two with industry, and two with agriculture – were soon collectively designated by the press as Mr. Bennett's New Deal legislation and were rather more formally grouped in a reference to
the Supreme Court for a test of constitutionality.

The fact that these government measures, once introduced,
were approved by the legislature is of no particular significance.
The attitude of the House is, however, worthy of note. The day
before the introduction of the unemployment and social insurance bill the House had unanimously concurred in a resolution
introduced by Mr. Woodsworth that a special committee be
appointed to recommend methods of amendment to the British
North America Act which would permit the national government to deal with "urgent economic problems which are essentially national in scope."[13] Similar resolutions, three of them
introduced by Mr. Woodsworth, had been rejected by the House
in 1924, 1925, 1927, and 1931. By 1935 Mr. Bennett, Mr. King,
and Mr. Lapointe all joined in urging that the question of

[12] The Employment and Social Insurance Act, *Statutes of Canada*, 1935,
c. 38; the Weekly Rest in Industrial Undertakings Act, *ibid.*, c. 14; the
Minimum Wages Act, *ibid.*, c. 44; the Limitation of Hours of Work
Act, *ibid.*, c. 63; a new section 498A of the Criminal Code, *ibid.*, c. 56,
s. 9; the Dominion Trade and Industry Commission Act, *ibid.*, c. 59;
the Natural Products Marketing Act, *ibid.*, 1934, c. 57, amended 1935,
c. 64; the Farmers' Creditors Arrangement Act, *ibid.*, 1934, c. 53;
amended 1935, c. 20.

[13] The complete resolution was, "That, in the opinion of this house, a
special committee should be set up to study and report on the best
method by which the British North America Act may be amended so
that while safeguarding the existing rights of racial and religious
minorities and legitimate provincial claims to autonomy, the dominion
government may be given adequate power to deal effectively with
urgent economic problems which are essentially national in scope."
Canada, House of Commons Debates, Jan. 28, 1935, 217. The Special
Committee of the House of Commons on the British North
America Act reported on June 19, 1935, merely urging the necessity
of a Dominion-Provincial conference on the matter. Cf. Claxton,
"Social Reform and the Constitution," p. 431.

amendment to the constitution be investigated. When it came to a consideration of Mr. Bennett's legislative proposals little opposition was voiced except concerning their constitutional validity. Regarding the reform legislation of the 1935 session as a whole the House was in general agreement on two points, first that the legislation was clearly necessary and, second, that it was certainly unconstitutional.

A brief reference to the judicial treatment of these measures is necessary, for it is related to later policy moves on the part of the federal government.[14] The eight measures came before the Judicial Committee of the Privy Council by way of appeals, after a reference by the Canadian government to the Supreme Court. On January 28, 1937, the Privy Council rendered its decisions on their constitutionality. The four labour laws and the Natural Products Marketing Act were declared *ultra vires* the dominion. The Farmers' Creditors Arrangement Act was declared valid as falling within the federal jurisdiction over bankruptcy and insolvency.[15] Section 498A of the Criminal Code relating to unfair trade practices was upheld as a proper exercise of criminal jurisdiction, and the Dominion Trade and Industry Commission Act was held valid, with the exception of one clause, as a measure for the regulation of trade and commerce supported also by criminal law.

The adverse decisions of the Privy Council may not have been unexpected. Yet there had been ground for the government's argument that all of the measures were constitutional. In support of the dominion's claim to jurisdiction it was argued that the four labour bills fell within five of the fundamental areas which were within the competence of the federal legislature: (1) the treaty-making or performing power of section 132 of the British North America Act, (2) trade and commerce, (3) criminal law, (4) taxation and (5) peace, order, and good government. If the federal powers in these areas, individually or

[14] For fuller discussion of the judicial features of the New Deal legislation see, e.g., Claxton, "Social Reform and the Constitution," and F. R. Scott, "The Privy Council and Mr. Bennett's 'New Deal' Legislation," *Canadian Journal of Economics and Political Science,* III, no. 2, May, 1937, pp. 234-41.
[15] Professor Scott comments on the decisions in the two agricultural acts as follows: "The Dominion, helpless though it may be by marketing legislation to save the farmer from economic destruction can wait with open arms to receive and comfort him on his reaching the point of insolvency." "The Privy Council," 241.

collectively, could not support the claim of federal jurisdiction in labour matters under the circumstances of the day, these powers would have to be recognized as remote from reality.

The mainstay of the new hope behind the labour legislation was section 132, the treaty-performing power. Three of the laws[16] were practical replicas of draft conventions drawn up at international labour conferences under the League of Nations, adopted under the labour provisions of the Treaty of Versailles, and ratified by the dominion parliament. When it was argued in the House that all of these laws would bear on property and civil rights in the provinces, Mr. Bennett was able to counter with a reference to the decisions in the Aviation case[17] and the Radio case[18] of 1932. In these the Privy Council had held, in effect, that property and civil rights did not prevent federal perform-ance of certain treaty obligations, and performance under con-ventions which could be shown to pertain to the furtherance of peace, order, and good government. Any hopes held for the larger view in the years 1935 to 1937 were, however, disap-pointed. The labour conventions, the Privy Council held, were not part of an Empire treaty; they were merely conventions which the federal government could fulfil only if it did not infringe upon the property and civil rights clause or any other part of section 92. Obviously the labour laws would not meet these exacting requirements and were therefore invalid.

The restrictive view of the dominion's treaty-performing power which was advanced by the Privy Council in 1937 came as a distinct shock to federal leaders. It constituted a flat denial of the national stature which Canadians had come to regard as an established and accepted fact.

The ups and downs of constitutional reform are not, however, the concern of this analysis. Mr. Bennett's New Deal legislation has been given more than passing mention because of its impli-cations for national policy. While the legislative program was initially sponsored by a Conservative Prime Minister and his party following, it was not at any time actively opposed by members of the Opposition. By the time the Privy Council gave

[16] The Minimum Wage Act, the Limitation of Hours Act and the Weekly Rest in Industrial Undertakings Act.
[17] In re Regulation and Control of Aeronautics in Canada (1932) A.C. 54.
[18] In re Regulation and Control of Radio Communication in Canada (1932) A.C. 304.

its decisions invalidating the bulk of the reform measures, the Liberals were in power. Their reaction to the decisions was to show every intention of securing a measure of constitutional reform which would make possible legislation at least similar to Mr. Bennett's. The Liberals appointed the Royal Commission on Dominion-Provincial Relations to prepare the ground for such reform by means of an exhaustive enquiry.

The Canadian New Deal legislation of the middle thirties represented the first clear-cut evidence of a widespread conviction which has persisted to the present time that the federal government must assume increasing responsibility for economic and social conditions in the dominion. Behind this conviction there was originally, of course, the economic distress of five depression years as well as the generally changing public opinion on the social obligations of government at all levels. One additional influence at work in Canada was a gradual recognition of the peacetime futility of the federal government, with the wheat economy and a transcontinental trading system established and with the new frontiers of economic advance entirely within provincial jurisdiction. If federal leaders had thought that the much-talked-of increase in Canada's international stature after World War I would serve as adequate compensation for domestic futility, they were brought up with a rude jolt by the Privy Council in 1937. The verdict of the Privy Council at that time was, in effect, that domestic constitutional disabilities effectively denied any Canadian claim to national status when it came to participation in international affairs.

Since 1937, not excluding the years of World War II, the dominion government has persisted in its efforts to enlarge the area of its responsibility in the field of social welfare. The Rowell-Sirois Commission recommended a substantial transfer of revenues and responsibilities from the provinces to the dominion. The repeated failure of dominion-provincial conferences to agree upon measures of constitutional amendment or modification which would effect the Commission's recommendations is well known. One item, the care of unemployed employables, was recognized as obviously unmanageable except under dominion control, and dominion jurisdiction was clearly unattainable except by constitutional amendment. On the basis of a Joint Address of the Commons and the Senate, the imperial parliament amended the British North America Act in 1940 to add "Unemployment Insurance" to the headings of section 91. The federal government proceeded immediately to enact the Unemployment Insurance Act to become effective in 1941. In 1944 the Family Allowance Act established a national scheme of cash allowances for children up to sixteen years of age, the payments to commence in July, 1945.

Tax-transfer and subsidy agreements with individual provinces have served since 1942 as a compromise in view of the failure of dominion-provincial conferences to secure over-all agreement. The old expedient of the grant-in-aid serves to expand the federal realm in areas such as public health and education. It may be that today a national health insurance plan is the only major social security scheme seriously considered and proposed by the dominion government which has been constitutionally impossible of achievement.

As mentioned earlier, there are two other areas in which the outlines of a new national policy are discernible. These are the field of monetary policy or monetary management and the field of agriculture. Discussion of these has been crowded out of the present paper and, in any case, they fully warrant analysis on their own account. Only one or two points can be made here regarding these areas of activity.

The entry of the dominion government into the field of monetary management was one of its new expansive efforts between the wars that was not blocked by constitutional restrictions. The establishment of the Bank of Canada in 1935 represented a constitutionally acceptable departure in the government's interpretation of its functions under the currency and banking clauses of section 91 of the British North America Act. The Bank was but newly organized when the Keynesian revolution in monetary or full-employment theory spread its influence throughout the western world. The staff of the Bank were young and remarkably receptive to the newest ideas pertaining to their task. Lord Keynes's *General Theory* may well have done more to restore vitality and a sense of purpose to the dominion government than any single incident since the gold strikes in the Yukon in the late 1890's. At times within the past ten years it has been a question whether all peacetime national policy might not be subsumed under the head of full-employment policy. When baby bonuses and agricultural price support legislation are in danger of being regarded as mere instruments for the maintenance of full employment it is possible to suggest at least a temporary distortion of the national perspective.[19]

The new national policy, like the old, is concerned with agriculture, but to quite a different degree and in quite a different way. The interest of the first policy was in agricultural development. It was the stimulating concern over a segment of economic life which was expanding at a rate far in excess of other segments of the economy. The national interest in Canadian agriculture over the past quarter-century, by contrast, has been in a segment of the economy which is expanding, if at all, at a rate far below that of the economy as a whole. The approach has of necessity been different. Without detailed analysis it can nevertheless be said that the major differences between the agricultural features of the old and the new national policies relate to a modification in the national view concerning the price system in relation to the agricultural economy. Price support and crop failure legislation had no place in the first national policy but may be regarded as an integral part of the second. The first national policy was concerned with an agricultural-commercial economy; the second will necessarily conform to the requirements of an economy which is becoming increasingly industrial-commercial.

---

[19] See, e.g., *Employment and Income with Special Reference to the Initial Period of Reconstruction*, presented to Parliament by the Minister of Reconstruction, April, 1945, p. 13 and *passim*.

PART FIVE

BIBLIOGRAPHY

Recent Contributions to
Economic History: Canada

W. T. EASTERBROOK

The present state of economic history in Canada contrasts
sharply with that of a quarter century ago. It could be written in
the 1930's that the most distinctive work in Canadian economics
was being done by economic historians concerned with the
study of transportation and tariffs, trade associations and agricultural organizations, money and banking.[1] There was at the
same time a close approach to a generally accepted framework
of analysis and interpretation and more than a suggestion of
synthesis in Canadian historical writings. This pre-eminence of
economic history and this unity of theme are now things of the
past. As to the first, the rate of progress in economic analysis
and statistics, in sociology and political theory, has brought with
it both a change in status and the prospect of extensive revisions,
factual and interpretative, of our views of the past. Similarly, a
former unity of approach resting on the economics of staple

Source: W. T. Easterbrook. "Recent Contributions to Economic History: Canada", *Journal of Economic History*, Vol. XIX, No. 1,
March, 1959, pp. 76-102. Reprinted by permission of the publishers.
    The Postscript on pages 288-92 bringing this essay up to date has
been specially prepared by the editors for this Carleton Library
edition.

[1] O. D. Skelton, "Fifty Years of Political and Economic Science in
Canada," *Royal Society of Canada Anniversary Volume, 1882-1932*
(Ottawa, 1932), p. 88.

production[2] has lost ground before the complexities of modern industrial change. For the economic historian these changes promise much for present and future research even if, at the moment, they bring small comfort.

The impact of new fashions in the social sciences[3] is felt by economic historians everywhere and calls for no comment here. On the other hand, the partial breakdown of staples economics throws into clear relief prevailing trends in Canadian thought and has its use in tracing recent developments in Canadian economic history. In the search for "the trend of continuity, the unifying generalization, which shall at last make history more than a 'shallow village tale,' ". . .[4] W. J. Ashley had been the initiator, and H. A. Innis (ably supported by his colleague, C. R. Fay) and W. A. Mackintosh broke trail, followed by a host of others who explored with few reservations the paths they laid down. Architecturally, theirs was an impressive achievement and an effective response to the needs of the time. Before the 1920's research in Canadian economics had been scattered, piecemeal, conducted with a few notable exceptions[5] by those lacking analytical interest or historical grasp. It was left to such scholars as Mackintosh of Queen's and Innis of Toronto to bring order out of chaos and to create in the process a national economics[6] adequate for the analysis of the problems

[2] See C. R. Fay, "The Toronto School of Economic History," *Economic History*, III (Jan. 1934), pp. 168-71. On "staples economics" he writes: ". . . the emphasis is on the commodity itself: its significance for policy; the tying in of one activity with another; the way in which a basic commodity sets the general pace, creates new activities, and is itself strengthened, or perhaps dethroned, by its own creation" (p. 171).

[3] See Herbert Heaton, "Clio's New Overalls," *The Canadian Journal of Economics and Political Science*, XX (Nov. 1954), pp. 467-77. See also G. A. Elliott, "On Some New Fashions in Economic Theory," *ibid.*, XX (Nov., 1954), pp. 478-92.

[4] W. J. Ashley, "On the Study of Economic History," *Quarterly Journal of Economics*, VII (Jan., 1893), p. 24.

[5] Among these must be listed Adam Shortt of Queen's, James Mavor of Toronto, W. C. Kierstead of New Brunswick. See C. D. Goodwin, "Canadian Economic Thought, 1814-1914" (Ph.D. dissertation, Duke University, 1958).

[6] See W. A. Mackintosh, "Economic Factors in Canadian History," *Canadian Historical Review*, IV (Mar., 1923), pp. 12-25. See also H. A. Innis, "Significant Factors in Canadian Economic Development," *ibid*, XVIII (Dec., 1936), pp. 374-84, and his "Transportation as a Factor in Canadian Economic History," *Proceedings of the Canadian Political Science Association*, III (1931), pp. 166-84.

of a nation moving slowly out of a prolonged phase of economic colonialism.

The publication in 1940 of Innis' *Cod Fisheries: The History of an International Economy*[7] and of the findings of the Royal Commission on Dominion-Provincial Relations[8] make this a notable year in Canadian studies. The first brought new perspectives to Innis' earlier work on transportation, the fur trade, and problems of staple production, and rounded out his basic researches on Canadian materials. The second was an impressive list of research monographs that in breadth of view, historical emphasis, and concentration on problems of national consequence display staples economics at its best. Ashley's plea for an underlying unity in the study of historical change had not gone unanswered.

These studies mark the high tide of political economy in Canada.[9] Canadian social scientists, long caught up in the problems of building a transcontinental economy in the face of regional divisions and the threat of United States' penetration at key points, had found the way to a sound interpretation of Canada's "old industrialism" of railways and wheat, iron and tariffs. National autonomy was to rest on a prairie agriculture geared to European markets, an eastern Canadian industry protected by high tariff walls against competition from the south, and a railway network that provided the economic ties of federal unity. This was the structure of the old fur trade writ large; to the 1930's it had all the appearance of a successful response to the challenge faced by Canada's first nationbuilders. Wheat was king, and railway investment, industrial protection, and transatlantic trade bowed to this staple's leadership in national development.

This hard-won unity of approach, for all its virtues, has fared badly in the past two decades. There had been the valid criticism

[7] Published in "The Relations of Canada and the United States Series" (Toronto: Ryerson Press; New Haven: Yale University Press, 1940).

[8] See *Report of the Royal Commission on Dominion Provincial Relations*, Book I, "Canada, 1867-1939" (Ottawa, 1940, and reprinted in the Carleton Library, Toronto, 1963); W. A. Mackintosh, "The Economic Background of Dominion-Provincial Relations" (published as Appendix III to the *Report*, and reprinted in the Carleton Library, Toronto, 1964).

[9] See W. T. Easterbrook, "Political Economy in a Staples-Producing Area," paper prepared for the Duke University Seminar on Commonwealth Studies, 1959 (mimeographed).

that concentration on export commodities and related aspects of Canadian economic history made for neglect of numerous and significant internal changes, but of greater consequence for its value as an interpretative theme is the rapidly changing structure of the Canadian economy. A transformation well under way before World War II has been greatly accelerated by war and postwar changes. Canada's new industrialism, with its new metals, new sources of power, and new means of transportation has radically altered the older wheat-railways complex. The continuing importance of export commodities in the country's national income suggests that the economy has yet to break clear of its staples phase of growth. Yet, advanced industrialism, with its changed market-resource-investment alignments, is raising problems that demand substantial revision of the staples thesis. Acceptance has given way to exploration, and, as a consequence, there are few indications now of any unity of thought or approach in a period reminiscent of the late nineteenth and early twentieth centuries in Canadian economic thought. It is likely that Innis' shift to communication studies reflected his awareness of the "increasing fragmentation of knowledge" that these changes were bringing with them and led to his search for "an integration of basic approaches" beyond the limited range of Canadian experience.

The absence of any dominant school in Canadian economic thought is perhaps to be expected at this time. It should provide no grounds for regret, for in view of the volume and quality of research now under way, there is a strong case to be made for a diversity of approaches. The modern period is probably best described as one of testing of hypotheses old and new, and of filling gaps left in the past as a result, at least in part, of undue reliance on staples economics. It is for some architect of the future to restore the broader philosophical view of resource-oriented growth which was ours not so long ago. There is good reason to believe that this "restoration" is more than a remote possibility. The present rate of advance in the social sciences far exceeds that of any time in the past, the groundwork for a new synthesis is being laid, and the climate of inquiry continues to be highly unfavourable to the narrow empiricism of the specialist and the expert.

As in any nation faced with the task of maintaining autonomy in the face of strong external pressures, defensive strategies
in Canada focus attention on questions of national significance
and blur distinctions between analysis and policy-making.
Research interest is drawn to issues of national policy whether
it centre on agriculture and the grain trade, banking, currency,
and capital movements, tariffs and immigration, the application
of advanced techniques to natural resources, or the course of
federal-provincial relations. Among Canadian economic historians, Vernon Fowke,[10] of the University of Saskatchewan,
has explicitly formulated his findings in these terms. Working
out of a background of studies in Canadian agricultural history,
with special emphasis on the great staple wheat, he is concerned
with the consequences of an industrial revolution based on
petroleum and natural gas, hydro-electric power, nickel, and
other metals for the prairie provinces and for the economy as a
whole. National policy, viewed as the design of creating a
national political and economic unit in British North America,
is examined from this point of view. Although Fowke finds few
clues as to the shape of things to come, no one has gone farther
than he in coming to grips with the difficulties of an economy
caught between two worlds. The essentially defensive aspect of
Canadian policy is analysed in terms of both its Canadian and
its larger continental setting.[11] Writing of the wheat economy,
and in similar vein, G. Britnell[12] confirms the view that the
Canadian West and, to a considerable extent, the Canadian
economy remain tied to the fortunes of the predominantly
wheat-growing areas. New resource developments are leaving
their mark, but external influences exerted by way of investment
and markets ensure a continued emphasis on the export of raw
and semi-processed materials. Staples economics, in short, is still
not without validity and relevance.

This theme of the economics of transition is treated in a

[10] Vernon Fowke, *The National Policy and the Wheat Economy* (Toronto:
University of Toronto Press, 1957).

[11] Vernon Fowke, "National Policy and Western Development in North
America," *The Journal of Economic History*, XIV (Dec., 1956),
pp. 461-79.

[12] G. Britnell, "Perspective on Change in the Prairie Economy," C.J.E.P.S.,
XIX (Nov., 1953), 437-54. See also his "Underdeveloped Countries in
the World Economy," C.J.E.P.S., XXIII (Nov., 1957), pp. 453-66.

different setting by J. H. Dales[13] in his recent study of hydro-electric power and industrial development in Quebec. "The hydro-electric industry constitutes a Great Divide in the economic development of Quebec, and by implication, of Canada. On the one hand it belongs to a young, pioneer, economy, it is one of that succession of 'staples industries' on which Canada's economic development has been based. . . . On the other hand, certain special features of the hydro-electric industry become apparent when we look at its market problems, and in seeking solutions to these problems the industry has pointed the way to a more mature, more diversified economy."[14] The industry is viewed as an agent in the promotion of Canada's twentieth-century industrial revolution. In its support of a more diversified and self-reliant economic growth, it acts as a revolutionary force leading to a new kind of economic development, even though it must be viewed against the background of staples production. In a study valuable for its contributions to locational theory and to entrepreneurial history, Dales makes excellent use of a frame of reference similar in outline to that of Fowke's. Both writers take up for examination the meaning of the new industrial technologies for the slow-changing structure of Canada's economy. One writer makes an "old" industry his starting point, the other a "new" one, but each looks down both sides of the "Great Divide" that separates the underdeveloped from the mature economy. There are other writers who adopt the same vantage point, but none whose writings illustrate so clearly the present state of economic history in Canada.

Although the economy is moving into a new era of growth, there has been no slackening of interest in the older staples industries, and in no area has greater advance been made than in the study of the fur trade. The twenty volumes of "The Hudson's Bay Series" (edited by E. E. Rich), first launched by the Champlain Society and now continued by the Hudson's Bay Record Society, contain a wealth of material on the company and on related developments. They include a number of introductory essays of a quality unsurpassed in Canadian writings. Apart from this series, an authoritative, well-documented study

[13] J. H. Dales, *Hydroelectricity and Industrial Development: Quebec, 1898-1940* (Cambridge: Harvard University Press, 1957).
[14] *Ibid.*, p. 182.

of the achievements and strategies of the "Great Monopoly" is
J. S. Galbraith's recently published, *The Hudson's Bay Company as an Imperial Factor, 1821-1869*.[15] Narrative in style and
rich in historical detail, it is valuable as an account of a political
and economic organization whose long rule over roughly one
quarter of the continent has left its stamp on the present Canadian economy. There is no suggestion of revision of present
interpretations of the fur trade phase in Canadian history, but
the author's emphasis on developments in the Pacific coastal
area improves prospects for a balanced treatment of his subject.
Another and more general study of the fur trade is Marjorie
Campbell's *The North West Company*,[16] the great rival of the
Hudson's Bay organization up to 1821 and the leader in Canada's transcontinental expansion in the early nineteenth century.
In her detailed treatment of personalities, problems, and the
factors back of the submergence of this organization in that of
its rival, the author has prevented any similar submergence of
the North West Company in Canadian fur trade literature.
Although H. A. Innis' *The Fur Trade in Canada* (1930 and
1956) remains the standard interpretative work in this field, its
theme has been amplified and enriched by a more detailed
treatment of extensive documentary sources.[17]

Closely related to the fortunes of the transcontinental fur
trade was the balance of sea power in the Atlantic region. In his
Empire of the North Atlantic[18] Gerald Graham writes of the
past four centuries as one clearcut epoch of history in which
exercise of sea power by the ship of war was the determining
influence in the shaping of the North Atlantic empire. Economic
historians will find slim treatment of the economic aspects of
the subject, but the study serves as a useful counter to the
tendency to overlook the vital importance of naval power to the

[15] Toronto: University of Toronto Press, 1957. See also his "Hudson's
Bay Company Under Fire, 1847-1862," *Canadian Historical Review*,
XX (Dec., 1949), pp. 322-35 and his "Land Policy of the Hudson's
Bay Company, 1870-1913," *ibid.*, XXII (Mar., 1951), pp. 1-21.

[16] Toronto: The Macmillan Company of Canada, 1957.

[17] A more complete bibliographical account of writings on the fur trade
and other staples would entail reference to the publications of provincial and dominion archives. On the fur trade, the issues of *The British
Columbia Quarterly*, ed. Willard Ireland, should at least be given
honourable mention.

[18] Gerald Graham, *The Empire of the North Atlantic: The Maritime
Struggle for North America* (Toronto: University of Toronto Press,
1950).

outcome of continental rivalries. The author's highly competent presentation does much to compensate for past neglect of this aspect of international conflict. A useful supplementary study is P. W. Bamford's review[19] of the obstacles to French naval supremacy in this part of the world. His close scrutiny of French colonial policy of the seventeenth and eighteenth centuries throws new light on the factors back of French weakness in North America. More directly related to the Canadian scene is Albert Faucher's article, "The Decline of Shipbuilding at Quebec in the Nineteenth Century,"[20] which treats of the trading organization and the timber trade of this area and the consequences of steam power for a port whose iron men had so long manned wooden ships. A welcome addition to the literature of the Atlantic region is C. R. Fay's[21] delightful volume of essays on Newfoundland, past and present, a collection which reveals Fay at his storytelling best. An enthusiastic guide, he invites the reader to explore the neglected archives of Newfoundland's history. Few aspects of the island's past are left untouched in this lively guidebook for future historians of this area.

Unlike the North Atlantic, the North Pacific has fared poorly at the hands of economic historians, but G. R. Elliott's[22] study of the relationship between frontier conditions and forms of enterprise draws attention to the economic factors that contributed to the outcome of conflict in this area. In spite of the strength of continental influences in Canadian growth, such additions to our knowledge of events on the margins of the continent do much to preserve a balanced treatment of Canadian development. They, like Innis' *Cod Fisheries*, underline the significant part maritime areas have played at times in Canadian history.

Nevertheless, in a nation that has been a transcontinental entity over the large part of its history, her fortunes tied closely to the production and export of a limited number of continental resources, the major determinants of growth must be sought in the continent itself. Agriculture, for a time a mere appendage of

[19] P. W. Bamford, *Forests and Sea-Power: 1660-1789* (Toronto: University of Toronto Press).

[20] C.J.E.P.S., XXXIII (May, 1957), pp. 195-215.

[21] C. R. Fay, *Life and Labour in Newfoundland* (Toronto: University of Toronto Press, 1956).

[22] G. R. Elliott, "Frontiers and Forms of Enterprise: The Case of the North Pacific, 1785-1825," C.J.E.P.S., XXIV (May, 1958), pp. 251-61.

the fur trade, has long served as a key to studies of regional and national development. For eastern Canada F. Letourneau[23] provides a narrative treatment of agricultural change in Quebec over the period 1605-1950; the author writes with love and affection of the lives, traditions, and organizations of those whose descendants he sees as eventually tilling all the arable land of Canada. More objective and analytical is Charles Lemelin's[24] examination of the impact of new industries on the agriculture of the province. His account contains an enlightening discussion of the nature and consequence of the Quebec farmers' resistance to technological progress and an analysis of the problems arising from the absence of structural change in farm enterprises that function apart from developments in the industrial sector of Quebec's economy. A. Faucher and C. Vaillancourt[25] take up the co-operative movement in Quebec in a volume that tells us much of Alphonse Desjardins, founder of the first *caisses populaires* in North America and pioneer in the co-operative movement; there is useful material on European savings and credit co-operatives, on which Desjardins drew for inspiration, and on contrasts between Quebec's *caisses populaires* and the credit unions of Europe and western Canada. Agriculture in Lower Canada over the period 1792-1815 is the subject of an informative article by R. L. Jones,[26] author also of a first-rate study of Ontario's agricultural development, 1663-1880. His competent and comprehensive treatment of agricultural progress in terms of markets, labour and capital, technology and types of farming, transportation factors, and United States influence on the industry[27] fills a large gap in the literature of this period.

[23] F. Letourneau, *Histoire de l'agriculture (Canada français)* (Montreal: L'Imprimerie Populaire, Limitée, 1950).

[24] Charles Lemelin, "The State of Agriculture," in Jean C. Falardeau, ed., *Essays on Contemporary Quebec* (Quebec: Les Presses Universitaires Laval, 1953), ch. iii, pp. 55-56. See also A. Faucher, "Co-operative Trends in Canada," *The Annals of the American Academy of Political and Social Science*, CCLIII (Sept., 1947), pp. 184-89.

[25] A. Faucher and C. Vaillancourt, *Alphonse Desjardins: Pionnier de la coopération d'épargne et de crédit en Amérique* (Lévis: Editions le Quotidien, Ltée, 1950).

[26] R. L. Jones, "Agriculture in Lower Canada, 1792-1815," *CHR*, XXVII (Mar., 1946), pp. 33-51.

[27] R. L. Jones, *History of Agriculture in Ontario, 1663-1880* (Toronto: University of Toronto Press, 1946).

To the west, W. L. Morton[28] has written at length of the agriculture of the Red River colony, the passing of the old order of the hunt and subsistence agriculture, and the transition to sedentary commercial farming. More recent developments are outlined in his history of Manitoba and in his volume, *The Progressive Party in Canada*, an informative account of farm protest movements over the period 1896-1935.[29] Western agriculture is also given prominent place in Vernon Fowke's studies of the relationship between agricultural expansion and government developmental policies. In his *Canadian Agricultural Policy, The Historical Pattern*[30] Fowke argues that such considerations as defence of empire, provisioning of the staples trades, and the incentives offered to industry, commerce, and finance by an expanding agricultural frontier, rather than farmers' influence or pressure, have determined governmental policy. His more recent work on national policy[31] amplifies this argument and relates its themes to present-day advances in the exploitation of nonagricultural resources. Also written with an emphasis on the wheat economy is D. A. MacGibbon's[32] study of the grain trade, a history and analysis of trade policies in relation to the changing structure of agricultural markets. Closely associated with the grain trade over a long period, the

[28] W. L. Morton, "Agriculture in the Red River Colony," *CHR*, XXX (Dec., 1949), pp. 305-21. See also his "Introduction" to E. E. Rich, ed., "London Correspondence Inward from Eden Colville 1849-1852," in *Publications of the Hudson's Bay Record Society*, XIX (London, 1956), xiii-cxv, and W. L. Morton, ed., "Alexander Begg's Red River Journal, and Other Papers Relative to the Red River Resistance of 1869-1870," in *Publications of the Champlain Society*, XXXIV (Toronto, 1956), pp. 1-148).

[29] W. L. Morton, *Manitoba: A History* (Toronto: University of Toronto Press, 1957); *The Progressive Party in Canada* (Toronto: University of Toronto Press, 1950).

[30] Toronto: University of Toronto Press, 1946. See also W. M. Drummond, *Canadian Agricultural Development 1850-1900*, paper prepared for the Conference on Research in Income and Wealth, Sept. 4-5, 1957. National Bureau of Economic Research, New York (mimeographed).

[31] V. Fowke, *The National Policy and the Wheat Economy* (Toronto: University of Toronto Press, 1957).

[32] D. A. MacGibbon, *The Canadian Grain Trade 1931-1951* (Toronto: University of Toronto Press, 1952), a sequel to his *The Canadian Grain Trade* (Toronto: Macmillan Company of Canada, 1932). On the co-operative marketing of wheat, see W. K. Rolph, *Henry Wise Wood of Alberta* (Toronto: University of Toronto Press, 1950), a biography of a leading figure in the establishment of the wheat pools.

author writes with authority of the shift from free to compulsory marketing of wheat and other grains.

Geography and market factors have combined to give transportation a central place in Canadian economic history. A. W. Currie's *Economics of Canadian Transportation*,[33] a study of principles rather than historical development, stamps him as worthy successor to W. T. Jackman. But for the economic historian, his recently published, staunchly empirical study of the Grand Trunk Railway,[34] financial failure and public asset over a period of seventy years, will be of greater interest. This railway, a pioneer in design, management, and finance, provides an excellent case study in Canadian transportation and financial history, and the author has made the most of it. He has also broken new ground in communications history in his review of Canadian postal arrangements since the Confederation.[35] More limited in its treatment and scope as a study in transportation history is Howard Fleming's account of the Hudson Bay Railway,[36] the century-long dream of a short northern route for the province of Manitoba and the Northwest. Although exaggerating the importance of the Bay Railway movement as a political force, it has much useful detail on this competitor of the St. Lawrence system. Another dark corner in Canadian transportation development has been explored in Hugh Aitken's highly competent study of the Welland Canal Company,[37] a volume that brings into clear relief the problems of Canadian enterprise in the early decades of the nineteenth century. Economic and political issues are brought to a focus in a thorough examination of the investment setting of Upper Canada in this period. On the national level a review of transportation's role in Canadian history and an accompanying analysis of the rate structure as it affects the various regions of the country is contained in H. A. Innis' memorandum on transportation appended to the *Report*

---

[33] A. W. Currie, *The Economics of Canadian Transportation* (Toronto: University of Toronto Press, 1954).

[34] A. W. Currie, *The Grand Trunk Railway of Canada* (Toronto: University of Toronto Press, 1957).

[35] A. W. Currie, "The Post Office Since 1867," c.j.e.p.s., XXIV (May, 1958), pp. 241-50.

[36] H. Fleming, *Canada's Arctic Outlet, A History of the Hudson Bay Railway* (Berkeley and Los Angeles: University of California Press, 1957).

[37] H. G. J. Aitken, *The Welland Canal Company: A Study in Canadian Enterprise* (Cambridge: Harvard University Press, 1954).

of the Royal Commission on Transportation, 1951.[38] The report itself contains useful material on the evolution and present condition of Canada's freight-rate structure.

Recognition of the importance of tariffs and commercial policy is apparent in a number of first-rate studies in this area. Although mainly concerned with the effect of tariffs on various groups and industries, O. J. McDiarmid's[39] study of Canadian commercial policy puts the tariff problem in historical perspective; quantitative as well as policy aspects of the tariff are detailed in each of the principal phases of Canadian tariff history. D. R. Annett's[40] volume on the historical role of preferences in Canadian policy reviews tariff-making in general and assesses the significance of the factors that have determined its course. Commercial relations with the United Kingdom and the United States are related to the objectives of a national policy designed to cement imperial ties and to ensure a better balance on trading account with the United States. The study is valuable for the perspective it provides on present-day discussion of trading relationships with the United States and the Commonwealth. More strongly in the historical vein, somewhat less policy-oriented, is Gordon Blake's[41] recent study in the same field. Blake provides a detailed review of customs administration in the French and British regimes and in pre-Confederation Canada, followed by an analysis of customs changes since Confederation. Changes in customs administration are closely related to economic and political conditions in a country that has run the gamut of customs-tariff experience. A neglected aspect of Canadian tariff policy, the influence of hidden or indirect protectionism, is examined by G. A. Elliott[42] in a volume that provides ample material for a better-balanced interpreta-

[38] H. A. Innis, "Memorandum on Transportation," in *Report of the Royal Commission on Transportation, 1951* (Ottawa: King's Printer, 1951), pp. 294-307. See also J. C. Lessard, *Transportation in Canada* (Ottawa: Queen's Printer, 1958).

[39] O. J. McDiarmid, *Commercial Policy in the Canadian Economy* (Cambridge: Harvard University Press, 1946).

[40] D. R. Annett, *British Preferences in Canadian Commercial Policy* (Toronto: Ryerson Press, 1948).

[41] G. Blake, *Customs Administration in Canada: An Essay in Tariff Technology* (Toronto: University of Toronto Press, 1957).

[42] G. A. Elliott, *Tariff Procedures and Trade Barriers: A Study of Indirect Protection in Canada and the United States* (Toronto: University of Toronto Press, 1955).

tion of Canadian tariff history over the past four decades.

On Canadian banking and fiscal development R. C. McIvor[43] has met a long-felt need in his authoritative treatment of the subject in its historical and contemporary aspects in a volume that admirably rounds out the pioneer work of Adam Shortt and the later contributions of F. A. Knox and C. A. Curtis.[44] Beginning with a survey of monetary difficulties in New France, McIvor reviews developments in British North America to the formation of the first commercial banks. Banking history is traced through the nineteenth century to the present. There are useful chapters also on war finance and recent experiments in monetary-fiscal policy and control. History and analysis are linked in a study that relates financial changes to the evolving structure of the economy. In a more descriptive treatment of Canadian banking history, A. B. Jamieson's[45] study of chartered banking has chapters on banking organization, the creation and absorption of various banking institutions, and on changes in banking legislation. Central banking in Canada has a short history, but E. Neufeld's[46] review of the Bank of Canada's operations over the past two decades traces with great competence the evolution of this institution, although no attempt is made to place the bank in its broader economic setting. On the role of capital in Canadian growth Clare Pentland[47] has opened a promising new lead in an article on this theme, in which structural changes in the economy are related to problems of capital supply in the nineteenth century. His discussion of the difficulties facing a young country in its search for long-term capital to meet the needs of an emerging industrial economy provides fruitful insights into another neglected phase of financial history.

A major work in Canadian public finance is J. H. Perry's

[43] R. C. McIvor, *Canadian Monetary, Banking and Fiscal Development* (Toronto: Macmillan Company of Canada, 1958).

[44] See C. A. Curtis, "Evolution of Canadian Banking," *The Annals of the American Academy of Political and Social Science*, CCLIII (Sept., 1947), pp. 115-24.

[45] A. B. Jamieson, *Chartered Banking in Canada* (Toronto: Ryerson Press, 1955).

[46] E. P. Neufeld, *Bank of Canada Operations, 1935-1954* (Toronto: University of Toronto Press, 1955).

[47] C. Pentland, "The Role of Capital in Canadian Economic Development Before 1875," c.j.e.p.s., XXVI (Nov., 1950), pp. 457-74.

two-volume study, *Taxes, Tariffs, and Subsidies*,[48] in which the author treats of "the efforts of men to establish institutions of government in Canada and to clothe them with the financial resources which provide them strength and vitality" (I, 3). Although extending back to 1650, the study concentrates on the development since Confederation of a tax structure within a federal system. The history of taxation at three levels of government – federal, provincial, and municipal – and of the interrelations between these is recounted in a work notable for its lucid handling of a complex subject. Its wealth of historical data alone makes it an indispensable item in the economic historian's reading list. An added contribution is his article on the price of provincial autonomy,[49] a brief but balanced review of past developments and present problems in federal-municipal finance in Canada. D. C. MacGregor presents a brief but penetrating outline of trends in Canadian public finance and fiscal thought from a long-period point of view.[50] Not without historical interest, but with primary emphasis on administrative techniques and contemporary aspects of governmental operations, are studies by K. G. Crawford, H. L. Brittain, and A. H. Birch.[51]

Labour history in Canada owes much to the work of H. A. Logan. Since his first definitive study in this field, *The History of Trade Union Organization in Canada* (1928), the author has produced two volumes which round out several decades of research in labour movements and problems. His *Trade Unions in Canada: Their Development and Function*[52] is a detailed

[48] J. H. Perry, *Taxes, Tariffs and Subsidies: A History of Canadian Fiscal Development* (2 vols.; Toronto: University of Toronto Press, 1955). See also his *Taxation in Canada* (Toronto: University of Toronto Press, 1953), a study of the salient features of the present tax system in Canada, and J. H. Perry and Milton Moore, *Financing Canadian Federation* (Toronto: Canadian Tax Foundation, 1953).

[49] In C.J.E.P.S., XXI (Nov., 1955), pp. 432-45.

[50] D. C. MacGregor, "Trends in Canadian Public Finance," *The Annals of the American Academy of Political and Social Science*, CCLIII (Sept., 1947), pp. 105-14.

[51] K. G. Crawford, *Canadian Municipal Government* (Toronto: University of Toronto Press, 1954) and the same author's "Some Aspects of Provincial-Municipal Relations," C.J.E.P.S., XVI (Aug., 1950), pp. 394-407. See also H. L. Brittain, *Local Government in Canada* (Toronto: Ryerson Press, 1951); A. H. Birch, *Federalism, Finance and Social Legislation in Canada, Australia and the United States* (Toronto: Oxford University Press, 1955).

[52] H. A. Logan, *Trade Unions in Canada: Their Development and Function* (Toronto: Macmillan Company of Canada, 1948).

account of the Canadian labour movement since its beginnings early in the nineteenth century. Facts are given precedence over generalization or interpretation in a volume that omits little on labour organization and conflict and the external influences that have helped to shape labour history. Equally valuable is his study[53] of state assistance and collective bargaining over the period 1943-1954, a detailed review of labour legislation, its administration, and the issues at stake in collective-bargaining arrangements. Stuart Jamieson[54] has recently dealt with a similar theme in his study of industrial relations, a compact, well-written volume that puts heavy stress on the influence of developments on the labour front in the United States and their significance for Canadian labour and governmental policies. Salient points of similarity and contrast between the Canadian labour experience and that of the United States are underlined in a concise, comparative study that reveals much about the history and problems of Canadian labour in a continental setting. J. T. Montague[55] also takes up the question of the influence of the United States in his article on international unions and their implications for the Canadian trade-union movement. More than two-thirds of Canadian workers belong to such unions. Montague takes the position that, with competent leadership in Canadian ranks, Canadian unions can function effectively within international unions in spite of the lack of constitutional safeguards to protect Canadian minorities. More limited in scope, but highly informative, is D. C. Master's study of the Winnipeg general strike, a significant though unfortunate episode in labour history.[56]

Although immigration and population studies have not been stressed in recent years, D. C. Corbett[57] has made an important contribution in this field in his work on Canadian immigration

[53] H. A. Logan, *State Intervention and Assistance in Collective Bargaining: The Canadian Experience 1943-1954* (Toronto: University of Toronto Press, 1956).

[54] S. Jamieson, *Industrial Relations in Canada* (Ithaca: Cornell University Press, 1957).

[55] J. T. Montague, "International Unions and the Canadian Labour Movement," C.J.E.P.S., XXXIII (Feb., 1957), pp. 69-82.

[56] D. C. Masters, *The Winnipeg General Strike* (Toronto: University of Toronto Press, 1950).

[57] D. C. Corbett, *Canadian Immigration Policy: A Critique* (Toronto: University of Toronto Press, 1957). See also his "Immigration and Economic Development," C.J.E.P.S., XVII (Aug., 1951), pp. 360-68.

problems. Immigration and population changes over the past century are viewed in the light of their lessons for present immigration policy in a critical analysis that does much to clarify a topic that has become a highly controversial one of late. Emphasis on the relation between population change and economic development adds much to the value of his work. Mabel Timlin[58] attacks this question of population change and economic growth from a strongly Keynesian point of view. On the quantitative aspects of Canadian immigration and population history there is no scarcity of material and the principal sources are noted in the "borderlands" section of this paper.

For the demographer, French Canada continues to serve as a useful case study, and J. Henripen,[59] writing of the demography of this area since the seventeenth century, discusses the consequences of the slow shift from acceptance of nature to birth control. M. Lamontagne and J. C. Falardeau[60] trace the life cycle of urban families in Quebec and underline "the paradox of a North American society dramatically engaged in the process of remaining true to symbols of social stability while immersed in often unnoticed violent industrial and social change" (p. 247). N. Keyfitz[61] deals at greater length with Quebec's demographic development since 1871, with rural-urban shifts and occupational patterns, and the consequences of these for the French farmer. On Canadian demographic trends in general the late Burton Hurd has reviewed long-term changes in the principal phases of growth.[62]

It is only recently that industrial studies and business history have begun to receive the attention of the economic historian, but there are indications that this very large gap in Canadian

[58] M. Timlin, *Does Canada Need More People?* (Toronto: Oxford University Press, 1951).
[59] J. Henripen, *"From Acceptance of Nature to Control,"* c.j.e.p.s., XXIII (Feb., 1957), pp. 10-19, and reprinted in *French-Canadian Society*, vol. I (Toronto: Carleton Library, 1964), pp. 204-216.
[60] M. Lamontagne and J. C. Falardeau, "The Life Cycle of French-Canadian Urban Families," c.j.e.p.s., XIII (May, 1947), pp. 233-47.
[61] N. Keyfitz, "Population Problems," in J. C. Falardeau, ed., *Essays on Contemporary Quebec* (Quebec: Les Presses Universitaires Laval, 1953), ch. iv, and reprinted in *French-Canadian Society*, vol. I (Toronto: Carleton Library, 1964), pp. 216-244.
[62] B. Hurd, "Demographic Trends in Canada," *The Annals of the American Academy of Political and Social Science*, CCLIII (Sept., 1947), pp. 10-15. For a more strongly analytical view of population change see V. W. Bladen, *An Introduction to Political Economy* (Toronto: University of Toronto Press, 1956), ch. v, pp. 94-123.

literature is being narrowed. Apart from Dale's volume on the hydroelectric industry, O. W. Main's[63] study of the Canadian nickel industry and W. G. Phillips'[64] history of the farm-implement industry make welcome additions to the literature of this field. The former examines forms of entrepreneurial behaviour in a historical setting in which strong elements of monopoly are present. Monopolistic-competition theory is applied to empirical data in work that puts emphasis on the process of decision-making under conditions of uncertainty. The history of this major international industry provides abundant material for a study of business strategies applied in the face of frequently adverse economic and political changes. Although denied access to company records, Main has made excellent use of the materials available to him. Phillips' study, a companion piece in the "Canadian Studies in Economic Series," traces the rise and growth of the industry in two lengthy historical sections and reviews the changing pattern of competition in the industry over the past few decades. On the pulp and paper industry J. A. Guthrie[65] has supplemented his *Newsprint Industry* (Cambridge, Mass., 1941) with a more recent volume on the economics of pulp and paper, a useful study of the industry in its continental aspects. The development of the oil and gas industry, a relative newcomer to Canada, has been analysed by Hugh Aitken in a brief but informative study.[66]. . . A valuable addition to the industrial history of Quebec is a recent survey of long-period industrial change in this province by A. Faucher and M. Lamontagne.[67] Slow progress in 1939 is contrasted with the

[63] O. W. Main, *The Canadian Nickel Industry: A Study in Market Control and Public Policy* (Toronto: University of Toronto Press, 1955).

[64] W. G. Phillips, *The Agricultural Implement Industry in Canada: A Study in Competition* (Toronto: University of Toronto Press, 1956).

[65] J. A. Guthrie, *The Economics of Pulp and Paper* (Pullman: State College of Washington Press, 1956).

[66] H. G. J. Aitken, *The Oil Industry in Canada*, 1956 (mimeographed). See also Eric J. Hanson, *Dynamic Decade* (Toronto: McClelland & Stewart, 1958), a study of the impact of oil and gas developments on the economy of Alberta.

[67] In *Essays on Contemporary Quebec*, chs. i-ii, Chap. ii, "History of Industrial Development" has been reprinted in *French-Canadian Society* (Toronto: Carleton Library, 1964), pp. 257-271. See also comments by O. J. Firestone, pp. 38-44 of this volume. B. S. Kierstead in his *Theory of Economic Change* (Toronto: Macmillan Company of Canada, 1948, pp. 291-313), presents a comparative view of selected maritime industries in the interwar period of this century. For a general survey of industrial expansion see W. T. Easterbrook, "Industrial Development in Canada," *Encyclopedia Americana*, V, pp. 347-53.

remarkable industrial expansion of the period 1939-1950. The factors back of this virtual explosion are examined in a study admirable for its interpretative value and its stress on the continental influences in industrial growth. Too much is made perhaps of economic and technological factors, but the work is a valuable offset to the heavy emphasis placed in most studies on cultural and social elements in the Quebec scene.

Historical investigation of the problem of concentration of enterprise in Canada has not been stressed in Canadian studies, but V. W. Bladen[68] in his work on combines in Canadian experience has drawn attention to an aspect of economic organization that has been of the greatest significance from the beginnings of Canadian economic history. Gideon Rosenbluth's[69] analytical study of concentration in Canadian manufacturing, although primarily a short-run view, is useful for the light it throws on trends and determinants of concentration and for its comparative view of Canadian and American experience in this sector. For the most part, however, problems of competition and monopoly in Canadian development have yet to be subjected to the long-period study and analysis that their importance merits.

These contributions to industrial history and organization are flanked by a number of business and industry studies directed mainly at the general reader, but not out of place on the academician's bookshelf. The most prolific of business historians is M. Denison.[70] He has had more success than most in gaining access to company records. His *Harvest Triumphant* is a nar-

[68] V. W. Bladen, *An Introduction of Political Economy* (3d, ed.; Toronto: University of Toronto Press, 1956), ch. viii. See also his "Monopoly and Competition in Canada," in *Monopoly and Competition and Their Regulation* (London: Macmillan Co., Ltd., 1954), ch. i. See also V. W. Bladen and S. Stykolt, "Combines and the Public Interest: An Economist's Evaluation," in *Anti-trust Laws: A Comparative Symposium* (Toronto: Macmillan Company of Canada, 1956), pp. 45-90.

[69] G. Rosenbluth, *Concentration in Canadian Manufacturing Industriés* (Princeton: Princeton University Press, 1957). See also review article based on this publication by S. Stykolt, "The Measurement and Causes of Concentration," C.J.E.P.S., XXIV (Aug., 1958), pp. 415-19.

[70] M. Denison, *Harvest Triumphant: The Story of Massey-Harris: A Footnote to Canadian History* (Toronto: McClelland & Stewart, 1948). See also his *The Barley and the Stream: The Molson Story* (Toronto: McClelland & Stewart, 1955).

ative of the growth of the Massey-Harris enterprise. Technology and tariffs provide the backbone of the account, and a good eye for changing customs and colourful events adds to the interest of a good story well told. His *Barley and the Stream* describes the entrepreneurial achievements of the Molson family since its founding of the Molson Brewery in 1786; other family functions, including banking, distilling, sugar refining, and steam-boating also serve as reference points in a volume based on business records and correspondence. The romance of mining has drawn the attention of those who write for a wider public than university circles provide. Arnold Hoffman's *Free Gold*[71] is a lively account of major mining camps and leading personalities, and contains a wealth of material on changing conditions in the industry. D. M. LeBourdais, in *Metals and Men*,[72] similarly traces the history of mining, from the Cariboo of 1859 to the present, and includes a good deal of useful data. Less successful is his *Sudbury Basin*,[73] a chronicle of the activities of mining companies in the Sudbury district since its discovery in 1883. Leslie Roberts' *Noranda*,[74] although written in popular vein, is another volume of more than general interest. Merchandising has received very little attention to date, but C. L. Burton's[75] narrative of the rise of a Canadian merchant from country storekeeper to head of the Simpson merchandising enterprise marks an interesting beginning in this neglected area of business history. It is apparent that the chronicler has found easier access to company files than has the academic researcher; the success of the former, it is to be hoped, may promote in time a more favourable reception to the economic historian. The reluctance of firms under United States' control to open their files to the research student remains an obstacle not easily overcome.

Of the volumes in which the large view, spatial and temporal, of Canadian economic change is taken, none will have greater

[71] A. Hoffman, *Free Gold: The Story of Canadian Mining* (New York: Rinehart & Company, 1946).
[72] D. M. LeBourdais, *Metals and Men* (Toronto: McClelland & Stewart, 1957).
[73] D. M. LeBourdais, *Sudbury Basin: The Story of Nickel* (Toronto: Ryerson Press, 1953).
[74] Toronto: Clarke, Irwin & Company, 1956.
[75] C. L. Burton, *A Sense of Urgency: Memoirs of a Canadian Merchant* (Toronto: Clarke, Irwin & Company, 1952).

interest or appeal than that containing the published essays of H. A. Innis.[76] Twenty-eight items selected from the findings of a lifetime's research provide an essential background for an understanding of many phases of Canadian development. Few aspects of Canadian growth are overlooked in essays that, along with the author's *Fur Trade in Canada, Cod Fisheries,* and Part II of *Settlement and the Forest and Mining Frontier* attest to the quality and range of Innis' Canadian studies. . . . A set of scholarly essays drawn from many contributors is to be found in *Canada,*[77] a contribution to the "United Nations Series," that presents an authoritative survey of the factors, geographical and historical, economic and political, that lie back of the evolution of mid-twentieth-century Canada. On French Canada, Raoul Blanchard's geographical studies[78] contain historical chapters and a good deal of quantitative data, and *Notre milieu,*[79] a four-volume work edited by Esdras Minville, presents useful material on secular change, including time series of value to the economic historian of the region.

Writing on general economic history, M. Q. Innis, in her *Economic History of Canada,*[80] makes good use of the staples approach to Canadian history. There is a healthy emphasis on geographical and technological factors in a survey that ranges from the fishing industry of the sixteenth century to the minerals and newsprint of the present. The events of French and British rule, the extension of settlement in the Canadas, the appearance

[76] H. A. Innis, *Essays in Canadian Economic History,* ed., M. Q. Innis (Toronto: University of Toronto Press, 1956). See also D. G. Creighton, *Harold Adam Innis: Portrait of a Scholar* (Toronto: University of Toronto Press, 1957).

[77] Berkeley and Los Angeles: University of California Press, 1950. Part III of the volume contains a review of structural changes in the Canadian economy and useful material on regional aspects of growth. See also *Canadian Perspective: Some Aspects of Canada's Growth* (Toronto: Bank of Nova Scotia, 1957).

[78] The following studies of Raoul Blanchard have been published since 1945: *Le centre du Canada français, "Province de Quebec"* (Montreal: Librairie Beauchemin, 1947); *Montréal, esquisse de géographie urbaine* (Grenoble: Allier, 1947); *L'Abitibi-Temiscaminque* (Grenoble: Allier, 1949); *La Mauricie (Les Trois-Rivières* Editions du Vien Public, 1950).

[79] Esdras Minville, ed., *Etudes sur notre milieu* (4 vols.; Montreal: Ecole des Hautes Commerciales de Montréal, 1942-44). See in particular, I, ch. xv and II, ch. xiv.

[80] Toronto: Ryerson Press, 1943 and 1954.

of the railway and the steamship, wheat and industrialism are reviewed in a balanced treatment of change in each of the principal phases of Canadian history. A. W. Currie, in his *Canadian Economic Development*,[81] sets out the main features of the country's growth from the French regime to the present-day Canada of ten provinces. A valuable feature of his work is its detailed account of progress in the various regions of the country. A more recent addition to the literature of general economic history is Easterbrook and Aitken, *Canadian Economic History*.[82] This work traces the process of nation-building with particular references to its European background, the rise of a transcontinental economy, the influence of the United States, and the shift from the old industrialism to the new. Concern is with trends and patterns of change, and strategies of development and their outcome. D. G. Creighton's[83] *Dominion of the North*, though less slanted to the economics of change, is an indispensable item on the economic historian's reading list, for no one has explored so thoroughly the possibilities of the staples approach as a means of tracing the complex interrelations of politics and economics over the course of Canadian history.

In spite of the rate of progress in historical investigation on numerous fronts, it is apparent that important gaps remain. Our knowledge of manufacturing development[84] remains meagre, business history is barely underway, and many aspects of financial history other than commercial banking remain unexplored. The retail trade and marketing organization in general have received little attention, and problems of competi-

[81] Toronto: Thomas Nelson & Sons, 1942 and 1951.

[82] Toronto: Macmillan Company of Canada, 1956.

[83] D. G. Creighton, *Dominion of the North: A History of Canada* (Toronto: Macmillan Company of Canada, 1944 and 1957). See also the author's new edition of his *Commercial Empire of the St. Lawrence* (Toronto: Ryerson Press, 1937), now entitled *The Empire of the St. Lawrence*, an interpretation based on the idea of the St. Lawrence as the inspiration and basis of a transcontinental system.

[84] Studies for the Royal Commission on Canada's Economic Prospects, although looking to the future rather than the past, range over the major sectors of Canadian manufacturing and industry. Surveys of the forest and mining industries, primary iron and steel, secondary manufacturing, the automotive industry, agricultural and industrial production, electrical manufacturing and electronics, and primary textiles promise much for our knowledge of the contemporary scene, and incidentally draw attention to the trend aspects that still await study.

tion and monopoly are dealt with very largely in their contemporary setting. Very little has been done on the growth of Canadian economic thought apart from the occasional survey. The relationship between law and economics in Canadian history remains a dark corner. Nevertheless, here and there gaps are being filled and the rate and volume of research under way far exceed that of any time in the past. And progress on the "borderlands" of economic history, in statistics and economic analysis, sociology and political theory, promises much for the future of the subject in Canada. Numerous studies, not primarily historical in nature, are rich in data and in suggestive hypotheses of value to students of secular change.

In none of the "borderlands" has progress been more rapid than in the statistical realm. Research in the quantitative aspects of change has yielded a wealth of material that remains to be drawn upon by the historically inclined. In some instances the gap between quantitative and institutional approaches to history has been effectively bridged. In Kenneth Buckley's[85] study of capital formation in Canada, 1896-1930, the first six chapters are devoted to historical aspects of the subject, with a strong emphasis on quantitative analysis. Changes in the major sectors of investment are treated in relation to structural changes in the economy. Over the period under survey, wheat production is seen as a prime mover in growth and railway investment, and urban development and long-building cycles in Canadian cities are analysed largely in this context. Penelope Hartland Thunberg's[86] discussion of rates and determinants of economic growth over the past century provides new perspectives on change, along with a sound emphasis on the importance of Canada's "southern exposure." Her statistical account of the more important long-period changes in balance of payments

[85] K. Buckley, *Capital Formation in Canada, 1896-1930* (Toronto: University of Toronto Press, 1955). See also his "Capital Formation in Canada," in *Problems of Capital Formation* [*Studies in Income and Wealth, XIX*; National Bureau of Economic Research, New York] (Princeton: Princeton University Press, 1957), pp. 91-145.
[86] Penelope Hartland Thunberg, "Factors in Economic Growth in Canada," *The Journal of Economic History*, XV (Mar., 1955), pp. 13-22. See also her "Canada's Balance of Payments Since 1868," Conference on Research in Income and Wealth, Sept. 1957, National Bureau of Economic Research, New York (mimeographed). F. A. Knox provides a more general review of Canadian experience in "Canada's Balance of International Payments," *The Annals of the American Academy of Political and Social Science*, CCLIII (Sept., 1947), pp. 134-42.

and in capital movements is good grist for the historian's mill. Similarly, O. J. Firestone's[87] researches on Canadian economic development since 1867 have contributed greatly to our statistical knowledge of salient elements of growth. Changes in the country's national production and wealth and in factors bearing on these are subjected to close scrutiny of structural and quantitative changes that have too long been treated as matters apart. A general survey of Canadian growth, presented by J. M. Smith,[88] contains a useful statistical summark of growth experienced by a number of leading Canadian industries since 1926.[89]

A wealth of statistical material closely linked to economic growth in its theoretical aspect is contained in a volume by W. C. Hood and Anthony Scott[90] on output, capital, and labour in the Canadian economy. Although emphasis is placed on forecasts of development in the next quarter century, the study makes excellent use of available quantitative indexes of long-period change; a section devoted to a synoptic view of growth is particularly valuable in this respect. In its linking of quantitative and historical aspects of growth few Canadian studies attain the high quality of workmanship displayed in this volume. An intensive study of a limited period is V. W. Malach's[91] analytical treatment of the major cycle 1921-1933, in which the

[87] O. J. Firestone, *Canada's Economic Development, 1867-1952, with Special Reference to Changes in the Country's National Production and National Wealth*, paper prepared for the Third Conference of the International Association for Research in Income and Wealth, Castelgondolfo, Italy, Sept. 1-7, 1953 (mimeographed). See also his *Canada's Changing Economy in the Second Half of the Nineteenth Century*, paper prepared for the Conference on Research in Income and Wealth, Williamstown, Mass., Sept. 4-5, 1957 (mimeographed).

[88] J. M. Smith, *Canadian Economic Growth and Development from 1939 to 1955* (Ottawa: Queen's Printer, 1957).

[89] A more complete bibliographical account of statistical investigation than can be given in these pages would contain numerous references to the publications of federal and provincial government agencies. Publications on private and public investment, national accounts, income and expenditure, and Canada's balance of international payments merit more attention than can be given here. The close co-operation of government departments is in good part responsible for the rate of progress made in recent years toward a more adequate treatment of Canada's growth in the twentieth century. Special mention should be made of the *Reference Papers* of the Dominion Bureau of Statistics, each of which is a short monograph.

[90] W. C. Hood and A. Scott, *Output, Capital and Labour* (Ottawa: Queen's Printer, 1957).

[91] V. W. Malach, *International Cycles and Canada's Balance of Payments, 1921-1933* (Toronto: University of Toronto Press, 1955).

international aspects of short-run oscillations are stressed. Capital theory as applied to change has attracted few historians, but recent studies in this area should arouse their interest. Anthony Scott's[92] study of the economics of conservation applies capital theory and welfare analysis to an old historical problem and contains a useful historical survey of natural-resource policies in Europe, the United States, and Canada. More interesting in some respects is Burton Keirstead's[93] volume on profits and income distribution, a work that goes far to make the term "dynamics" acceptable to his historical brethren. The author's reflections on entrepreneurial expectations, on the nature of uncertainty as a factor in decision-making, and on the relationships between cycle and long-term trend make this a contribution of more than theoretical value. Historical illustrations and practical applications add to its utility for the historian who would come to terms with the theorist on questions of common interest. Another work, primarily theoretical in appeal, but of interest because it represents a rare exercise in the area of Canadian economic thought, is I. Brecher's[94] study of changes in monetary and fiscal policy over the period 1919-1939. Chapters on the "thought environment" of the 1920's, the "Great Depression" and the changes it wrought in monetary theory and practice, and the re-orientation of fiscal thinking that had occurred by the end of the 1930's provide material of value to those who would pursue the topic from a longer-run point of view.

Similarly, progress in sociology and political science is making its contributions to the study of long-period economic change. Studies by S. D. Clark[95] on the role of religious institutions and thought in economic development do much to fill this gap in Canadian writings. Centralization in religious organization has checked the growth of secular interests and

[92] A. Scott, *Natural Resources: The Economics of Conservation* (Toronto: University of Toronto Press, 1955).

[93] B. S. Keirstead, *An Essay in the Theory of Profits and Income Distribution* (Oxford: Basil Blackwell, 1957).

[94] I. Brecher, *Monetary and Fiscal Thought and Policy in Canada, 1919-1939* (Toronto: University of Toronto Press, 1957).

[95] S. D. Clark, "The Religious Sect in Canadian Economic Development," c.j.e.p.s., XII (Nov., 1946), pp. 439-53; and "The Religious Factor in Canadian Economic Development," *The Journal of Economic History*, VII (Dec., 1947), pp. 89-103. See also his *Church and Sect* (Toronto: University of Toronto Press, 1948).

forms and hereby weakened materialistic influences in national development. Sectarianism in Canada, unlike in the United States, has been a force too weak to break through traditional ways opposed to the dominance of economic interests. "In contrast with the United States, the sects have been much less important in breaking down the hold of organized religion and thus in releasing the energies of the population from religious pursuits."[96] Religious organization is seen as one line of defence against external pressures and as a response to the cultural and political insecurity that afflicts exposed areas; this insecurity has meant dependence on isolation and a strengthening of religious forms. This theme of church and sect is also treated with reference to economic growth in backward areas in general.[97]

On the political-science front, a contribution that makes light of the distinction between politics and economics is M. Lamontagne's[98] volume on the evolution and problems of Canadian federalism, a study of the role of the federal government in Canadian economic development that reviews the antecedents of Canada's federation of 1867, the nature of the political structure that emerged at that time, the period of federal government leadership to the 1920's, the rise of provincial autonomy in the next decade, the consequences of the economic crisis of the 1930's, and the return of the federal government to leadership. The state of public finance is a leading theme throughout, in a study that closely relates political changes to economic conditions in each of the main phases of federal-provincial relations. Taking up a similar theme, J. R. Mallory[99] in his volume on social credit in Alberta deals with the political and constitutional aspects of the search for a new national policy to take the place of that which had so effectively

[96] S. D. Clark in *The Journal of Economic History*, VII (Dec., 1947), p. 102.
[97] S. D. Clark, "Religion and the Economic Backward Areas," *Papers and Proceedings of the 63rd Annual Meeting of the American Economic Association, Chicago, Dec. 30, 1950*, XLI (May, 1951), pp. 258-65.
[98] M. Lamontagne, *Le fédéralism canadien: évolution et problems* (Quebec: Les Presses Universitaires Laval, 1954). On the economic and political forces and aspirations behind the movement for autonomy in the western provinces at the turn of the century, see C. C. Lingard, *Territorial Government in Canada: The Autonomy Question in the Old North West Territories* (Toronto: University of Toronto Press, 1946).
[99] J. R. Mallory, *Social Credit and the Federal Power in Canada* (Toronto: University of Toronto Press, 1954).

served the national interest to the 1920's. The growing economic and political power of the provinces in the interwar period raised new and difficult problems for a federal government faced with increased collective responsibilities; an older federal structure that had lost much of its coherence and viability faced the challenge of conditions that strengthened regional tensions within the nation. The conflict between dominion and provinces occurred in its sharpest form in Albertan politics, and Mallory has made effective use of the details of this conflict in his study of an attempt to add new dimensions to the old two-party system. No work to date has analysed so effectively the complex interrelations between political aspirations, constitutional processes, and economic interests in the Canada of these decades. C. B. Macpherson,[100] also writing in the "Social Credit Series," relies on a class-interest hypothesis in his account of the evolution of social credit, which he views as the expression of a quasi-party system. He regards this as a deviation from the two-party alignment and an arrangement that enables one party to exercise political monopoly in a structure in which minority rights are preserved. There is much in Canadian politics to support the view that this form of monopoly is not uncommon in provincial and federal areas of government, and Macpherson has done much to clarify its nature and significance. These political studies, in touching on many aspects of economic interest, have greatly improved prospects for an integration of economic and political approaches to historical change in Canada.

Progress in these "borderlands" confirms the view that the achievement of a new and more comprehensive synthesis in Canadian economic history must rest on the contributions of social scientists working beyond the confines of their respective specialisms. There are, it must be admitted, few clues as to what form this synthesis may take, but indications of a growing community of interest, based on a substantial and increasing volume of research across the social sciences, promise much for revisions now under way. Modification of the staples theme in the light of this program has its suggestions for future research. Kenneth Buckley, in a recent paper on the role of staples

[100] C. B. Macpherson, *Democracy in Alberta: The Theory and Practice of a Quasi-Party System* (Toronto: University of Toronto Press, 1953)

industries, takes the view that following 1820, when fur gave way to timber and wheat, there was a rapid increase in the total of economic activity unrelated to staples production. The difficulty of determining the contribution of the staples industries to the growth of the national economy after this date leads him to suggest an alternative general concept of "economic opportunity," used without reference to determinants of change, and a greater concentration "upon what has happened to the measurable dimensions of productive capacity by areas, industries and in the country as a whole in the course of their growth through time."[101] Although it would put aside many of the more interesting questions of economic development, the suggestion should be of value to those who choose to concentrate upon the quantitative aspects of change. As such, it points less to a displacement of the staples thesis than to a means of supplementing it.

And there are other lines of inquiry. Writings on the applicability of the frontier thesis to Canadian experience point to new and fruitful lines of inquiry. M. Zaslow,[102] in his discussion of the frontier hypothesis, stresses the difficulty of utilizing this theme in Canadian studies. Canada's brief frontier experience, her close ties with Europe, the importance of external influences, and the viability of French Canada's culture have made the frontier influence a weak force in Canadian history. S. D. Clark,[103] consistent with his views on the conservative forces of religion in Canada, goes farther in his stress on the persistence of authority and its supports in Canadian development. A highly centralized federal system emerged in Canada as a response to the necessity of defending exposed frontiers against expansionist influences from the south. The frontier as a force in development could be tolerated, even encouraged, in the United States; in Canada it represented a threat too great to be allowed free expression. J. S. M. Careless[104] argues that

---

[101] Kenneth Buckley, *The Role of Staple Industries in Canada's Economic Development, The Journal of Economic History*, XVIII (Dec. 1958), 429-50.

[102] M. Zaslow, "The Frontier Hypothesis in Canadian Historiography," *CHR*, XXIX (June, 1948), pp. 153-66.

[103] S. D. Clark, "The Frontier and Democratic Theory," *Transactions of the Royal Society of Canada*, XLVIII, Series III (June, 1954), pp. 65-75.

[104] J. S. M. Careless, "Frontierism, Metropolitanism and Canadian History," *CHR*, XXXV (Mar., 1954), pp. 1-21.

metropolitanism rather than frontierism must be accepted as the central thesis in Canadian history. In Canada, as in the United States, the political and economic power of the urban centre as the focus of decision-making in national affairs has made it the principal agent of expansion.

These views, along with recent discussion of concentration in the Canadian economy, strengthen the impression that the Canadian structure has, from the beginning, been centralized in form and authoritarian in outlook. Only for a short-lived period in the maritime areas could the frontier be said to have exerted much influence. Although this proposition can be reconciled with the staples hypothesis, it does draw attention to our limited knowledge of the role of the metropolitan centre as a guiding force in development. Very little has been done on the strategies by which economic control was so effectively maintained over a transcontinental system. Histories of the fur trade, banking, land policy, and transportation provide clues to an understanding of this process, but little attention has been given to the rise of the city, its enterprisers, and its institutions. It is clear that the political scientist has made considerably greater progress in coming to grips with the nature and determinants of centralism in Canadian life than has the economic historian. The Laurentian school of Innis, Lower, and Creighton pointed the way, but the urban centre as the locus of concentration, particularly in business life, has virtually escaped investigation.

There is another area of inquiry that is beginning to invite exploration. A review of recent contributions to Canadian studies reveals a growth preoccupation with Canadian development in continental terms, expressed less in terms of relationship between the economies of Canada and the United States than in comparisons that reveal strong elements of unlikeness in growth experience. Reference has been made to the views of Fowke on continental expansion, to those of Logan and Jamieson on labour history, to Faucher's treatment of industrialism in Quebec, and to Clark's comments on the religious factor. In these, as in many of the studies noted above, there are numerous references to United States' development and its contrasts with that of Canada. This increasing tendency to view change in a North American context has its suggestions for those who would bridge Dales's "Great Divide," or in other words, who would treat of the impact of the new industrialism on a structure still embedded in the old.

This search for a larger view of Canadian economic history is not a new search. Innis' international view of the *Cod Fisheries* and J. B. Brebner's classic *North Atlantic Triangle*[105] remain as guides to future investigations, but in spite of the continuing importance of empire ties and the growing interest in Commonwealth relations, for the economic historian at any rate, the inescapable fact of economic integration with the United States demands formulation of views of secular change in a continental framework. The metropolitan hypothesis suggested by Careless and others must be tested in these terms, for many of the strategies of investment in Canadian resource exploitation are devised in controlling centres to the south of the border, and no political or other defences appear likely to upset this relationship. The essentially defensive aspect[106] of Canadian policy is apparent from the beginnings of Canadian economic history, but it is only recently that this has received its due as a unifying theme in Canadian studies, even though staples economics lends itself to this line of treatment. United States investment and trade policies clearly imply the continuance of Canada's role of supplier of materials for its gigantic industrial apparatus. Escape from this design promises to be more difficult than that of the colonies to the south who once broke loose from a not wholly dissimilar imperial design.

H. G. J. Aitken[107] writes of the changing structure of the Canadian economy in these terms and W. T. Easterbrook[108]

[105] J. B. Brebner, *North Atlantic Triangle: The Interplay of Canada, the United States and Great Britain* (New Haven: Yale University Press and Toronto: Ryerson Press, 1945; reprinted in the Carleton Library, Toronto, 1966).

[106] See H. G. J. Aitken, "Defensive Expansion: The State and Economic Growth," in Aitken, ed., *The State and Economic Growth* (New York: Social Science Research Council, 1959), pp. 79-114, and reprinted in this volume, pp. 183-221.

[107] H. G. J. Aitken, *The Changing Structure of the Canadian Economy with particular Reference to the Influence of the United States*, paper prepared for the Duke University Commonwealth Studies Center, Summer 1958 (mimeographed). See also M. Lamontagne, *The American Economic Impact on Quebec*, a paper prepared for the same center, Summer 1958 (mimeographed).

[108] W. T. Easterbrook, "Long-Period Comparative Study: Some Historical Cases," *The Journal of Economic History*, XVII (Dec., 1957), pp. 571-95.

takes a similar view in a comparative survey of the two economies. The extent of United States influence is the subject of a recent volume on Canadian-American economic relations by I. Brecher and S. S. Riesman.[109] In a detailed review of changes over the past four decades the authors deal with business cycle transmission, the extent of non-resident ownership and control of Canadian industry, and the course of commercial relations between the two countries. In general, writings on the continental and defensive elements in Canadian growth, such as revisions of the staples theme and reflections on metropolitan influence, are in the stage of hypotheses to be tested, tentative views that require elaboration and, incidentally, close reference to work under way on re-interpretations of United States economic development.

It is too early to discard the staples thesis, but the explorations of the past two decades point the way to more inclusive and more comprehensive treatments of historical change than those provided by staples economics. Awareness of an incomplete pattern precedes strategic acts of synthesis; recent progress confirms the view that this awareness exists and the conclusion that the search for a "new" economics as effective as the "old" is well advanced. The "integration of basic approaches" that Innis sought is unlikely to be achieved by any one discipline or school of thought or to rest on any strongly nationalistic version of Canadian history. The evidence suggests that the work of the economic historian is a necessary, though not sufficient, condition of this achievement.

POSTSCRIPT

Two massive studies of the fur trade have contributed greatly to our knowledge of the place of this staple in economic history. In his study of the Hudson's Bay Company, E. E. Rich[110] has presented a detailed account of the interplay of business, politics and personalities in the history of the great Company. His evaluation of old-world policies and practices which largely determined the fortunes of the trade provides a balanced inter-

[109] I. Brecher and S. S. Riesman, *Canada-United States Economic Relations* (Ottawa: Queen's Printer, 1957).

[110] E. E. Rich, *Hudson's Bay Company, 1670-1870*. Volume I, 1670-1763, Volume II, 1763-1870 (London: Hudson's Bay Society, 1958-9).

pretation of events in which developments in North America are placed in their wider setting. Paul Chrisler Phillips'[111] well-documented narrative of the fur trade in North America describes the role of the trade in the colonization of the continent, the rivalries of Canadian and American entrepreneurs, and the development and outcome of the trade in the Oregon country, in the Mississippi valley and on the Pacific coast. With its wealth of detail, the study represents the most complete and comprehensive account of the contributions of the trade to continental expansion.

A most welcome development has been the publication of *Historical Statistics of Canada.*[112] This major contribution to scholarship in the social sciences brings together a wide range of statistical time series along with descriptive material, covering where possible the period from 1867 to 1960. Both by what it contains and by the gaps it discloses, it promises to give new emphasis to quantitative economic history in Canada. The "new economic history," with its central emphasis on quantification, has had little impact yet on Canadian studies; Edward J. Chambers and Donald Gordon, however, provide a highly controversial essay in this field in their "Primary Products and Economic Growth" (*Journal of Political Economy*, August 1966, pp. 315-31.

G. E. Britnell and V. C. Fowke offer a brief survey of the role of agriculture in Canadian history in Part 1 of their volume *Canadian Agriculture in War and Peace 1935-50.*[113] R. E. Caves and R. H. Holton have made a distinguished contribution to Canadian studies in their volume *The Canadian Economy: Prospect and Retrospect.*[114] Part 1 of this study admirably demonstrates the value of the staples theory as a unifying theme. Chapters on growth patterns in Canada's four major regions provide new material on regional aspects of Canada's development. A Twentieth Century Fund study of Canada's needs and resources contains a useful summary of economic

[111] Paul Chrisler Phillips, *The Fur Trade.* Two volumes (Normal, Oklahoma: University of Oklahoma Press, 1961).

[112] *Historical Statistics of Canada.* Editor, M. C. Urquhart; Assistant Editor, K. A. H. Buckley (Toronto: Macmillan Company of Canada, 1965.

[113] Stanford University Press, 1962.

[114] *Harvard Economic Studies,* Volume CXII (Cambridge: Harvard University Press, 1959.

development since World War II.[115] A valuable addition to Canadian regional studies is made by André Raynauld in his volume on Quebec, Part 1 of which presents a descriptive analysis of the development of the economy over the period 1870-1955.[116] On Canadian economic thought, C. D. W. Goodwin traces the transplantation of economics to Canada from England, Scotland, France and the United States and describes the evolution of economic thought in Canada to the First World War. A fresh interpretation of New France, stressing the limited development of its economy, is offered by Jean Hamelin,[117] while the economic development of Quebec from 1760 to 1850 receives a lengthy and penetrating analysis from Fernand Ouellet.[118]

A collection of readings by L. A. Skeoch contains a brief summary of the history of combines policy.[119] Education, which had been completely neglected by Canadian economic historians, is the subject of a monograph by Gordon W. Bertram.[120] Class structure, élite groups, and a host of other important topics are dealt with in a brilliant, baroque volume by John Porter.[121] Relevant documents in the history of money and banking are contained in a collection by E. P. Neufeld.[122]

Articles of interest to the economic historian include the following: on imigration, Mabel Timlin, "Canada's Immigration Policy, 1896-1910" (*Canadian Journal of Economics and Political Science*, November 1960, pp. 517-32), D. M. McDougall, "Immigration into Canada, 1851-1820" (*Canadian Journal of Economics and Political Science*, May 1961, pp. 162-75) and

[115] G. W. Wilson, H. S. Gordon, S. Judek and A. Breton, *Canada: An Appraisal of its Needs and Resources* (Toronto: University of Toronto Press, 1965).

[116] A. Raynauld, *Croissance et Structure Economique de la Province de Québec* (Ministère de l'Industrie et du Commerce, Province de Québec, 1961).

[117] Jean Hamelin, *Economie et Société en Nouvelle-France* (Québec: Les Presses Universitaires Laval, 1960).

[118] Fernand Ouellet, *Histoire Economique et Sociale du Québec 1760-1850* (Montreal: Fides, 1966).

[119] L. A. Skeoch (ed.), *Restrictive Trade Practices in Canada* (Toronto: McClelland and Stewart Ltd., 1966, pp. 2-20).

[120] Gordon W. Bertram, *The Contribution of Education to Economic Growth*, Staff Study No. 12, Economic Council of Canada (Ottawa: Queen's Printer, 1965).

[121] John Porter, *The Vertical Mosaic* (Toronto: University of Toronto Press, 1965).

[122] E. P. Neufeld, *Money and Banking in Canada*, Carleton Library, 1964.

J. Pickett, "An Evaluation of Estimates of Immigration into
Canada in the Late Nineteenth Century" (*Canadian Journal of
Economics and Political Science*, November 1965, pp. 499-508);
on the capital market, I. M. Drummond, "Government Securities
on Colonial New Issue Markets" (*Yale Economic Essays*, Spring
1961, pp. 137-75) and "Life Insurance Companies and the
Capital Market, 1890-1914" (*Canadian Journal of Economics
and Political Science*, May 1962, pp. 204-24); on capital formation, J. Pickett, "Residential Capital Formation in Canada,
1871-1921" (*Canadian Journal of Economics and Political
Science*, February 1963, pp. 40-58); on the labour market, H. C.
Pentland, "The Development of the Capitalistic Labour Market
in Canada" (*Canadian Journal of Economics and Political
Science*, November 1959, pp. 450-61); on business history,
A. W. Currie, "The First Dominion Companies Act" (*Canadian
Journal of Economics and Political Science*, August 1962, pp.
387-404); G. F. McGuigan, "The Emergence of the Unincor-
porated Company in Canada" (*University of British Columbia
Law Review*, April 1964, pp. 31-57) and H. G. J. Aitken,
"Government and Business in Canada: An Interpretation" (*The
Business History Review*, Spring 1964, pp. 4-21); on the quan-
titative dimensions of economic growth, O. J. Firestone, "Devel-
opment of Canada's Economy, 1850-1890" in *Trends in the
American Economy in the Nineteenth Century*;[123] on the fur
trade, E. E. Rich, "Trade Habits and Economic Motivation
among the Indians of North America" (*Canadian Journal of
Economics and Political Science*, February 1960, pp. 35-53) and
J. F. Crean, "Hats and the Fur Trade" (*Canadian Journal of
Economics and Political Science*, August 1962, pp. 373-386);
on mining, W. D. G. Hunter, "The Development of the Canadian Uranium Industry: An Experiment in Public Enterprise"
(*Canadian Journal of Economics and Political Science*, August
1962, pp. 329-52); on business cycles, Edward J. Chambers,
"Late Nineteenth Century Business Cycles in Canada" (*Canadian Journal of Economics and Political Science*, August 1964,
pp. 391-412) and K. A. J. Hay, "Early Twentieth Century
Business Cycles in Canada" (*Canadian Journal of Economics
and Political Science*, August 1966, pp. 354-365); on combines
policy, D. F. Forster, "The Politics of Combines Policy: Liberals
and the Stevens Commission" (*Canadian Journal of Economics*

[123] Princeton University Press, 1960, pp. 217-52.

and Political Science, November 1962, pp. 511-26; on internal migration, Kenneth Buckley, "Historical Estimates of Internal Migration in Canada," (*Canadian Political Science Association, Conference on Statistics,* 1960, *Papers,* edited by E. F. Beach and J. C. Weldon) and Charles M. Studness, "Economic Opportunity and the Westward Migration of Canadians during the late Nineteenth Century" (*Canadian Journal of Economics and Political Science,* November 1964, pp. 570-84; on manufacturing, J. H. Dales, "Estimates of Canadian Manufacturing Output by Markets, 1870-1915" and Gordon W. Bertram, "Historical Statistics on Growth and Structure in Manufacturing in Canada, 1870-1957," *Canadian Political Science Association,* Conferences on Statistics, 1962 and 1963, *Papers,* edited by J. Henripin and A. Asimakopulos; on the National Policy, J. H. Dales, "Cost of Protectionism with High International Mobility of Factors (*Canadian Journal of Economics and Political Science,* November 1964, pp. 512-25), "Some Historical and Theoretical Comments on Canada's National Policies" (*Queen's Quarterly,* Autumn 1964, pp. 297-316), and Peter Russell (ed.) *Nationalism in Canada;*[124] on transportation, John Lorne McDougall, "The Relative Level of Crow's Nest Grain Rates in 1899 and 1965" (*Canadian Journal of Economics and Political Science,* February 1966, pp. 46-54).

---

[124] McGraw-Hill, 1966. See in particular J. H. Dales, "Protection, Immigration and Canadian Nationalism," R. Craig Brown, "The Nationalism of the National Policy," and M. H. Watkins, "Technology and Nationalism."

SUGGESTIONS FOR
FURTHER READING

The following highly selective list represents the results of important research that has been or is currently being done in Canadian economic history. The most recent survey of the economic development of Canada is W. T. EASTERBROOK and H. G. J. AITKEN, *Canadian Economic History* (Toronto, 1956). An excellent economic history of Canada in the period between Confederation and the Second World War is found in Book I of the Report of the Royal Commission on Dominion-Provincial Relations, 1940 (Rowell-Sirois Report). An abridgement of this work is available in the Carleton Library (1963).

The Canadian experience in economic development is treated in O. J. FIRESTONE, *Canada's Economic Development, 1867-1953* (London, 1958); R. E. CAVES and R. H. HOLTON, *The Canadian Economy: Prospect and Retrospect* (Cambridge, 1959) and G. W. WILSON, H. S. GORDON, S. JUDEK and A. BRETON, *Canada: An Appraisal of Its Needs and Resources* (Toronto, 1965). The research studies of the Royal Commission on Canada's Economic Prospects (Gordon Commission), which reported in 1957, are also invaluable aids to an understanding of recent economic history in Canada. Another royal commission, that on Health Services (1964) attempted to analyse and project the economic growth of Canada: T. M. BROWN, *Canadian Economic Growth* (Ottawa, 1965).

The foundations of Canadian economic history are discussed in P. CAMU, E. P. WEEKS and Z. W. SAMETZ, *Economic Geography of Canada* (Toronto, 1964). Statistical material on economic growth is brought together in *Historical Statistics of Canada*, edited by M. C. URQUHART and K. A. H. BUCKLEY (Toronto, 1965). For the period after 1960 the reader is referred to the *Canada Year Book* or the *Canadian Statistical Review*, both published in Ottawa by the Queen's Printer.

The role of capital in Canadian economic history is described in K. A. H. BUCKLEY, *Capital Formation in Canada, 1896-1930* (Toronto, 1955) and H. G. J. AITKEN, *American Capital and*

Canadian Resources (Cambridge, 1961). The standard work on Canadian banking is R. C. MCIVOR, *Canadian Monetary, Banking and Fiscal Development* (Toronto, 1958). See also E. P. NEUFELD, *Money and Banking in Canada* (Carleton Library, 1964). All forms of transportation are discussed in G. P. DE T. GLAZEBROOK, *A History of Transportation in Canada* (Carleton Library, 2 vols., 1964).